33025477

CW00347633

TERROR FROM THE SKY

This book is dedicated to the men and women of the Royal Air Force who since the Great War have fought to keep Britain and the world free from tyranny. Especially to the pilots, ground personnel, controllers and observers who carried out their duty with dedication, skill and bravery.

TERROR FROM THE SKY

The Battle against the Flying Bombs

By

Graham A Thomas

Pen & Sword
AVIATION

First Published in Great Britain in 2008 by
Pen & Sword Aviation
an imprint of
Pen & Sword Books Ltd
47 Church Street
Barnsley
South Yorkshire
S70 2AS

Copyright © Graham A Thomas, 2008

ISBN 978-1-84415-684-9

Pen & Sword Books Ltd incorporates the Imprints of Pen & Sword Aviation,
Pen & Sword Maritime, Pen & Sword Military, Wharncliffe Local History,
Pen & Sword Select, Pen & Sword Military Classics and Leo Cooper.

For a complete list of Pen & Sword titles please contact
PEN & SWORD BOOKS LIMITED
47 Church Street, Barnsley, South Yorkshire, S70 2AS, England
E-mail: enquiries@pen-and-sword.co.uk
Website: www.pen-and-sword.co.uk

Contents

Acknowledgements

I would like to thank the people at the National Archives and the Imperial War Museum for being so helpful, the people at the Royal Air Force Museum for their help and those people such as Wendy English who provided their recollections of life under the reign of terror from the doodlebugs. I would like to thank Dave Sanderson from 96 Squadron Association who provided a unique insight into the Squadron; Graham Berry, related to Joseph Berry, who had the highest score against V1s; John Kendall, the son of Squadron Leader Philip 'Joe' Kendall; Tony Harper of 1 Squadron Association; Adrian Cooper from 501 Squadron Association; and Christer Landberg, webmaster for The Hawker Tempest Page.

Foreword

The Airborne Terrorist Attacks by Craig Cabell

Some nights, though, I could not remember my prayers even. I could only get as far as 'On earth as it is in heaven' and then have to start all over and be absolutely unable to get past that.

Now I Lay Me from *Men Without Women*, Ernest Hemingway

Having studied a great many reports concerning terrorist attacks on London during the Second World War by V1s and V2s, I welcome this book. I am a great believer in the difference made by the RAF in countering the strikes on London from these despicable beasts. Many people do not share my view, drawing the very oblique opinion that the threat was only thwarted when Allied troops raided areas in Europe that were making and firing the things. Thank God Graham A Thomas has stepped forward to bring weight to the thoughts of people like myself – a student of the Second World War – and also, the people who were there too. I refer here to Flight Lieutenant Raymond Baxter of 602 Spitfire Squadron, among others, who dive-bombed V2 rocket sights – and the odd V1 rocket sight – in late 1944 through to March 1945. When I spoke to Baxter about the 'difference made by the RAF', he was convinced it was great. When I told him that Alanbrooke thought the RAF made little difference, he said, 'Typical bloody soldier.'

One can view a CGI movie of Operation *Big Ben*, the anti-V2 Spitfire Missions, on the internet, or one can buy a classic war movie called *633 Squadron* and see the difficulties the RAF faced when carrying out special missions in their quite primitive aircraft. However, one must still marvel at the bravery and never-say-die attitude possessed by the British pilots of the Second World War; whether or not you agree with Graham's angle in this book, you cannot fail to be impressed by the fearlessness and the selflessness of those magnificent men who flew to ease the suffering of a nation.

Furthermore, the operations fought over Britain to save civilian suffering have hardly been mentioned before and, like Operation *Big Ben*, the story must now be fully told.

With this book, I believe, Graham has gone a long way in achieving that. His love of aviation and the brave men who flew has been echoed throughout his work and, if his work makes the student of twentieth century warfare stop and consider for one moment the difference made – outside the Battle of Britain – by the RAF, then I know Graham will be a happy man.

I applaud this book, its vital sentiment and important statistics and reminiscences. Through my work – ongoing – concerning Operation *Big Ben*, my studies of Alanbrooke, Montgomery and Ismay, also my knowledge of the Joint Planning Staff of the War Cabinet, I *know* the British Government were petrified of the threat of V1s and V2s. The only thing they could do was to send the RAF in because they couldn't get troops deep enough into enemy territory to knock out launching areas, let alone factories. But the RAF did their best to do that. Actually, not just that, they knocked out heavy vehicles, bridges, railway lines, all manner of things that could transport vital components of V1 and V2 machines. If they saved a dozen people by slowing down the Nazis then surely that is a significant victory. Think about it: twelve people. Forget the statistic, think of twelve members of your family standing talking in a living room and then being blown to bits for no bloody reason at all. Think how angry you would be at the injustice. Well, dear reader, it happened on more than one night during the latter stages of the Second World War. Forget the statistics, think of people's lives. Now understand where this book is coming from.

This book is a brave work that flies in the face of the soft answer as to how the V-threat was countered. It explains that the British Government hid their fears from the public eye because they didn't want blind panic; *the government couldn't truly counter the technology and believed the war was beginning to move out of their control as a consequence.* Hence covert RAF missions such as Operation *Crossbow* and Operation *Big Ben* and, if anyone wants to challenge the success of these missions, I beg them to get back in the classroom and reassess the significance of the RAF during the Second World War. I think they will be genuinely surprised.

Let us not underestimate the horror of those airborne terrorist attacks and the bravery of the men that desperately tried to counter them despite huge difficulties. What difficulties? Well, please read on ...

There was a grim determination in me, a kind of dark coldness that had taken over from the rage to stifle any other emotion. Sure, I was scared, but for the first time ... I felt I was in control.

'48, James Herbert

Craig Cabell
London, May 2007

Author's Note

Terror from the Sky is about the battle against the flying bomb. This was, essentially, an air battle against a pilotless, jet-propelled robot aircraft that caused destruction and havoc on London and the surrounding areas. This tiny aircraft with its pulse-jet engine brought fear into the hearts of most Londoners when the jet engine cut out and there was a silent pause before the explosion murdered innocent people.

To document the bravery and courage of the pilots who flew against these fast little devils I have gone to the sources, combat reports, log books, squadron histories, official documents and to people who were actually there listening to the terrible wail the V1s made as they approached our shores.

To put the terror into context I look at the experiences of ordinary people having to deal with the menace of the flying bombs, like the reminiscence of my mother that opens the book. Quotations from people like Air Marshal Sir Arthur Tedder show the initial attitude towards the coming menace and then the dreadful realisation that they had completely misjudged the German capability.

But the main body of this book covers the day-to-day round-the-clock flying and fighting the pilots of the Tempest Wing, the Mosquito crews, the Spitfire pilots and other squadrons endured to try to stop the V1 attacks.

This is not meant to be an academic work but a living, breathing account of a few months in the summer of 1944 when the outcome of the war could have been far different. This is the account from the pilot's point of view, sitting in the cockpit of the high-speed

Tempest diving down on a V1 in the dark of night firing short bursts until the missile exploded.

It was a hazardous time and the pilots flew day and night to try to counter the V1 attack. If not for their efforts many more V1s would have reached their targets and many more civilians would have died. These pilots were fighting to save lives and prepared to make the supreme sacrifice to do so. At the same time they were flying state-of-the-art fighters in the Tempest but without any electronic aid for night-fighting. It was down to being in constant contact with the controllers on the ground directing them towards the coordinates of V1s approaching London and, as always in those days, the main piece of equipment was the Mark 1 eyeball.

This book is also about the beginning of the rocket as a weapon of terror. The V1 was the first successful cruise missile. One merely has to look at the battle between Hezbollah and the Israelis in 2006 to see that the use of rockets as weapons of terror hasn't changed that much since the Germans began firing off their V1 and V2 vengeance weapons.

This was the beginning of the world we know today.

Graham Thomas
Salisbury 2007

Introduction
The Battle Begins

The doodlebug was terrible. One came over our house making that awful sound. When it was making the buzzing sound you knew you were safe but when it stopped that was when you had to worry. The sirens were going off and we ran down to the shelter at the bottom of our garden. The old couple next door didn't. Suddenly, the noise stopped and there was this terrific bang. When we came out of the shelter the house next door was gone completely and all the windows and doors in our house had been blown out. The damage was so bad we had to move onto father's boat for six months until they found us some housing. The old couple were killed outright.

Daphne Shuffell, survivor of a buzz bomb attack.

On 23 August 1944 Spitfire pilots from 402 Squadron saw something they had never seen before. Aircraft without pilots and without propellers shot past them at great speed as they crossed the coast of Britain. The huge flame that came from the back of their pulse-jet engines identified the unknown aircraft as V1 flying bombs.

The three doodlebugs roared in at around 400 mph when the Spitfires, out of Hawkinge, flying at 4,000 feet caught sight of them. Flying the new Mark XIV, with the Rolls-Royce Griffon engine, this version of the mighty fighter could just about catch them. The enemy buzz bombs were cruising at around 3,000 feet when the Spitfires attacked, diving on them.

The greatest danger to the pilots was the flying bombs exploding so close to their aircraft and blasting the pilot and his aircraft out of the sky.

1

The principal weapons against the V1 menace were Spitfires, Mosquitoes and the mighty Tempests – the only fighters that could out fly the doodlebug. Towards the end of the battle Mustangs were brought into the fray and with their engines boosted they were able to catch and destroy the V1s but they did so in limited quantities. The Tempest was the fighter of the moment. In the end the number of flying bombs destroyed by fighters and by anti-aircraft (AA) guns was almost equal but the Tempest wing had the largest tally out of all the ground and air units involved in defending the skies over Britain against this new menace.

The V1 was the first of Hitler's secret 'vengeance' or reprisal weapons that he believed would turn the tide of the war. It was the very first of what we know today as the cruise missile. It had a rudimentary guidance system and flew on a specified course. Unlike today's highly computerised cruise missiles that can fly over the contours of the terrain towards their targets, the V1 was launched in the direction of London and pretty much stayed on that course. But the objective was the same – to create terror in the population.

Known as a *Vergeltungswaffen*, the first flying bomb landed in Britain one week after D-Day on 13 June 1944. Called the buzz bomb because of the buzzing noise of its pulse-jet engine, it caused terror in the hearts of people when it came over. As long as the engine sounded people were safe, but when the engine cut out the V1 went into a dive and that silence, dreaded by all, resulted in a massive explosion.

Jointly designed by Robert Lusser of Fieseler and Fritz Gosslau of the Argus engine factory, the V1 was a development managed by the *Luftwaffe* and designated the Fi 103. Constructed mostly of sheet metal, the V1 was a simple device and usually took around fifty man-hours to assemble.

Once the missile had been launched and was clear of the ramp an autopilot kicked in that regulated height and speed using a weighted pendulum system designed to get fore and aft feedback that controlled the V1's pitch. A gyro magnetic compass, which was set prior to launch by swinging in a hangar, helped to create a reaction between yaw, pitch and roll while the fore and after pendulum plus the feedback from the magnetic field kept the gyroscope trued up. Because of this interaction there was no need for a banking mechanism and once the V1 reached the target the fuel ran away from the pipes as the V1 descended and the power cut out. The V1 had two fuses, one in the belly and one in the nose, so there was usually an explosion when the missile crashed.

Intelligence reports had already shown that the Germans were working on radical projects as early as late 1942. Reconnaissance photos and reports from agents working behind the lines indicated the existence of 'ski-ramps' on the French coast generally directed towards London. Several intelligence reports had been received since 1942 about German long-range rocket experiments and Prime Minister Winston Churchill ordered investigations into the German rocket developments be instigated right away. Soon he received reports on German experiments with jet-propelled aircraft, airborne rocket torpedoes (V1s) and heavy rockets all taking place on the German Baltic coast at Peenemünde.

It was here, at the German's top-secret research establishment at Peenemünde in early 1942 that the first test flight of the V1 took place, which showed the Germans they still had to work out guidance and stabilisation problems. These were finally resolved when a V1, modified for manned operation, was flown by test pilot Hanna Reitsch. Fighting the controls, she managed to bring the V1 down to a successful landing and brought back the data the engineers needed to redesign the stabilisation system.

As intelligence reports mounted, Churchill was advised to order Bomber Command to attack Peenemünde. At the same time, the Home Office was preparing plans to evacuate women and children from London and Morrison shelters were moved into the capital city. Since the Blitz after the Battle of Britain in 1941–2 had ended the people of London had started to breathe more easily. Life had become a little better without the incessant drone of enemy bombers overhead and the explosions night after night. Little did people know they were about to face another Blitz.

The intelligence reports about the enemy's secret weapons projects came from a wide variety of sources. For example, the person who spotted a tiny aircraft sitting on a ramp that was pointed out to sea at Peenemünde in a reconnaissance photograph was WAAF Constance Babington-Smith. Agent Michael Hollard, working in France, investigated a large building under construction near Rouen. Hollard managed to get a job at this installation and spotted a ramp that was being built facing towards London. He found similar structures as he cycled around northern France. The evidence could not be denied.

So on 17 August 1943 Bomber Command attacked Peenemünde with nearly 600 bombers, destroying assembly shops, labs and killing several high-ranking scientists. Forty-one bombers did not return to base. Rather than end the rocket production, the raid forced the Germans to move their work into the Harz Mountains, right inside a mountain itself, making their work impervious to Allied bombs.

In order to handle the flying bombs, the Germans created the special unit 155th *Flakregiment*, commanded by Colonel Wachtel. The German designation for the V1 was FZG-76. Fully loaded, the V1 weighed in at 2,150 kg (4,750 lb). The length was 7.90 m (25' 11"), the wingspan was 5.37 m (17' 7") and the height was 1.42 m (4' 8"). The V1's power plant was an Argus As14 pulse jet putting out 660 lb of thrust. The top speed of the V1 was 410 mph and it had an amatol warhead of 830 kg (1,832 lb).

Most of the 10,500 V1s that were fired at England up until 29 March 1945 were launched by ramps. Some 1,200 V1s were launched by specially converted Heinkel III twin-engined bombers after August 1944 when the launching sites were overrun. Almost 7,000 were considered as 'hits' as they landed in England with more than half of those landing in Greater London. The fighters, barrage balloons and anti-aircraft fire accounted for more than 3,000 V1s shot down or destroyed.

Originally the range of the V1 was 150 miles but as the launch sites were being overrun in France the range was extended to 250 miles so they could be launched from Holland. Almost 30,000 V1s were manufactured.

The first V1 that exploded on British soil did so in the early hours of 13 June 1944. It happened around 0400 hrs when a Royal Observer Corps member stationed in Kent saw the bright yellow flame coming from the back of a V1.

In his memoirs Field Marshal Lord Alanbrooke states:

Last night the Germans used their pilotless planes (V1s) for the first time, but did little damage. Cherwell and Duncan Sandys came to COS [Chief of Staff's] meeting where we discussed action to take and decided that we must not let defence interfere with the French battle!

The man in charge of the V1s was Lieutenant-General Erich Heinemann and he ordered Wachtel to get all the sites working right away. Owing to a combination of defensive measures, mechanical unreliability and guidance errors, only a quarter of all the V1s launched ever got through to their targets but it was enough.

As the Allies moved forward, pushing out of the beachhead, they captured and destroyed the main sites in France that were aimed at England. The Germans then switched their tactics, using the sites still available to them to attack strategic Allied points in the Low Countries such as the port of Antwerp.

The only real defences against these fast-moving flying bombs were RAF fighters, barrage balloons and anti-aircraft fire. Destroying the V1s had to be done outside of London lest the stricken V1s exploded on the ground, achieving what they had been sent to do.

The Hawker Tempest was the main fighter used to combat the V1. By September 1944 there were more than 100 of them involved in the war against the flying bomb. Other aircraft such as the Spitfire XIV with its massive Griffon engine and the Merlin-powered Mustang III had to have their engines boosted to make them fast enough to catch the V1s. From June 1944 the Tempests shared night-time defensive duties with Mosquitoes.

Other American aircraft such as the P47M were also pressed into service and were virtually stripped of any extraneous equipment. Their fuel tanks were cut in half, their firepower halved and all external fittings and armour plating were removed to enable them to catch up with the V1s.

Chasing V1s could often be very chaotic and unsuccessful. Things got better when a defensive zone was set up from London to the coast allowing only the fastest fighters to operate. Tempests had the highest score of V1s shot down, more than 638 between June and mid-August 1944, with the Spitfires accounting for 303 and the Mustangs 232. Even the much-heralded jet fighter the Gloster Meteor, which was rushed half-ready into service to combat the V1s, managed to shoot down thirteen. Even though it had the speed, the Meteor's guns often jammed.

Two electronic countermeasure aids for anti-aircraft guns also helped to stem the V1 tide. One was an automatic radar-based gun-laying device developed in the US and the other was the proximity fuse, which was also an American development. Once these were brought into service the kill-rate increased dramatically from one V1 brought down for every 2,500 shells fired to one for every 100 shells fired.

Despite these developments high-speed aircraft were still combating V1s, mainly launched from Heinkels, up until March 1945.

The major V1 offensive began on 15 June 1944 when 244 were launched on London, with seventy-three landing in the city and another seventy-one outside the city. But more than 100 didn't get across the Channel. Wachtel knew the V1 was not completely ready and the number of bombs that crashed on take-off or never made it to Britain is a testament to the way the Germans rushed it into production. Hitler himself went to northern France to congratulate Wachtel, ordering all V1s to be launched against London. On 17 June one V1 smashed into the Guards Chapel at Wellington barracks, killing 121 people and wounding another sixty-eight. By the end of the next day more than 500 had been launched in total.

> *The staff meeting with PM at 5 pm attended by Tedder, Hill (from Stanmore), Pile (from ADGB), 3 Chiefs of Staff. Again, very few real decisions were arrived at. In my mind it is pretty clear and 3 essentials stand out:*
>
> *(a) Attacks by what can be spared from Overlord on launching sites*
> *(b) Barriers of fighters, guns and balloons in succession south of London*
> *(c) No sirens and no guns in London*
>
> *We shall, I hope eventually get these, but it will take time.*
>
> Lord Alanbrooke, *War Diaries 1939–45*

Although 617 Squadron, flying the Avro Lancaster heavy four-engined bomber, attacked V1 sites with special 12,000-lb bombs, by 29 June more than 2,000 flying bombs had been launched at London.

Lord Alanbrooke again:

> *Up early to find that a pilotless plane had struck the Guards Chapel, Wellington Barracks during Sunday Service and had killed about*

60 people! Amongst them to my great grief Ivan Cobbold! And on my own writing table was a letter from him written Saturday, sending me on a wire from the Duke de la Luna who is fishing at Cairnton and asking me to lunch this week! It all gave me a very nasty turn, and I cannot get him and poor Blanche out of my mind.

As far as the fighters were concerned the standard form of attack was to dive on the V1s and open fire then turn and climb quickly away to avoid flying into the debris. Some pilots, however, developed the method of flying alongside the V1, sliding a wingtip under the wing of the V1, then just tipping it over, upsetting its internal gyros so the flying bomb was knocked off course.

While the Allies overran the land-based sites the *Luftwaffe* switched to firing the V1s from the Heinkels that would usually operate over the North Sea. The *Luftwaffe* also proposed a piloted version of the missile, which presumably would have been a one-way trip for the pilot. From July 1944 to January 1945 V1s were launched by airborne Heinkels and there was a proposal to use the Arado 234 jet bomber as a launching vehicle for V1s. This would have been either by towing the missiles or in a piggyback arrangement with the V1 on top of the aircraft. Fortunately, this was never used.

By 5 July 1944 more than 2,500 people had been killed. The Air Ministry in the Strand suffered a direct hit with 198 people dead. Roughly 5,500 people died in London and another 16,000 were injured as a result of the V1 attacks.

In his memoirs Field Marshal Lord Alanbrooke wrote about the excitement at the cabinet meeting in preparation for Churchill's speech on the V1. Churchill wanted reprisals on small towns in Germany as a deterrent but Alanbrooke was against it.

The Germans, fully realise that we are at present devoting nearly 50% of our air efforts in trying to stop these beastly bombs, added to which about 25% of London's production is lost through the results of these bombs! They won't throw away these advantages easily. I am afraid however that Winston's vindictive nature may induce him to try reprisals. I hope we shall succeed in stopping him.

Alanbrooke's final entry on 19 July on the V1 was a personal one.

A nasty disturbed night with about a dozen flying bombs in the vicinity. The nearest landed 150 yards away at about 0300 hrs. It displaced the window frame of our sitting room and blew a lot of glass out of the surrounding houses. I heard it coming, thought it was coming unpleasantly close, so slipped out of bed and took cover behind my bed on the floor to avoid glass splinters.

CHAPTER ONE

Preparing for the Storm

Before we get to the day-by-day accounts of the doodlebug war it is necessary to put those operations into context. Air Marshal Roderick Hill KCB, MC, AFC, ADC in his report 'Air Operations by Air Defence of Great Britain and Fighter Command in connection with the German Flying Bomb and Rocket Offensives, 1944–1945' outlined the state of Allied Air Forces in the period leading up to operations against the flying bomb, which coincided with the landings in Normandy by Allied Forces.

In his report, Sir Roderick Hill set out the details surrounding the battle of the flying bombs and it is this report we shall use as a base on which to build the day-to-day battles against the V1.

In the build-up to the D-Day landings in western Europe the Allied fighter, tactical reconnaissance and bomber forces in the UK were combined into one force under the command of Air Chief Marshal Sir Trafford Leigh-Mallory KCB, DSO called the Allied Expeditionary Air Force. Part of this force was set aside for the air defence of the UK under the command of Air Chief Marshal Sir Roderick Hill.

This new force was a successor to Fighter Command and was called the Air Defence of Great Britain (ADGB), coming into being on 15 November 1943 and lasting through until 14 October 1944 when the Allied Expeditionary Air Force ceased to exist and everything reverted back to Fighter Command. Sir Roderick Hill was Air Officer Commander-in-Chief ADGB and then for Fighter Command through to the end of the war.

He was responsible for the air defence of Great Britain and Northern Ireland while commanding Nos 9, 10, 11, 12, 13, 60 and 70

Groups, as well as having operational control of AA Command, the Royal Observer Corps, Balloon Command and any other elements of air defence formerly under the control of Fighter Command. One other key responsibility included the development of interception methods and apparatus for eventual use in the ADGB and other theatres.

Although some of the squadrons in ADGB would play a part in the D-Day landings the role of ADGB remained a defensive one. 'The Overall Air Plan issued by the Air Commander-In-Chief showed that my most significant responsibility even in that phase would be to stand guard over the bases,' Hill wrote in his report on the ADGB. The challenge he faced with limited resources was to ensure the UK was securely defended so it could be used as a base for the operations leading up to D-Day and afterwards.

In order to succeed with this task some reorganisation of the limited resources available to ADGB was needed. In Scotland, for example, No. 14 Group was amalgamated with No. 13 Group. By 6 June 1944 the number of fighter groups had been reduced to four and the number of active sectors from nineteen to fourteen, which was less than half of those in existence at the end of 1941. Sir Roderick's basic strength was fixed at ten day-fighter squadrons and eleven night-fighter squadrons. He also had another six night-fighter squadrons under his command from 85 Group, which were earmarked for the defence of the bases in Europe as the Allies moved out of their beachhead. Also earmarked for 85 Group were another six day-fighter squadrons, which were to be used to keep German aircraft from attacking the lodgement area in Normandy as well as performing other tasks as the need arose directly out of the operations in Europe. So, ADGB was responsible for the air defence of Great Britain, the lodgement area in Normandy and the waters in between.

In addition, Sir Roderick Hill also had fifteen more day-fighter squadrons that had been lent to the Second Tactical Air Force for the duration of the assault on Europe but which, in an emergency, would be used for the air defence of No. 11 Group in Kent. The total number of squadrons that ADGB could call upon for defending British skies was forty-eight, which was less than half the number considered necessary for air defence at the end of 1941 when the main theatre of war at that time was the Russian Front.

But much progress had been made in fighter interception, especially at night, since the Battle of Britain ended. 'The German Air Force was known to have lost a great deal of its hitting power since those days and its offensive spirit had declined,' Sir Roderick reported. Also, technical advances in methods and equipment on which the elements of air defence relied had been made since 1941. 'Against this I had to reckon with the psychological difficulty of maintaining the fighting spirit of men placed on the defensive while their opposite numbers were fighting an offensive battle.'

Despite this and the limited resources available to him Sir Roderick was confident it would be enough to roll back anything that the Germans could throw at them.

The Allies were expecting a German air offensive against the UK to begin on or around the D-Day landings according to Sir Roderick Hill and these attacks were likely to consist of orthodox aircraft as well as the secret weapons. More than likely these two types of attacks would occur simultaneously. That was the expectation and estimate by the Allies.

Although the Allies knew the numbers of the German bomber force, they didn't know how they would be used so they had to make some assumptions. The first of these assumptions was that the Germans would make minor daylight attacks along the south coast before D-Day and then on the beaches and anchorages afterwards. They also assumed that during the weeks preceding D-Day the Germans would make night-bombing attacks of up to fifty long-range bomber sorties a night for two or three nights a week, increasing to 150 sorties a night for short periods. The most probable targets for these attacks would be ports, troop and war materiel concentration areas on the south coast.

However, all of this was just theory but early in 1944 the Germans mounted several attacks on London and other cities, later known as the 'Baby Blitz'.[1] 'Thanks to the watch we were able to keep on its movements, these attacks did not take us by surprise,' Sir Roderick wrote in his report. 'The defences were ready.'

The Germans used their fastest bombers for this blitz and only stayed over England for very short periods. They suffered more casualties at the hands of the RAF during these raids than the Germans themselves were able to inflict upon Bomber Command's long night flights over Europe. Faced with the organised and technologically superior defences the German navigation, target marking and bombing proved to be poor indeed, making the attacks virtually useless.

Sir Roderick wrote:

After this experience, I felt confident that we should be able to deal with any attempt by the German bomber force to interfere with the concentration of the Anglo-American land, sea, and air forces in preparation for the assault.

Attacks by the German secret weapons were something else again. By the end of 1943 few doubted that the Germans were preparing novel and disturbing means of aerial attack. A mass of information collected over a long period of time pointed to a long-range rocket of some kind and a pilotless aircraft. In his report, Sir Roderick states that this conclusion made the Allies more sure that the secret weapons would be used when they obtained evidence of new constructions in northern France they called ski sites[2] that were meant for launching the V1.

Sir Roderick had two methods of defence against the V1s. The first was a defensive offensive against the sites where the missiles were made or stored, the launch sites and the communications between them such as roads or railways. This of course was provided that these sites could be found. The other method was to attack the bombs once they were airborne.

The Chiefs of Staff decided to concentrate on the first method of attack in early December 1943. The Second Tactical Air Force and the US Ninth Bomber Command began bombing raids on the 'ski sites' on 5 December 1943. Also, RAF Bomber Command and the American Eighth Bomber Command were involved in these attacks. By the end of that year some 3,216 tons of bombs had been dropped on these sites. This amount of explosive was approximately the weight that fell on London in an average fortnight during the Blitz of 1940–41.

The effect of the bombing as far as the Air Ministry was concerned was that only twelve sites had been destroyed and a further nine damaged.[3] But since the Allies had discovered eighty-eight sites in total by that time and suspected there was as many as fifty other sites, the neutralisation of all of them would be a long drawn-out affair lasting several months.

While these attacks were going on plans were being made by Sir Roderick and his staff officers to combat the problem of defending the country against pilotless aircraft. A document was given to Sir Roderick that outlined everything that was known at the time of the V1s. Sir Roderick wrote in his report:

According to this document, these missiles flew at something between 250 and 420 mph, at a height which might be anything from 500 to 7,000 feet. I was to assume that an attack by two missiles an hour from each of 100 sites might begin in February 1944.

The estimates provided to Sir Roderick were too broad to make detailed planning possible. On 20 December the Air Ministry replied to a questionnaire from Sir Roderick's staff saying that they believed the V1s would probably fly at an average speed of 400 mph and at a height of 7,500 feet. But these estimates were later reduced to 350 mph at 7,000 feet, then 330 mph at 6,000 feet. As the bombing of the 'ski sites' got under way the estimates as to when the flying bomb campaign would start were also revised by the Chiefs of Staff.

Although Sir Roderick states in his report that he and his staff worked very closely with the head of Anti-Aircraft Command General Sir Frederick A Pile GCB, DSO, MC and his staff we shall see in later chapters that this close relationship was not quite as close as Sir Roderick wrote in his report. Pile was General Officer Commanding, Anti-Aircraft Command and as Sir Roderick wrote 'helped in the preparation of all detailed plans which involved guns and searchlights as well as fighters'.

So as the plans were being prepared and the bombing campaign against the 'ski sites' got under way it became clear to Sir Roderick that to provide the Chiefs of Staff and the Air Ministry with a detailed plan of the defence against the flying bombs would take several weeks. Instead, he submitted an outline plan that had as its fundamental premise that a pilotless aircraft was still an aircraft and would be vulnerable to the same basic methods of attack. Sir Roderick wrote:

As there was no crew such an aircraft could not be made to crash by killing the pilot. It would be incapable of retreat or evasion. Never-theless if the missile should prove in practice as fast as was believed

at first, the performance of the fighters on which we normally relied
would be inadequate.

The problem was that their information was incomplete so it
would make no sense that any of the normal methods of defence
used against ordinary aircraft be excluded when attacking the
flying bombs.

While the bombing campaign against the 'ski sites' was
achieving some results, Sir Roderick was completing his plan
along with General Pile and on 2 January 1944 presented the plan
to Sir Trafford Leigh-Mallory, the Air Commander-in-Chief, who
approved it and passed it onto higher authority. The good results
being achieved by the bombing offensive meant that the likelihood
of imminent attack by the Germans was receding. Twenty days
later the Chiefs of Staff decided that the date for being ready
for attacks by the flying bombs could be put back until March.
Operations for the landings in Europe began in April 1944 and
they were faced with the possibility that the German flying bomb
campaign might start while these preparations were going on or
even while the landings were taking place.

Early in February the Chiefs of Staff asked Sir Roderick to
come up with a plan that simultaneously provided for defence
against the flying bombs and the needs for offensive operations.
Sir Roderick and General Pile then overhauled their plan to ensure
that it would meet the needs of defending Britain against the V1
using resources not directly required for the European operations.
This modified plan was named the *Overlord/Diver* plan, which was
approved, and on 4 March 1944 Sir Roderick Hill had copies of the
plan sent to the Commands and the Groups that would be directly
involved in the battle.

It was also the plan that was used when the attacks began some
three months later. Regarding this new plan, Sir Roderick stated that:

A Commander must not only take into account a number of factors,
political as well as military and logistic, which are governed by the
capabilities of his own side, he must also reckon, first and last and all
the time, with what the enemy may have up his sleeve.

The bombing offensive of the 'ski sites' was achieving its
objectives by March 1944. Although the Air Ministry revised its

estimate of the scale of the enemy attack of flying bombs, the broad concepts that built the defensive measures adopted by the British remained basically unchanged.

Both plans had a lot in common, including the ability of the radar station chains to pick up the flying bomb in the same way they would detect ordinary aircraft. Sir Roderick believed that the radar stations would be able to differentiate between pilotless aircraft and conventional aircraft piloted by a man. Their flight behaviour could be tracked and should prove to be different as flying bombs would not take evasive action as a piloted aircraft would. There was also the Royal Observer Corps who would have been able to recognise the flying bombs and the noise they made.

From the first, the principal objective of both the outline plan of December and the *Overlord/Diver* plan was the defence of London as most of the 'ski sites' were aimed at the capital. However, they also had to plan for the defence of Bristol as some of the sites near Cherbourg were aimed at that city, while there was also the possibility that the Germans would aim some of the flying bombs at the southern ports where preparations for D-Day were taking place.

Sir Roderick planned fighters to be the first line of defence. For the defence of London during a daylight attack both plans saw the fighters of No. 11 Group patrolling at 12,000 feet along three patrol lines, 20 miles off the coast between Beachy Head and Dover, over the coastline between Newhaven and Dover and between Haywards Heath and Dover. Once the flying bomb attack began additional fighters would patrol along these lines at 6,000 feet while at night the fighters would patrol under the control of radar stations as well as under Sector Control.

For Bristol and the area around the Solent the fighters would be scrambled as per normal rather than mount standing patrols.

Guns and searchlights were planned to provide the second line of defence and the first line of the defence if the fighters were prevented from flying due to poor weather or any other factors.

Sir Roderick reported that:

For London General Pile and I proposed under the first plan to deploy 400 heavy A.A. guns in the folds and hollows on the southern slopes of the North Down where their radar equipment would be liable to the minimum of interference from 'jamming' by the enemy.

Another 346 guns were proposed for use on searchlight sites while 216 searchlights were to be used as well. For Bristol they planned ninety-six heavy AA guns and 216 light AA guns with 132 searchlights, while thirty-two heavy guns, 242 light guns and searchlights were to defend the Solent area.

The reason for presenting these two plans here is to illustrate how little real concrete evidence existed for the British. They were, to be blunt, groping in the dark because their intelligence was limited. They knew there would have to be risks as Sir Roderick stated.

Some risks would be involved in removing guns from places like Oxford, Birmingham and the Clyde to defend London, Bristol and the Solent against flying bombs. But the risk was one that I felt we should be justified in taking, since otherwise there was no possibility of finding the resources required for adequate defence against the threat from pilotless aircraft as we conceived it in December.

In February when they were drawing up the revised plan for defence against the flying bombs, the bombing missions on the 'ski sites' were successful, which gave Sir Roderick and General Pile the hope that they could reduce the number of guns and searchlights needed. The thinking was that so many of the 'ski sites' had been destroyed or put out of action that the Germans would not be able to mount a heavy attack. So they proposed that the number of heavy AA guns deployed in each of the sites in the belt defending London be reduced from eight to four, saving 208 guns. They also hoped that by the time the attack began the new American 90-mm guns with the SCR 584 radar would be available to replace the existing 3.7-inch guns with the GL Mark III radar. However, by the eve of the attacks the American guns had not yet arrived and the crews would have to be trained on them before they could be thrown into the fray.

Their revised plan also proposed reducing the number of light AA guns in front of London from 346 to 246. Other savings on the number of guns were also proposed. The reason for these reductions was to provide as much AA fire as possible for the preparations for *Overlord* against conventional enemy aircraft attack.

Should the V1s get past the fighters and the AA guns the third line of defence was the balloons and the plan envisaged a barrage of 480 balloons from Cobbam in Kent to Limpsfield in the west. As no balloons were needed for *Overlord* there was no need for a reduction in the number of balloons.

Armed with the revised plan they then waited for the German attack to begin. The plan was not a compromise as such as the defence of England was essential for the *Overlord* preparations. The number of guns to be deployed was no more than the bare minimum based on their knowledge and estimate of the German attack in the spring of 1944. 'I took the precaution of pointing out that if the pilotless aircraft should fly between 2,000 to 3,000 feet,' Sir Roderick stated in his report, 'the guns would have a very awkward task.'

When the attack started they soon found out that their estimates had been wrong. This was largely because the height at which the V1s flew had been substantially overestimated and the enemy's capabilities of launching the flying bombs had been under-estimated. When the attack came they realised they would need more guns than the revised plan called for and more guns than the original plan called for.[4]

There was one factor that the Allies had not counted on. Ironically, the success of the bombing raids against the 'ski sites' had forced the Germans to build new, less obvious launching sites that were hard to find, simpler in construction and con-cealed. These sites were dubbed 'modified' sites and the Germans began their building campaign in March 1944. By that time, the Air Ministry believed that only ten of the 'ski sites' remained operational.

The new sites were built out of prefabricated parts with very few buildings attached to the sites, enabling the Germans to complete these sites very quickly.[5] 'Unlike the "ski sites" they seemed to be intended as launching sites and nothing more,' Sir Roderick reported.

On 27 April 1944 the first of these new sites appeared on reconnaissance photographs. By the middle of May the Allies had located twenty sites and by 12 June they had located a total of sixty-six sites, forty-five of which were aimed at London. The rest were aimed at Bristol and the south-coast ports.

Bombing the new sites was also difficult. A Typhoon raid on 27 May proved to be almost useless as the site was difficult to see and the results were poor. Sir Roderick wrote:

> *The conclusion was that any stocks of pilotless aircraft held locally would not be kept on the sites themselves but would be stored elsewhere or dispersed in the wooded country amongst which all the sites were placed.*

No further bombing attacks were made on the new sites until the Germans starting launching the flying bombs from them. From May onwards very little was done to stop the Germans making their preparations. There were reasons for this. The first was that the new sites made very poor targets but one factor, according to Sir Roderick, was the success of the bombing campaign against the 'ski sites'. As these sites had been virtually neutralised the feeling was that the menace had been averted, at least for the time being, as Sir Roderick stated:

> *The threat from the new sites was underestimated, not in the sense of a failure to apprehend it intellectually, but in the sense that it was not felt as keenly as the original threat from the 'ski sites' had been six months earlier.*

Had the Allies understood the significance of the new sites they probably would have mounted the same vigorous bombing campaign as they had on the 'ski sites'. But they didn't. In fact, the Germans were left to carry on with their building programme unmolested by Allied bombers.

Looking back on events it is easy to see that the decision not to mount campaigns against the new sites was misguided and possibly wrong. But the decision was based on the knowledge they had at the time, on the fact that every available bomber and fighter was needed for the coming operations in Europe, that the destruction of the 'ski sites' had averted an imminent attack and that the new sites were difficult targets to hit. In fact, thirty-six hours before the first V1 was launched the existing intelligence suggested the new sites would not be ready for several weeks.

One of Sir Roderick's other responsibilities was to prevent enemy reconnaissance aircraft from getting to the area in the southern ports where the Allies were concentrating for D-Day. This responsibility was carried out so well that when the landings took place on 6 June 1944 they achieved complete tactical surprise according to Sir Roderick. 'Even on subsequent days when the Germans had time to appreciate what we were doing the air opposition was far from energetic.'

While the Air Commander-in-Chief and his staff were jubilant about the lack of enemy air response to the landings in Normandy, Sir Roderick and his staff were not so optimistic. 'So much was at stake for the enemy that we dared not believe he would let us have our own way,' Sir Roderick wrote. 'We could not help suspecting he still had something up his sleeve.'

CHAPTER TWO

Engagement

Indeed, the Germans did have something up their sleeves. On the night of 12/13 June 1944 shortly after midnight German long-range guns opened up and sent shells across the Channel. Eight fell on Maidstone, one at Otham and twenty-four at Folkestone. The effect of this bombardment was the belief for some people that the Germans were using some sort of new weapon that would create an atmosphere of uncertainty and rumour.[6]

On the same night an Me 410 flew over London and was shot down by AA fire near Barking.

Then at 0400 hrs the shelling stopped. A few minutes later an observer of the Royal Observer Corps (ROC) in Kent spotted an aircraft passing overhead that made a 'swishing sound' and had a bright glow coming from the rear. The ROC had been trained to recognise the flying bomb and so following his training he shouted 'Diver'[7] as the flying bomb shot by, heading over the North Downs until its engine cut out and it crashed exploding on the ground at Swanscombe near Gravesend at 0418 hrs. The observer said the flying bomb made a sound similar to a model T Ford going up a hill.

In the next few hours three more flying bombs came over and crashed at Cuckfield, Bethnal Green and Sevenoaks. In this first wave of attacks, six people were killed at Bethnal Green and nine injured.

Then the attack stopped, leading Sir Roderick Hill to conclude that such a small effort didn't justify the major redeployment of anti-aircraft defences as his revised plan stated. He therefore ordered that the plan should not be put into place until they knew what was going to happen. The V1s were to be engaged in the same way as ordinary aircraft with the existing defences in place. At the same, time several bombing raids on the supply sites for the new modified launching sites took place on 13, 14 and 15 June.

Despite these bombing raids the flying bomb attack began in earnest on the evening of 15 June and over the next twenty-four hours 200 flying bombs were launched against the south of England. '144 crossed the coasts of Kent and Sussex,' Sir Roderick wrote. '73 reached Greater London.'

The following morning a very different situation from 13 June stared the authorities in the face. Sir Roderick now felt that the revised *Diver* plan should be implemented as quickly as possible and this was agreed by the Chiefs of Staff. At a staff conference that afternoon attended by the Prime Minister and Minister of Defence the decision to redeploy the gun, searchlight and balloon defences to counter the attacks was taken. Also, it was decided that the guns inside and outside the London defensive area should continue to engage the flying bombs.

Sir Roderick gave the order for the *Diver* plan to be implemented that day and in the early hours of 17 June the first of the AA regiments began to move. Originally, the plan called for deployment of all the defences to take twenty-five days and the Air Ministry had expected to provide a month's warning. 'In the event we received no warning at all,' Sir Roderick wrote. 'Apart from that provided by the Germans themselves on the 13th of June.' The original timetable was thrown out and the deployment took only five days after the order had been given.

All the while the flying bombs were coming over at rate of about 100 per day. The fighters were destroying 30 per cent of that number while the rest of the defences were destroying another 8 to 10 per cent, but more than half were getting through to London. The scale of the attack showed that the static defences of guns, searchlights and balloons needed reinforcing. By 28 June 363 heavy guns and 522 light guns were in action with further light guns from the Royal Air Force Regiment, anti-aircraft tanks from the Royal Armoured Corps and rocket projectors in action against the doodlebugs.

Fighters of No. 11 Group (the Tempest V, Spitfire XIV, Spitfire XII, Spitfire IX and Mosquito night fighters) had been in action since the main attack began. On 16 June Sir Roderick defined their area of engagement as patrolling the Channel and the land between the coast and the southern limit of the gun belt. He prohibited them from passing over the gun belt unless they were actually chasing a V1. In good weather, the fighters were much more successful than the guns because they were hampered by the fact that the V1s were not flying at 6,000 to 7,000 feet as the Air Ministry had previously estimated but between 1,500 to 3,000 feet, making it much more difficult for the gunners to shoot them down.[8]

During bad weather, the guns became the first line of defence and the most effective way of bringing down the V1s. Also, in good weather the guns were to remain silent to give the fighters complete freedom of the air, whereas when the weather was bad the reverse took place, the guns had complete freedom of action and the fighters remained on the ground. When the weather allowed both guns and fighters to operate then the fighters operated in front of the gun belt and only flew into the gun belt when chasing a V1, otherwise the guns inside the gun belt could fire with impunity up to 8,000 feet. However, the light AA guns linked into the communications network were instructed to open fire on targets they could see provided no fighters were in the vicinity.

Sir Roderick drew up these rules of engagement to ensure that there was no interference between the fighters and the guns. He issued these rules of engagement on 26 June 1944 but they did not entirely achieve his aim.

The Allied air forces responsible for offensive countermeasures against the flying bomb began a series of bombing raids on the new launching sites in the first two weeks of the attacks and these raids destroyed several. But they did not reduce the scale of the flying bomb attacks on England. Sir Roderick wrote:

> *The factor limiting the German effort was not the number of sites available, but something else – most probably the rate at which the flying bombs could be supplied to the launching sites.*

The efforts of the strategic and tactical air forces against the flying bomb launching sites were seen as harassing the launch crews to lower their efficiency. 'It was arguable that the attacks on the "modified sites" amounted to locking the stable door after the horse had been stolen and were a waste of effort,' Sir Roderick wrote. After the war was over the Germans admitted that the bombing of the new launching sites made no difference to them at all.[9]

Intelligence reports showed that the key supply sites for the flying bombs were likely to be underground storage depots in the limestone quarries of the Oise valley as well as an abandoned railway tunnel in Champagne. These sites were duly pounded by bombs and fighter-bombers, which resulted in a noticeable decrease in the number of flying bomb attacks.

The Germans found alternative channels of supply and the scale of the flying bomb attacks increased. It became obvious to Sir Roderick and his staff that the efforts of the Allied air forces would not be able to stop the flying bombs completely. The land forces in France by the end of June had not yet broken out and were still in the lodgement areas, which meant that the capture of the launching sites was not around the corner. 'The preservation of thousands of lives, much valuable property and productive capacity would turn on our ability to provide an effective defence for London,' Sir Roderick wrote.

Up until the end of the first week in July roughly 100 flying bombs a day were still coming over. This number dropped to around seventy a day for the next ten days. This was partly due to a period of very good weather. The Germans saved their biggest efforts for days when the weather was so bad that effective fighter defences could not be mounted. But, it may also have been due to a successful night attack on the main storage depot on 7 July by Bomber Command.

During the five-week period that ended on 15 July 1944 almost 3,000 V1s came within the defences and a tenth of those were shot down into the sea by fighters, with the guns knocking down a few more into the sea as well. Of the remaining 2,500 or so that crossed the coast, fighters, guns and balloons accounted for roughly half over land, with the fighters claiming ten and the guns four for every one the balloons destroyed.

However, the overall average since the attacks began up until the 15 July was forty bombs a day getting through to London alone. 'London had endured heavier bombing than this in 1940,' Sir Roderick stated. 'But for various reasons an intermittent drizzle of malignant robots seemed harder to bear than the storm and thunder of the "Blitz".'

Between 13 June and 15 July 1944 3,000 people had been killed, more than 10,000 seriously injured and 13,000 homes irreparably damaged.

Since the beginning of the attacks the performance of the defences had steadily increased. In the first two weeks of July the fighters had performed particularly well but Sir Roderick believed they had reached the zenith of their performance with the existing methods. He believed that unless changes were made the performance of the defences would steadily decline.

To get a more intimate knowledge of the special problems of the arms involved he decided early on to share in the fighter operations as a pilot and used various aircraft to do it. His personal experience convinced him that the first problem the fighter pilots faced was the speed of the V1. Sir Roderick stated:

Most of the bombs seem to have left the launching site at about 200 mph. Their speed increased throughout their flight, reaching about 340 mph at the English coast and 400 mph or thereabouts over London.

The fastest aircraft Sir Roderick had at his disposal early in the attacks were a wing of Tempests and a wing of Spitfire XIVs. But as they couldn't be everywhere at once he borrowed a wing of Mustang IIIs from the Second Tactical Air Force. These proved to be 'very fast at the height at which the bombs flew and made a valuable contribution to the improved results achieved by the fighters after the first week in July'.

By 15 July, Sir Roderick had a total of thirteen single-engine fighter squadrons and nine Mosquito squadrons flying against the flying bombs. Six of those squadrons did other work, alternating between flying bomb duties and operations over the beachhead in Normandy.

To get as much speed as possible from the fighters used exclusively against the V1s ground crews were ordered to strip all their armour and all unnecessary external fittings, remove their paint and polish their external surfaces. The engines were also modified so they could use 150-octane fuel with a higher than usual boost. These changes managed to provide an extra 30 mph in speed for most of the fighters.

But they only had a small advantage of speed over the flying bomb according to Sir Roderick Hill. He states in his report that:

... they did have a margin. Even so it was no more than a fractional superiority hence the problem was essentially one of time and space.

For interceptions over the sea we used a method of close control from radar stations on the coast, or alternatively a method of running commentary. At best the radar chain could give about six minutes warning before the flying bomb reached the coast; but in practice the time available to [the] fighter was always less than this.

The reason was that the modified fighters could not be used closer to the French coast where they could be intercepted by German fighters. Their lack of armour would have meant greater risks for the pilots and increased losses for the RAF.

The Royal Navy came to the RAF's assistance by providing a chain of small craft sailing 3 miles apart from each other 7 miles from the French coast, each with observers on board. Pilots would be warned of flying bombs on their way by the observers firing off star shells or signal rockets. However, this system was not fully in place until the main attack ended.

Running commentary from radar stations and Royal Observer Corps Centres was used for interception over land with various devices such as signal rockets, searchlight beams and star shells to warn the patrolling pilots of approaching flying bombs. This system, however, had a weakness, which was that several pilots would go after the same flying bomb, as we shall see later in the book, leaving other bombs to slip through unmolested. The absence of low-looking radar over land at that time made close control very difficult.

The line from Cuckmere Haven and St Margaret's Bay was the area where most of the flying bombs crossed in from the Channel. The distance from the coast to the gun belt was about 30 miles, which the flying bombs crossed in five minutes. Pilots patrolling over land then had five minutes to select their targets, get in range and shoot them down before entering the gun belt. Even if pilots did enter the gun belt in pursuit of a flying bomb they only had an extra minute or so before the V1 would reach the balloon barrage and the pilot would then have to break off the chase.

Sir Roderick wrote:

There was rarely time for a stern chase unless the pursuer started with a substantial advantage in height. The most effective method was to fly on roughly the same course as an approaching bomb, allow it to draw level, and fire deflection shots as it passed, being careful not to fire when it was closer than 200 yards lest it should explode in the air and blow up the attacker.[10]

For a fighter flying directly behind a flying bomb the hot gasses pouring from the V1's jet engine made steady aim difficult so according to Sir Roderick short bursts and frequent course and aiming corrections were necessary. Several bursts were usually required to inflict enough damage to explode the bomb in the air or send it crashing down into the sea or into the ground.

If the fighters had a difficult task in destroying the flying bombs so did the guns. In theory, robot aircraft should have made ideal targets for the anti-aircraft guns as they flew on a predictable course and could not dodge and weave as ordinary enemy aircraft would. This advantage, however, was outweighed by the speed and height at which the flying bombs flew. They were too fast and too high to make good targets for the light AA guns and for the heavy AA guns they were too low and crossed the field of vision too quickly for the radar to be used.

By replacing the heavy mobile guns with static guns that could be electrically elevated and traversed these problems were minimised but the static guns needed concrete emplacements, which took time to install. A steel mattress, used instead of the concrete emplacements, was found to be a much quicker solution and the task of replacing the mobile guns with static guns mounted on these steel mattresses began at the end of June 1944.[11]

General Pile decided to move the radar sets from the valleys, where they had been originally placed because of the worry about jamming by the enemy, to more exposed higher ground where the contours of the land caused less interference. Successive bombing campaigns had, according to Sir Roderick Hill, deprived the Germans of the ability to jam the radar sets of the heavy guns so moving them to higher exposed ground proved less of a risk.

Also, General Pile decided to move the light AA guns from the searchlight sites to concentrate them in front of the heavy gun belt. By linking the lighter guns to the radar sets of the heavy guns they could fire at unseen targets as well as visual targets.

Also, the American SCR 584 radar sets and predictors began arriving towards the end of June, which contributed heavily towards the success of the anti-aircraft guns. A vigorous training programme was set up before this new equipment could be put into action.

As far as the balloon barrage was concerned sufficient density was needed for successful operations against flying bombs, but despite this bombs were still slipping through.

The double parachute links[12] used to arm the cables in normal balloon barrages had not been designed to cope with aircraft travelling faster than 300 mph. During the first few days of the attack the cables weren't armed but by 21 June all the cables had been armed.

To prevent V1s from getting caught in the barrage and going down in built-up areas the barrage itself was slightly adjusted. At the same time the decision to keep the balloons up all the time no matter what the weather was dropped. However, Sir Roderick states in his report that 'in order that our pilots should not lose their lives by colliding with the barrage we perpetrated a pious fraud on them by allowing them to believe the balloons would fly continuously.'

We have seen the practical problems facing the various arms of defence during the battle of the flying bombs but the biggest problem of all facing Sir Roderick and his staff was the degree of co-operation between the guns and the fighters. Against ordinary aircraft a working solution had been found between the two rival arms. But against the flying bomb a host of new difficulties presented themselves. 'It was sometimes hard for a pilot to realise he was approaching the gun belt in time to avoid infringing the rule against entering it,' Sir Roderick wrote. At the same time, the gunners could be blasting away at a flying bomb without realising that a fighter had legitimately entered the gun belt in pursuit of the same flying bomb. The guns would go on firing.

The gun crews on the coast had an even more difficult task because they bore the onus of ensuring that there were no fighters around before they opened fire. 'When the attention of the gunners was concentrated on their targets,' Sir Roderick wrote, 'it was only too easy for a fighter travelling at six miles a minute to enter the field of fire.'

On several occasions the fighters infringed the gun belt and there were many unintentional engagements by the anti-aircraft guns on the fighters, especially in middling weather when both guns and fighters were operating. 'Charges and counter-charges mounted,' Sir Roderick stated. 'I began to sense a rising feeling of deep mistrust between the pilots and the gunners.'

If things didn't change the situation would get worse. Sir Roderick continued:

> To all appearances the machine was growing more efficient. But this improvement brought me scanty satisfaction. I knew the point would soon be reached at which this friction would become the limiting factor and no further improvement would be possible.

Losing the spirit of co-operation between gun crews and pilots that had been built up over the years could only lead to the efficiency of the defences sharply declining.

Sir Roderick's solution to the problem was to give the fighters and the AA guns the freedom to work within their own spheres of operation. On 10 July he gave the order for the fighters not to enter the gun belt under any circumstances after 17 July. All the guns were then to be moved inside the belt so they could also operate within their own area of operation, creating a clear-cut situation. Giving the gunners a free hand in their own territory also meant that when they were not in action they could be training but the change reduced the area of operation for the fighters.

Sir Roderick wrote:

> To make this sacrifice clear to the pilots I instructed my Deputy Senior Air Staff Officer, Air Commodore G.H. Ambler, C.B.E., A.F.C. to prepare an explanation to be circulated to lower formations. At this stage no question of changing the geographical position of the gun belt had been raised.

But as we shall see in subsequent chapters there were strong arguments for moving the gun belt, principally put forward by Air Commodore Ambler. In the February *Diver* plan the guns had been placed in the North Downs to avoid the jamming of their radar by the Germans, which at that time was a very real threat. However, once the landings in Normandy took place successful bombing of enemy radar and radio stations had removed the jamming threat altogether.

With the jamming threat gone there was, by the middle of July, no need for the guns and their radar to be hidden in the Downs if they could be moved to a much better position. The idea was to move all the guns to the coast. This had some definite advantages. To start with the gunners could see their targets better and the effect of ground echoes on their radar was reduced to a minimum. But perhaps, most importantly, they could now use proximity fuses on their shells that they could not have used inland because of the danger to civilian life and property. Also, the majority of the bombs the guns brought down, if they were on the coast, would now fall harmlessly into the sea.

The disadvantage of moving the guns to the coast was that there would now be three operational areas, one for the guns and two for the fighters – in front of the coastal gun belt and behind it. This would also limit the effectiveness of the fighters. The move to the coast made the guns much more effective and the fighters less so.

Sir Roderick wrote:

Up till then the fighters had been by far the most successful weapon against flying bombs. Out of 1,192 bombs which had been destroyed or brought down up to sunrise of the 13th July, they had accounted for 883. No move which was to impair their effectiveness was to be undertaken lightly.

Interception over sea and interception over land had different sets of procedures and difficulties so the problem of having three different spheres of operation was not as bad as they first thought.

Air Commodore Ambler took on board the need for the guns to be put into one place but not on the Downs. On the morning of 13 July Ambler presented Sir Roderick with a formal paper detailing the advantages of moving the guns to the coast. He convinced Sir Roderick that the tactical theory behind the redeployment was sound. Sir Roderick knew a decision of either accepting the proposal or rejecting it had to be made that day. He called for a conference late that afternoon but spent the morning mulling over the proposal.

At the conference, the plan for moving the guns to the coast was endorsed by everyone present and adopted.

Sir Roderick took the responsibility of the success or failure of the scheme on his own shoulders and immediately gave instructions for the preparations of moving the guns to the coast to begin right away. 'During the following week vehicles of Anti-Aircraft Command travelled an aggregate distance of two-and-three quarter million miles in consequence of this decision,' he wrote. Ammunition and stores, weighing as much as two battleships, the guns themselves and 23,000 men and women were moved to the coast and enough telephone cable was laid that would stretch from London to New York.

By dawn of 17 July the heavy guns were in action and two days later so were the light guns.

Sir Roderick was fully aware of the risks he was taking and the detrimental effect the move would have on the effectiveness of the fighters. If things went wrong and the performance of the guns didn't improve he alone would be responsible for that disaster. The Air Ministry were not pleased.

They informed him formally a few days later that he should not have ordered a major re-deployment of the guns without consultation and approval from them.

However, within a few weeks Sir Roderick was vindicated as the number of flying bombs shot down by the guns dramatically increased. This increase showed how sound the decision had been that had come after Air Commodore Ambler's proposal. The Air Ministry sent a letter of congratulations to Sir Roderick's command at the close of the main attack.

CHAPTER THREE

Fighter Command (17 July to 1 September)

At dawn on 17 July the new system came into being. For the next six days 473 bombs came within the area of the defences but only 204 reached London. However, these figures were lower than the number destroyed during the last week of the old system. As critics predicted, the improved results from the guns and the denser balloon barrage did not outweigh the decline in the numbers of flying bombs destroyed by the fighters.

The improvement of the guns was encouraging and the decline of the performance of the fighters was what Sir Roderick had expected.

Between the sunset of 20 July to the sunset of 21 July all the services destroyed sixty bombs, with the gunners destroying twenty-three alone, the fighters only nineteen. It was now time to ensure that all the services were thoroughly familiar with the new system and all its nuances. Sir Roderick felt that it was his responsibility to do this.

One of his chief concerns now was the declining morale of the fighter pilots who had been curtailed by having their area of operations split in two.

He decided to set up the Sector Headquarters at Biggin Hill as a co-ordinating centre for the new *Diver* system where all the services would co-ordinate together to provide the maximum coverage. But the practical hour-to-hour supervision of operations left the staff here with little time to do anything else. Sir Roderick reported:

It seemed to me that the study and dissemination of tactical doctrine and the promotion of disciplined enthusiasm amongst pilots faced with a novel weapon ought to proceed from a rather higher level than that of a Sector Headquarters.

The solution was to give the Station and Squadron Commanders a direct lead to deal with the flying bombs. A pilot himself, Sir Roderick entered the fight against the flying bomb, flying several different types of aircraft as he gathered his information.

Sir Roderick claimed:

Trying to shoot down a missile travelling at six miles a minute while flying at the same speed and a height of a thousand feet across a narrow belt of undulating country bounded by balloons and guns was a business whose subtleties were not really appreciable from an office chair. I found that practical experience had its uses and it helped me to acquire a fund of tactical knowledge that I could hardly have gained any other way; above all it enabled me to talk on a basis of common understanding and endeavour with the pilots whose devotion it was my task to foster.

One advantage of getting rid of the inland gun belt was that it gave the searchlights more scope to assist the night fighters. Though the guns had been moved to the coast, the searchlights remained inland. By moving the guns to the coast, the headquarters of the AA batteries were brought much closer to the bases from which the fighters were operating. This meant that contact between battery commanders and station commanders would now be easy but when Sir Roderick visited the stations he saw that no advantage had been taken of this opportunity.

At the fighter stations Sir Roderick was shown fragments of shell casing, which the pilots claimed had come from the guns firing on them. On Sir Roderick's suggestion the RAF station commanders took the shell fragments round to the battery commanders to talk over their grievances and work out a working solution.

The mists of suspicion began to clear. When Sir Roderick went back to the same stations after the visits had taken place he was shown again aircraft that had suffered damage from the anti-aircraft guns but this time the reason was largely because the pilots had disobeyed the rules and flown too close to the guns. In the main, the pilots and gunners were beginning to work together and certainly beginning to understand each other's problems.

Sir Roderick wrote in his report of a particular sortie that he felt exemplified this new-found close co-operation.

Flying towards the south coast on the 28th of August, I could see over Romney Marsh a wall of black smoke marking the position of the Diver barrage. From time to time a fresh barrage would be added to repair the slow erosion of the wind.

On the far side of the barrage fighters were shooting down flying bombs into the Channel. On the nearer side more fighters waited on its fringe to pounce on the occasional bomb that got so far. The whole was as fine a spectacle of co-operation as any commander could wish for.

Two weeks after the redeployment of the guns the defences were destroying a much higher proportion of the flying bombs than those getting through. Indeed, during a week of bad weather that hampered the effectiveness of the fighters, the guns continued to bring down flying bombs and for the first time exceeded the rate at which the fighters destroyed them.

By the middle of August the overall performance of the defensive system was surpassing all previous achievements, especially so with the guns. Whatever the weather, the defences could confidently destroy one half to three quarters of all the flying bombs heading for Britain. 'Indeed, it has been calculated that during the last three weeks of this phase only one out of every seven bombs that the enemy launched actually reached London,' Sir Roderick wrote.

So effective were the defences that by the last few days of August only an occasional bomb got past them. Sir Roderick wrote:

It is fair to claim that almost complete ascendancy over this novel and ingenious weapon had been gained when, at the beginning of September, the capture of the launching areas by our Armies ended the main attack.

CHAPTER FOUR

Overview from SHAEF

The flying bomb menace opened up in real earnest on the night of the 15 June,' wrote Air Marshal Sir Arthur Tedder in his memoirs. At the time of the doodlebug menace he was Deputy Supreme Commander under Eisenhower. 'The enemy had chosen his moment well for the main sites in the Pas de Calais were covered with cloud.'

Operation *Crossbow* was the code name for the Allies' response to the V1 flying bomb menace. Specifically, it was the name for the destruction of the V1 launching sites and the air defence of Great Britain.

On the evening of 16 June Tedder attended a meeting called by Churchill to discuss Operation *Crossbow*. Churchill, according to Tedder, would not allow the threats from the flying bombs and the intelligence reports regarding the V1 to hamper the battle in Normandy. But that attitude didn't last long and by the morning of the 18 June Eisenhower himself had decreed that the flying bombs must be the Air Force's top priority. In a directive to Tedder, Eisenhower stated 'these targets must take priority over everything except the urgent requirements of the battle.'

But as the fighting in Normandy continued, the officers at Supreme Headquarters Allied Expeditionary Forces (SHAEF) struggled with the conflicting demands of fighting in Normandy, fighting in other theatres such as Africa, Italy and the war in the Far East. What were the priorities – the oil targets, the *Crossbow* sites, or the extermination of the *Luftwaffe*? Air Marshal Arthur Harris, head of Bomber Command, and General Spaatz, Commander of the US Air Forces in Europe, had no problems carrying out their duties and orders from those higher up such as Eisenhower and

Tedder, but they both longed for the kind of operations that would secure a quick victory. Indeed, Spaatz urged Eisenhower to make a policy decision that whenever the weather permitted the Allies should concentrate on the operations needed to wipe out the German Army's ability to wage war. In his memorandum to the Supreme Commander Spaatz suggested that the main objective must also be to neutralise the *Luftwaffe* and that these kinds of operations should take priority over all others.

Eisenhower, according to Tedder, disagreed. Tedder wrote:

> The 'Crossbow' sites must remain our first priority. When the entire strategic forces could not be used against 'Crossbow' we should attack the aircraft industry, oil and the production of ball bearings and vehicles.

But all targets had to give way to the needs of the land battle when the use of strategic air power was needed.

Tedder thought that air power could reduce but not eliminate the threat from the flying bombs. At the time when Churchill was considering reprisals against the Germans, Tedder strongly advised against it. The idea was that if the attacks from the flying bombs continued, a public announcement would be made that selected German towns would be targeted and wiped out. Tedder wrote:

> It would be a mistake to enter into negotiations with the enemy, for such a course would provide the Germans with invaluable proof that the flying bombs were achieving success and that their decision to start the attacks had been right.

By July nearly 40 per cent of the bomber force had been diverted to attacking *Crossbow* targets. On 5 July 1944 the Chiefs of Staff rejected out of hand a proposal to use gas on *Crossbow* installations, along with rejecting the bombing of small towns as reprisals. Eisenhower himself rejected the idea of reprisals and told Tedder to continue to oppose them in meetings with Churchill and the Chiefs of Staff. Air Chief Marshal Sir Charles Portal, Chief of the Air Staff, indicated to Tedder that the Air Ministry was under heavy pressure about the percentage of the bomber effort being used against *Crossbow* targets.

By 6 August Tedder wrote that there had been no change in the priority allotted to *Crossbow* targets. However, the fact that more bomber effort had not been allocated to *Crossbow* was down mostly to poor weather, which had only provided fleeting opportunities and a lack of targets. Tedder wrote:

> *As our Intelligence improved, I hoped we should be able to evolve a more satisfactory target system. Until then, I feared that our efforts were bound to be rather piecemeal and unsatisfactory.*

The only real solution to the flying bomb problem was overrunning the launching sites in France and by July as the Americans broke out of Cherbourg and the British captured Caen, real hope for stopping the flying bomb menace grew.

There was also the importance of bombing the six liquid oxygen plants that were within range of Allied bombers at that time. Both the V1 and the V2 depended on liquid oxygen and cutting off or destroying their supply would also help to end the scourge.

Tedder wrote in his memoirs that by August 1944 the flying bomb menace had killed more than 5,000, seriously injured more than 15,000 and slightly injured more than 20,000. Some 30,000 homes had been destroyed. One would have thought that figures like these, though we don't know how inflated they are, would be an incentive to continue the *Crossbow* attacks. However, it was not as simple as that. Tedder wrote:

> *Air Chief Marshal Harris pointed out on the 18 August the extreme difficulty of bombing accurately the flying bomb and rocket installations.*
>
> *Against these targets Bomber Command had already carried out nearly ten thousand sorties, losing the better part of 100 aircraft and 650 personnel. Nearly 36,000 tons of bombs had been dropped. Harris did not think that we had achieved a result commensurate with the effort. On the other hand the scale of the attack combined with the needs of the battle had caused us to take virtually the whole of Bomber Command and much of the American effort away from German targets for some 3½ months.*

By late August Allied troops were in Paris with Northern France and Belgium soon liberated reducing the argument for a massive offensive, in terms of *Crossbow*, to irrelevance.

CHAPTER FIVE

The Tempest Wing

B efore we get into the day-to-day operations of Fighter Command against the doodlebugs, it is essential to look at the period from the fighter pilot's point of view. What better person then, to promulgate this point of view than Wing Commander Roland Beamont who in February 1944 was tasked by Air Marshal Sir Hugh Saunders, Air Officer Commanding of No. 11 Group, to form No. 150 Wing with the new Hawker Tempest fighters?

The new Wing was based at Newchurch in the heart of Romney Marsh near Dungeness with the role of providing fighter cover over the Normandy invasion and if necessary switch at a moment's notice to defending London against the expected onslaught by the Germans' latest secret weapon, the flying bomb.

In his book *The Years Flew Past* published by Airlife Publishing Ltd, Beamont described how he, as Wing Leader of 150 Wing, had known of the coming attacks by some sort of secret German weapon. However, he had been unable to obtain any form of technical or operational information on the new enemy that would have helped to create interception methods and tactics that might have saved the lives of those pilots killed when the flying bombs blew up around them. No such information was divulged.

It was not until 16 June 1944 that the flying bomb campaign for 150 Wing kicked off. The Tempests were ordered on standing patrols along the Channel coast as a wave of doodlebugs came pouring in between Beachy Head and North London targeted for Central London.

Leading a section of Tempests, Beamont radioed in for more information. The Controller replied that all they knew was that the targets were flying at 2,000 feet!

That first day of operations the Newchurch Wing destroyed eleven flying bombs and by the end of the week, according to Beamont, they had destroyed 100. Beamont wrote:

This was a significantly higher success rate than any of the other fighter units, and an order of magnitude improvement on the initial performance of the AA command whose thinly dispersed gunsites and outdated manually directed 3.7 guns and relatively ineffective Bofors had them struggling to get into even double figures each week in June and early July.[13]

The success rate of the Newchurch Tempests gained official notice and Beamont was summoned to report to 11 Group with recommendations on countering the German offensive. His first suggestion was banning the slower fighters over the Kent and Sussex areas, which were getting in the way of the squadrons actively involved in defending British skies. According to Beamont these slower fighters were achieving few successes.

His second recommendation was for the AA guns to be concentrated on a narrow coastal belt. He also suggested that the fastest fighters, the Tempests, Mustangs and Spitfire XIVs, intercept the flying bombs over the Channel or between a concentrated gun belt and the London balloon belt to avoid being shot down by the guns.

To help the pilots' first sightings of the flying bombs Beamont also suggested that the Observer Corps fire signal rockets towards the incoming V1s as the converging smoke trails would help in identification.

All his measures were implemented in July 1944, increasing the success rate dramatically.

By June, waves of hundreds of V1s were falling on London, which was now in crisis,[14] according to Beamont. This month, the fighters destroyed 925 while the guns destroyed 312.

According to Beamont, there was a distinct rivalry between HQ ADGB (Air Defence of Great Britain) and the RAF Tempest Wing. At the beginning of the battle, Beamont received a terse signal from HQ ADGB that stated that 'pilots were not to claim the destruction of flying bombs as victories as having no pilots the V1s could not be compared with the destruction of manned aircraft.'

For Beamont this seemed completely illogical as he explains in his book.

Were not RAF and Allied fighters frequently credited with victories over Europe against Arado and Bucker trainers, Me 108 and Caudron Goeland light transports and Ju 52 troop transports, all of which were completely defenceless, whereas the Fieseler V1 carried 1,800 lb of Amatol high explosive which could often bring down the attacking fighter as it exploded under the fighter's cannon fire.

Beamont passed on HQ ADGB's comments, which created unease and anger in the squadrons that their efforts in combating the menace were so unappreciated.

Beamont states in his book that casualties from wild AA fire missing the V1s but hammering the Tempests continued to mount. Some of these fighters were brought down in flames in Kent and Sussex in full view of people and questions were asked in parliament.

The adverse publicity understandably embarrassed the AA service but rather than remedy their problems, Beamont was instructed to visit the AA Command area headquarters at Hastings to, as he described, 'make peace'. He felt that the boot should be on the other foot since it was his pilots that were being shot down. Travelling with Newchurch Commandant Wing Commander 'Digger Aitkin', he arrived at the AA/HQ Mess. They were introduced to General Pile who insisted that the RAF and especially Beamont's fighters stop their complaints even though Beamont had made none outside of official channels. His response to Pile's allegations was the hope that the cause of the complaints would be removed by the gunners ceasing to fire at the fighters. Unfortunately, this did not go down well and he and Aitkin left as soon as they could.

The fight against the V1 was an intense day and night operation by pilots and ground personnel alike. Pilots flew no fewer than four sorties a day, with many at night destroying two or more doodlebugs in a single sortie.

Oddly enough, as the continued success of the fighters increased more criticism of their efforts was levelled at them. Beamont wrote that several Spitfire squadron leaders had been heard to say, 'that true fighter pilots should not be employed in shooting down flying bombs, but they should be reserved for the pure and glorious activity of one-to-one air combat.'

It was his opinion that these sentiments were said out of envy because, with the exception of the new Spitfire XIV, the Spitfires in operation at the time had been found wanting against the V1. Perhaps this is the reason why the speed and specifications of the V1 seem to be so contradictory. It depends on who is telling the story, a Spitfire pilot or a Tempest pilot!

The acrimony continued. Beamont and his pilots in early July attended a Field Investiture where they received awards from King George VI, although there had been no prior warning of these 'Immediate Awards' at all. He later read in the *London Gazette* that he had received the awards for forming and leading a fine fighting unit, the Newchurch Wing of Tempests. But the article made no mention of the V1 battle that was costing lives.

The rumour mill continued to churn and Beamont writes that there was conflict in the Services in high places over the conduct of the V1 battle. In fact, General Sir Fredrick Pile wrote a memorandum in September 1944 that stated:

> *There is no doubt in my mind which needed the greater courage – to stand on a gunsite and fire at a directly approaching flying bomb with the knowledge that it will hit you if you bring it down or to fly an aircraft at a suitable distance behind the bomb and shoot it down. Any pilot who shot down a large number of V1s could count on receiving yet another decoration.*[15]

This inter-Service rivalry was compounded by Churchill himself in a memorandum to the RAF Chiefs of Staff that said:

> *You have no grounds to claim that the RAF frustrated attacks by V weapons – so far as the flying bombs were concerned the RAF did their part but in my opinion their efforts rank far below that of the AA artillery.*[16]

The Tempests of the Newchurch Wing accounted for more than a third of the V1s shot down by all the fighters, destroying more than 638. Although warm acknowledgements of their efforts came from No. 11 Group Headquarters as well as from Sir Ernest Gowers

(Regional Defence Commissioner for London on behalf of the London Town Clerks), nothing came from ADGB HQ.

Another big player in the Tempest Wing was Squadron Leader Joseph Berry who took over command of 501 Squadron on 10 August 1944. At that time the Squadron had flown some 200 sorties and only destroyed three flying bombs.

Beginning the day after his arrival, the Squadron destroyed eight flying bombs on the night of 11 August. On two occasions Berry managed to destroy a flying bomb with a one-second burst, firing only sixty rounds at the target. During the night, the Squadron mounted regular patrols so that aircraft would be airborne when flying bombs were spotted. Night-flying training was also maintained so the pilots could feel at home in the Tempests flying in the darkness of night.

On 12/13 August the Tempests were patrolling the inland area of the south and south-east coast when Berry attacked a single flying bomb, destroying it with a long burst from his cannon. That same patrol Flight Lieutenant Robb attacked two Divers with bursts from his cannon but he did not see the results of his attacks on either target. Confirmation of their destruction came later after several enquiries.

On the night of 14 August patrols were maintained except for a short period when roaming barrage balloons made flying in darkness extremely dangerous for the Tempest pilots.

On 19/20 August a section of 501 Squadron was scrambled to intercept some flying bombs. Berry was up flying two patrols in a Mosquito to see the effect of searchlight dousing and flying bomb interception from the Mosquito pilot's point of view. On one of those patrols he took off at 2310 hrs and chased a doodlebug, firing at it as he did, but he was not able to destroy it. However, later that morning he was back in his Tempest and attacked one Diver and destroyed it.

So important was the need to counter the V1 menace that Squadron Leader Berry was ordered to London to have a chat with Churchill's Ministers about what the Government expected of the Squadron. The role of 501 Squadron against the night intruder, they told him, had come from Churchill himself. In effect, the Squadron had to consider itself expendable and must try to intercept the V1s in every weather condition even though other squadrons were grounded. This chilling message of expendability was reinforced when the Secretary of State for Air, Sir Archibald Sinclair, arrived at the base for a visit. He reiterated the Ministers' words, saying that the morale in London was so low due to the V1 that the Government was treating the situation very seriously. They were prepared to sacrifice several pilots for every V1 shot down.

At the height of the doodlebug war Squadron Leader Berry was interviewed by the BBC and described how he shot down the dreaded V1 flying bombs. The transcript of his interview was published in the *Listener Magazine* in July 1944.

The interviewer described the V1s as robots, saying that shooting one of them down should have been easy meat, as the robot could not take evasive action or fire back at its enemies.

But as the article suggested, it was a different story when the Germans started sending the V1s over at night. The only thing the pilots could see was the jet of flame coming from their jet engines.

To start with, some of our day fighter pilots were sent to intercept these robots. Normally, these day fighter pilots in their Tempests and Spitfires are crack shots but it soon became apparent that they were not sufficiently at home in the dark clouds of night.

But the urgency of the situation demanded results and the RAF top brass, as Berry put it during the interview, convened to see if some of the night fighter pilots could be converted to flying the Tempest. Some, as Berry indicated, were skeptical about the plan. Berry himself had reservations because he was involved right from the outset. 'Because I had some experience of attacking doodlebugs in daylight, I can tell you that flying against them by night proved even more dangerous,' he said.

However, their initial skepticism proved to be unfounded and the night fighter pilots soon began to take a toll of the V1s in their Tempests. The RAF pilots flying against the V1s and the AA gun crews trying to shoot them down from the ground knew almost nothing about the flying habits of the doodlebugs or their construction so experimentation was the order of the day. By experimenting and swapping experiences the pilots were able to work out the best method of destroying them or shooting them down.

Every evening during the summer of 1944 at the early phase of the battle with the flying bombs a council of war took place on the lawn of a little cottage in southern England. Here, pilots, including Wing Command Beamont and Squadron Leader Berry, compared their experiences on operations against the V1. They worked out different methods of attacking the V1s, discussing them one evening then trying them out in the air the following day, then reporting back that evening.

According to Squadron Leader Berry, no one worked harder than Beamont during this experimental phase of the battle. Berry said Beamont flew day after day from dusk till dawn, trying to work out the best method of attack. It evolved into the approach from the astern at an acute angle.

It may sound simple now but clearly it was not. It took some of the most experienced fighter pilots several days to get the best angle and the best manner of attack. Once they did, the results were immediate. 'The bag went up hand over fist,' Berry said to the BBC interviewer, 'and the casualties dropped equally sharply.'

As the war against the doodlebug advanced, pilots were able to expend less and less ammunition shooting down the flying bombs. Some managed to get their attacks down to 150 rounds for each flying bomb destroyed, compared with the 500 rounds they had fired at the beginning of the flying bomb menace.

The technique was to patrol higher than the path of the average flying bomb at 5,000 to 6,000 feet. The doodlebugs usually came across the English coast between 2,000 and 3,000 feet. The first thing the pilots saw during the dark night was a small light, like a shooting star coming in from the sea, then the searchlights would pick up the bomb, showing the direction that it was coming from, and the AA crews would open up.

While the barrage was going on, the pilots waited for those bombs that got through the curtain of flak. During the interview Berry said they would then make a diving turn going after the flying bomb, 'finishing our dive just behind the bomb and opening fire at a range of 250 yards.'

Even though the V1 was a robot aircraft it didn't go down easily. It took a lot of punishment and the best way to shoot it down was to aim at the propulsion unit, as Berry indicated during his BBC interview. 'If your range and aim are dead on you can see pieces flying off the jet engine and the big white flame at the end goes out and down goes the bomb.'

Sometimes, the V1s would dive straight into the ground and explode but at other times their sensitive gyros would be damaged and the bomb would start giving off a weird and bizarre display of acrobatics before finally falling to the earth. Sometimes, the bombs would just explode in mid-air and pilots had to be alert to avoid the debris. 'The flash is so blinding that you can't see a thing for about 10 seconds,' Berry recalled. 'You hope to be the right way up when you are able to see again.'

On one occasion one of the flying bombs Berry chased and attacked caught fire, diving on an operational airfield, which had its lights blazing in the night. He closed in behind the V1 and fired a long burst from his four cannon and the bomb finally burst into flames, exploding into pieces, much to the relief of the flying control officer who had been watching it on the airfield with mounting dread as the bomb came closer. 'Fragments of the bomb were blown into my aircraft and one went into the air intake, jamming the throttle, which was almost wide open,' Berry said. He flew home at full speed, unable to do anything, and managed to land his Tempest safely.

During that same interview Berry mentioned one of the most famous incidents concerning the destruction of doodlebugs. During a busy sortie, when pilots were chasing and attacking several bombs, their ammunition could easily run out. Such was the case with a Polish pilot who, with his ammunition spent, was still chasing a V1 heading inland towards London. Having a sudden flash of inspiration the pilot flew alongside the flying bomb, gently eased his wing tip under the wing of the V1 and gave his aircraft an upward flick, which turned the bomb on its back and sent it smashing into the empty countryside where it exploded.

Pilots from other squadrons began to copy the same delicate manoeuvres very successfully, to the point where in some cases they could turn the bomb around and send it back towards its base in the Pas de Calais. Imagine the surprise and shock of the Germans when they saw their V1 heading back the way it came.

After the interview Berry continued to fly night patrols against the V1, scoring another seven that helped to bring 501 Squadron's total up to forty V1s destroyed in the month of August 1944.

As the Germans switched to air launching their V1s from airfields in Holland and Germany, 501 Squadron moved to Bradwell Bay on 22 September 1944. This enabled the Squadron to launch patrols against the Heinkel units launching the V1s from the air.

On the night of 28 September 1944, Squadron Leader Berry led two other Tempests on a Ranger sortie over Holland and Germany towards the Rhine to attack the Heinkel airfields. But due to poor visibility, low cloud and rain, the attack was cut short.

Over the next few days the weather began to clear and it was decided that another attempt should be made to knock out the airfields of Bomber *Gruppen* III/KG3.[17] On 2 October, Berry took off at 0535 hrs, leading Flight Lieutenant EL Williams and Flight Lieutenant CA Hansen to attack the airfields and any other ground targets of opportunity between (Bad) Zwischenahn and the Rhine. The importance of Zwischenahn in North Western Germany was twofold; it was a He 111 H-22 airfield and it had a nearby rail yard where trains were bringing the V1s to the airfields.

At first light, the three Tempests roared across the Dutch coastline, at 50 feet, tearing along at 400 mph, heading towards Meppel. Turning north-east they flew towards Veendam, flying fast and low towards their targets.

East of Veendam, the pilots ran into intense light machine-gun fire from enemy soldiers alerted to their presence. Despite their speed, several shells ripped into Berry's Tempest, rupturing his glycol tank. Suddenly the controls went tight in his hands; he pulled the stick back to gain height, struggling to keep the Tempest in the air, leaving a white vapour trail of glycol behind him. Over the R/T the other two Tempest pilots heard their leader calmly say, 'I've had it chaps, you go on.'

Two miles east of the 'Gazelle' radar station, Berry's Tempest flipped over onto its back and dived straight into the ground, crashing in flames. Berry had no time to bale out. As the pall of smoke rose into the air, the two other Tempest pilots circled overhead looking for signs of life. Unable to stay long, they flew a couple of quick circuits then roared away, carrying on with their mission.

On the ground, the head teacher of the junior school in the little Dutch village of Kibblegaarn, Mr A Jager, had been in the school when Berry's aircraft had narrowly missed crashing into it. He ran towards the crash site followed by the farmer who owned the field Berry had crashed in, Mr S de Lange, and managed to pull Berry from the blazing Tempest, desperately trying to extinguish the flames from his burning uniform. Berry was already dead when they pulled him free. His identification documents had been destroyed in the fire and at the time his identity was unknown but one clue, which helped to identify him, was a cigarette case with the initials 'JB' engraved on it. Before the Germans arrived to salvage anything from the wreckage, the villagers managed to spirit away Berry's body.

Squadron Leader Joseph Berry was buried in a quiet plot in Scheemda and the inscription of the wooden cross above the grave simply read 'Unknown RAF'.[18]

The war against the flying bomb took its toll on some of the RAF's best pilots. What follows is a day-by-day account of the operations by the Tempest squadrons, Mosquito squadrons, Spitfire squadrons and the Anti-Aircraft Command operations against the German flying bombs from the point of view of the pilots flying fast, heavily armed fighters, the best of the day, desperately trying to stop the V1 menace.

CHAPTER SIX

Tempests to the Rescue: 501 Squadron

No. 501 Squadron entered the battle against the flying bombs in August 1944. On 5 August Flight Sergeant RW Ryman scrambled from Manston, climbed to 6,000 feet and was vectored onto a flying bomb coming in over Hythe. He rolled into a dive, giving chase. 'I dived on it from its starboard side coming to line astern,' he reported. 'I closed to 50 yards giving it a burst. I saw strikes and it caught fire.'

Reducing his airspeed he fired several short bursts and broke off as the V1 blew up in mid-air at 1853 hrs.

Before dawn on 7 August Flying Officer RC Deleuse was patrolling over Folkestone when he was vectored onto coordinates near Dymchurch where V1s were approaching. Spotting one, he gave chase but lost sight of it. Returning to Dymchurch he picked up another V1, seeing the glow from its jet engine. It was flying at 3,000 feet at 315 mph as Deleuse gave chase. 'I fired a 1 second burst followed by a 3 second burst from astern,' he reported. 'The propulsion unit burst into flame and I saw it crash and explode between Tenterden and Appledore at 0601 hours.'

Under Berry's command the tally against flying bombs increased dramatically. Beginning the day after his arrival, the Squadron destroyed eight flying bombs on the night of 11 August.

Flying Officer RG Lucas was on patrol between 2335 and 0135 hrs when Wartling Control vectored him onto a V1, which was coming in over Hastings at 4,000 feet at 350 mph. Chasing it, he dived on the target, rapidly closing. He fired five one-second bursts from

250 yards away, south of the Marker Balloons and west of West Malling. 'I saw pieces fall off. The Diver exploded on the ground 8 miles west of south west of West Malling,' Lucas wrote in his combat report.

On the night of 11/12 August Flying Officer BF Miller (American) shot down three V1s. While patrolling over the Tonbridge area, he was vectored onto his first flying bomb by Wartling Control at 0117 hrs, coming in at 2,000 feet at 350 mph. Diving on the target, he closed to 50 yards, firing three two-second bursts. 'Pieces flew off and the Diver went down and crashed 8 miles east of Tonbridge,' he reported.

Eight minutes later he saw the glow from a V1's jet engine crossing in at the same speed and height as the first one. Peeling off, he attacked from 100 yards away and sent the V1 crashing into the ground and exploding a few miles north-east of Tonbridge. Ten minutes later he was on the tail of another flying bomb coming in at 8,000 feet at 280 mph. 'I attacked and fired 4 two-second bursts from 500 yards astern and I saw the Diver explode on the ground at 0135 hrs approximately 30 seconds after my last burst.'

That same night Flying Officer EL Williams was vectored onto a V1 by Wartling Control, coming in over Hastings at 360 mph at 2,100 feet. At 2318 hrs he intercepted the V1. He dived on the target, bringing his Tempest in behind it, firing two three-second bursts from 500 yards away, but seeing no results by the light of the jet engine. Breaking off he climbed rapidly away, turning to see the V1 losing height. 'The light went out 200 feet above the ground,' he reported. 'I saw the Diver explode on the ground 7 miles west of West Malling at approximately 2320 hrs.' He saw the explosions from two other flying bombs crashing near West Malling.

Three V1s were destroyed by Flight Lieutenant H Burton on the same evening. He tells the story of the first one.

> I saw a Diver which had come in 10 miles east of Beachy at 2,000 feet speed 320 mph. I attacked from astern and fired 4 2-second bursts from 200 yards. Strikes were seen and the Diver crashed south of Malling inside the outer circuit light and exploded on the ground at 2305 hrs.

He picked up the glow from the jet engine of the second V1 20 miles south-west of West Malling, travelling at 380 mph at 3,000 feet. Bringing his Tempest in behind the target, he lined the glow up in his sights and fired two two-second bursts of his cannon. As the V1 approached balloons, Burton pulled the stick back, climbing and turning the Tempest tightly to avoid collision. As he did he saw the flying bomb hit the ground and explode 10 to 15 miles north-west of West Malling.

At 2312 hrs Burton spotted the glow from his third flying bomb, travelling at 390 mph at 4,000 feet. Diving on the target he brought the Tempest in fast behind it, throttling back a little and closing to 100 yards. He fired a three-second burst on a 40-degree deflection shot, which obtained no results. 'I fired another 1 second burst from behind at 200 yards range and exhausted my ammunition,' he reported. The V1 went straight down through the Balloon Marker lights and exploded on the ground 10 to 15 miles north-west of West Mallling.

The following evening, 11/12 August, Squadron Leader Berry roared into the night sky from RAF Manston at 2200 hrs. He climbed away rapidly, his No. 2 tucked in beside and behind him. Vectored by Wartling Control onto a V1 coming in over Rye at 400 mph at 2,000 feet, he could see the glow from the target's jet engine. 'I immediately closed in and from 150 yards I opened fire,' he reported. 'I saw strikes on the motor and the Diver crashed 4 miles west of Sandhurst at 0123 hrs.'

On his second patrol he was heading back to base when Wartling Control advised him that the weather over Manston was awful. 'I flew over, headed to divert to Ford and on the way there trade was reported coming in over Dungeness,' he reported. 'I saw one Diver and turned in behind it.' The V1's height was 1,600 feet at 190 mph. From 300 yards away he fired two short bursts but saw no results. He fired another burst from 250 yards away and the flying bomb exploded in mid-air, approximately 6 miles south-west of West Malling at 0613 hrs.

During that same patrol Flight Lieutenant RLT Robb attacked two flying bombs with bursts from his cannon but he did not see the results of his attacks on either target. Confirmation of their destruction came later after several enquiries.

On 13 August Squadron Leader Berry destroyed another V1. Wartling Control vectored him onto an approaching V1 north of Hastings, flying at 330 mph at 1,800 feet. Dropping in behind the V1 he fired short bursts from 250 to 50 yards away, seeing his cannon shells hammer the target. Balloons forced Berry to break off the engagement as the V1 dropped to 1,200 feet and 280 mph. It crashed at 2255 hrs near Sevenoaks, bursting into flames on impact.

On the night of 14 August patrols were maintained except for a short period when roaming barrage balloons made flying in darkness extremely dangerous for the Tempest pilots. But, when the balloon danger had gone, the Tempests were back up in the air and Flight Lieutenant Burton chased a flying bomb over Hastings into the balloon barrage, firing at it as he did. However, the doodlebug remained unharmed and continued on its journey.

In the early hours of 14 August, Flight Lieutenant Robb picked up a V1 illuminated in searchlights north of Hastings. Rolling into a dive he gave chase, coming in behind the flying bomb that was travelling at 380 mph at 2,000 feet. Firing three short bursts from 600 yards away the jet engine flickered. 'I broke away as another aircraft appeared to be about to attack,' he wrote. 'The Diver caught fire and exploded on the ground just inside the balloon area at 0047 hrs.'

Two hours later he was back on patrol again. He fired at a V1 north-east of Hastings with five bursts from his cannon but had to break off the attack due to engine trouble. The V1 was seen to crash at West Malling at 0418 hrs.

On 18 August Flying Officer WF Polley was directed by Wartling Control onto three V1s coming in over Folkestone at 0305 hrs, flying at 2,000 feet and around 280 mph. 'As I came into a turn astern the searchlights doused and I closed the range to 300 yards and gave a 2 second burst,' Polley reported. Seeing no results he closed to 80 yards and fired a four-second burst. 'I broke away and saw the Diver explode beneath me on the ground.'

On 19/20 August a section of 501 Squadron was scrambled to intercept some flying bombs. Squadron Leader Berry flew two patrols in a Mosquito to see the effect of searchlight dousing and flying bomb interception from the Mosquito pilot's point of view. On one of those patrols, while flying the Mosquito UP-U, he took off at 2310 hrs and chased a doodlebug, firing at it as he did, but he was not able to destroy the enemy rocket. However, later that morning he was back in his Tempest VSD-Q and climbed rapidly away at 0615 hrs, leading a section to intercept more flying bombs.

There were reports of two V1s coming in over Dungeness and as they roared into the morning sky, Biggin Hill Control vectored them onto the targets. 'I was six miles north of Rye when I saw a Diver coming in just over cloud at 2,400 feet at 380 mph,' Berry wrote in his report. Bringing his Tempest in behind the V1 he put on more speed, closing the gap. Then, 200 yards away, he pressed the firing button, sending a hail of shells hammering onto the target. 'The Diver exploded in the air at 0635 hrs and crashed South of West Malling.'

Later in the evening of 19 August Flight Lieutenant Burton took off from Manston at 2205 hrs, vectored by Wartling Control between Folkestone and Dungeness. 'I saw about 6 Divers approaching the coast,' he reported. 'One at least was destroyed by AA fire.' Peeling off, he dived on one V1 flying at 2,000 feet at 340 mph, coming in fast, behind and above.

I overshot and turned to starboard slightly coming in again from astern. I closed to 250 yards and opened fire with my port cannon as my starboard cannon had jammed.

His cannon shells plastered the V1's main wing, sending it crashing into the ground at 2325 hrs. It exploded in the Tunbridge Wells area.

Flying Officer Deleuse had a busy day on 24 August as he shot down a Diver at 0610 hrs. Wartling Control put him onto the target, which was approaching Rye flying at 400 mph at 3,000 feet. He reported that:

The flames from the propulsion unit seemed to be brighter than usual as though it had been hit by AA fire. But it was still travelling level on its course. I attacked from astern with a 3 to 4 second burst.

His cannon fire slammed into the V1, setting it on fire as it dived into the ground and exploded 5 miles north of Rye.

At 0120 hrs on 27 August, Flying Officer Lucas climbed his Tempest rapidly into the air from Manston on an anti-Diver patrol when he was vectored onto a V1 by Wartling Control, coming in over Dungeness at 340 mph. Diving down to 3,000 feet he brought the Tempest in behind the V1, closing the gap to 300 yards, firing several short bursts of cannon fire. The V1 went straight down, crashing south of Maidstone at 0150 hrs.

On the last day of August 1944 Squadron Leader Berry destroyed another V1. Taking off from Manston at 0540 hrs he climbed to height, picking up Wartling Control over Ashford. He was vectored onto a V1 coming in over Sandwich at 3,000 feet flying at 250 mph. Turning, he put the Tempest into a dive coming in dead astern of the flying bomb, slightly above it. In his report he wrote:

I closed in to 300 yards and fired a short burst which knocked pieces off the propulsion unit. I fired again from 150 yards and saw more strikes and the Diver exploded on the ground in the Faversham area at 0550 hrs.

On 5 September Flying Officer Deleuse and Flying Officer KV Panter were scrambled from Manston under North Weald Control and vectored just north of Felixstowe. Panter reported:

I saw a Diver coming in at 400 mph at 1,000 feet. I got into position for attack as it crossed the coast and fired from 250 yards astern and the Diver exploded at 0550 hrs on the ground.

Flying Officer Miller was scrambled under Trimley Control from Bradwell Bay on 16 September at 0600 hrs. Climbing to 7,000 feet, he was vectored onto some V1s coming in over Felixstowe and saw the glow from the engine of one coming in at 340 mph at 2,500 feet. He wrote in his combat report:

I dived down on it and closed from 500 yards astern and opened fire. I saw strikes on the tail unit. Control told me to break off the engagement and I did so. I saw the Diver losing height and explode on the ground near RAF Castle Camps 30 seconds after my attack at 0606 hrs.

Climbing, he turned the Tempest back towards Bradwell Bay, catching sight of a V1 coming in on the same course as the one before at 340 mph. Peeling off, he dived on the target closing to 500 yards. He fired several short bursts of his cannon until he was 50 yards away, when the V1 blew up in mid-air. Kicking his rudder, he turned hard and climbed away to avoid the debris.

Gradually, as the launching sites were overrun by the Allied armies fighting their way through northern France, the Germans switched their tactics. This meant that 501 Squadron was relocated to meet a new challenge – the aircraft-launched V1.

As we have seen in the previous chapter the Squadron moved from Manston to Bradwell Bay near Southend on 22 September 1944 to enable the pilots to destroy airborne-launched V1s more easily.

Early on 29 September, Flight Lieutenant RJ Lillwall, while on patrol under Trimley Control, was vectored onto a V1 coming in at 500 feet at 250 mph. Seeing the glow from the jet engine, he rolled into a dive, bringing his Tempest in behind the V1, 600 yards away. Closing the gap to 100 yards he fired five short bursts of his cannon at the target. 'On the last burst I saw strikes on the Diver and as I overshot it climbing, it exploded 100 feet below me and slightly behind at 0545 hrs.'

October 1944 was a very busy month for the Squadron and also very sad. On 2 October Squadron Leader Berry was killed in action while attacking the Heinkel airfields.

On 5 October Flying Officer JAL Johnson shot down a flying bomb while on anti-Diver patrol under Trimley Control. He took off from Bradwell Bay, climbing his Tempest rapidly into the evening sky. He caught sight of the glow from a V1's jet engine and gave chase, diving on it as it approached the coast at 400 mph. Manoeuvring his Tempest in behind the target, he fired three short bursts from 400 yards away, seeing pieces fly off the jet engine. Suddenly, the V1 slowed as the engine went out and Johnson overshot it. Climbing, he turned tightly and saw the flying bomb explode on the ground below him at 2140 hrs.

Flight Lieutenant AT Langdon-Down was on anti-Diver patrol flying at 4,000 feet on the night of 12/13 October when Trimley Control vectored him onto a V1 coming in from the east at 350 mph between 1,500 and 2,000 feet. Peeling off, he rolled the Tempest into a dive, bringing his mighty fighter in behind the flying bomb. 'I fired two short bursts from 400 to 500 yards and saw strikes on the Diver,' he reported. 'It lost height and blew up just before hitting the ground.'

Early in the morning of 13 October, Flight Lieutenant R Bradwell was patrolling at 4,000 feet when Trimley Control told him two V1s were coming in at 1,500 feet. Turning, he put on more speed and saw the glow of the two flying bombs, like shooting stars tearing low across the landscape. Diving rapidly, he came in behind the first one, which was travelling at 360 mph. 'I closed in dead astern,' he wrote in his report. 'I fired four long bursts. The flame went out and the Diver went down and exploded on the ground at 0505 hrs approximately.'

The following day, Warrant Officer E Wojczynski was scrambled at 0330 hrs, roaring into the early morning air from Bradwell Bay. He had been vectored by Trimley Control onto a flying bomb coming in at 1,000 feet at 300 mph. Giving chase, he pushed the Tempest into a dive, coming in behind the V1 and closing to 800 yards when he fired a single burst without results. 'I closed in to 300 yards down to 150 yards and gave a long burst,' he reported. 'The Diver went down and exploded on the ground at 0345 hrs.'

Early in the morning of 15 October, Flying Officer McKenzie was patrolling when he caught sight of the glow from a flying bomb's engine coming in below him, already engaged by AA fire. This V1 was travelling at 400 mph so when the flak stopped, McKenzie flying above the target, rolled his Tempest into a dive to gain more speed and came down fast, bringing the fighter in behind the target, the glow from the V1 in his sights. He reported during debriefing:

> I made two attacks. On the second attack I gave a long burst at close range and saw strikes and the Diver caught fire and began losing height and finally crashed, exploding on the ground at 0150 hrs.

Eighteen minutes later he had destroyed a second flying bomb in much the same way as the first.

Pilot Officer RH Bennett and Flying Officer WF Polley took off from Bradwell Bay at 1845 hrs on the 16 October on anti-Diver patrol. In the summer evening light, they were vectored by Trimley Control onto the coordinates of a V1 coming in over Clacton at 1,500 feet and 450 mph. Both Tempests were at 6,500 feet. Bennett wrote in his combat report:

> I dived down and from 1,000 yards astern opened fire and continued firing. Flying Officer Polley flew alongside the Diver giving me the range. The Diver was hit and began to climb and I kept firing at it. At 4,000 feet the Diver exploded in mid-air over North Weald at 2050 hrs approximately.

Warrant Officer E Wojczynski attacked a flying bomb coming in near Clacton on the morning of 17 October. Flying at 3,000 feet he caught sight of the V1 below him at 1,000 feet flying at 370 mph. Diving, he lined the glow from the jet exhaust up in his sights as he positioned his Tempest behind the target from 700 yards away. Firing two three-second bursts of his cannon he saw no results so he closed to 300 yards and thumbed the firing button again. This time his cannon shells tore into the jet engine, putting it out. 'I broke off the engagement at the call-off line,' he reported. 'In the turn I saw the Diver explode on the ground west of Rockford at 2213 hrs approximately.'

The night of 21/22 October saw Flying Officer Johnson destroy two V1s. He saw the first Diver crossing in nearly over Bradwell, flying at 1,500 feet between 360 to 380 mph. Diving on it, he fired several bursts from his cannon. 'I saw blue strikes on the Diver and the light went out,' he reported. 'It crashed south of Chelmsford.'

Climbing up to 4,000 feet he turned back onto the patrol line and saw the glow of another V1 coming in at 380 mph at 1,000 feet. Giving chase, he brought his Tempest down fast behind the V1, firing several bursts. He saw blue strikes in the darkness all over the V1, which went straight down into the ground, exploding on impact.

Flight Lieutenant R Bradwell destroyed a V1 in the early hours of 24 October while on anti-Diver patrol. Vectored onto the coordinates by Trimley Control, he picked up the V1 illuminated in the searchlights coming in at 380 mph. Giving chase, he pushed the throttle forward, diving the Tempest on the target. Manoeuvring behind the flying bomb he fired several short bursts at the target until it crashed into the ground, exploding at 0100 hrs.

Flying Officer Bennett, who had taken off with Bradwell, saw a V1 coming in over the coast near Harwich travelling at 280 mph[19] at 500 feet. 'I chased it and closing fired three long bursts, observing strikes and the Diver crashed in a position due west of North Weald at 0115 hrs.'

Very late in the evening of the next day, Flight Lieutenant Birbeck with his No. 2 roared off the runway from Bradwell Bay, climbing to 2,000 feet, when Trimley Control vectored them onto some trade approaching the airfield. Birbeck reported:

I saw a Diver illuminated in the searchlights approaching base height 100 feet speed 370 mph. I closed in astern after a long chase and fired 4 bursts at 600 yards. When I was about to fire again the Diver caught fire and dived into the ground exploding south west of Chelmsford at 0100 hrs.

Before it crashed, pieces flew off the V1 showering Birbeck's Tempest causing some slight damage but he managed to land safely back at Bradwell Bay.[20] This very low high-speed chase must have been very hairy indeed when pursuer and target could not have been more than 100 feet above the trees!

At 1825 hrs Flying Officer RC Stockburn was on an anti-Diver patrol when Trimley Control vectored him onto a V1 coming in very low. Flying through a hail of flak, the V1 emerged from the AA fire still on course and at speed. Stockburn rolled into a dive, bringing his Tempest in behind the target, and fired a number of short bursts. He takes up the story.

I noticed that the propelling unit was emitting flames from the side. I continued firing and the Diver continued on course. I broke away as the Diver went through cloud but on emerging from the cloud the Diver almost immediately exploded in mid-air at a height of 500 feet at 1940 hrs.

That same evening Flight Lieutenant Robb destroyed a V1 over Chelmsford. While patrolling under Trimley Control Robb saw a patch of searchlights on some cloud and flew towards it. He wrote in his report:

My height was 4,000 feet and as the Diver passed under my port wing I started to dive, then levelled out at 1,200 feet which was the Diver's height. My speed was then 430 mph and I overshot.

Pulling up, Robb throttled back and closed on the flying bomb near the Chelmsford beacon.

I fired three bursts from 400 yards and saw strikes on the first burst. On the second burst a small flicker of flame appeared and on the third burst the Diver exploded in mid-air at 1942 hrs.

The peace of the early morning on 30 October was shattered with the call to scramble at 0500 hrs. Engines burst into life and two Tempests roared off the ground at Bradwell Bay, climbing rapidly into the air to intercept a V1. Flight Lieutenant Williams and his No. 2 were vectored onto a flying bomb by Trimley Control, which was approaching the base at 360 mph at 800 feet. Williams climbed to 1,000 feet then turned as the Diver passed below him. Bringing his Tempest in behind the flying bomb firing three short bursts, Williams saw his cannon shells hammer the target on the first and second bursts. The third burst of cannon fire caused the flying bomb to catch fire and crash into the ground where it exploded on impact at 0518 hrs south-west of Chelmsford.

From October 1944 the flying bomb menace was greatly reduced. By this time most of the launching sites had been taken over by the Allies and all that was left to the Germans were the airborne launches from Heinkel bombers. But most of the airfields these aircraft came from were under attack by Allied air forces so the V1 attacks became fewer and fewer. Still, the RAF kept squadrons back to deal with the remnants of the doodlebug menace and 501 Squadron was one of them.

For example, on 8 November 1944 Flight Lieutenant Bradwell was on an anti-Diver patrol when searchlights picked up a V1 coming in at 800 feet at 300 mph.

As the evening light was fading, Bradwell came in behind the V1, keeping the glow from the jet engine in sight. He fired a single short burst from minimum range and the V1 lost speed but continued on course. Re-engaging, Bradwell began to weave his Tempest from side to side to avoid overshooting. In his report he recorded:

> I gave 3 shorts bursts at close range. After the last burst the flame went out. The Diver crashed and exploded on the ground south west of Great Dunmow at 2045 hrs approximately.

The following evening Flight Lieutenant Bradwell was up again, this time with Flying Officer Panter as his No. 2. They climbed rapidly into the gloom of the evening sky, scrambled by Trimley Control onto a V1 coming in north of Clacton travelling at 220 mph at 800 feet. Bradwell reported:

> I went down to attack but because of the slowness of the Diver I had great difficulty to prevent overshooting. I fired a number of bursts

*while weaving and when I was nearly out of ammunition and the
Diver did not seem to be hit I called Flying Officer Panter to take
it on.*

As Bradwell broke off the attack Panter could see that the V1
was going down. To help it on its way, Panter dived on the target,
firing two short bursts from his cannon. This time there was no
doubt as his shells peppered the flying bomb and the V1 went
straight down, exploding just before it hit the ground south of
Chipping Ongar.

In the opening days of December 1944 V1s were increasingly
rare, but on 5 December Squadron Leader A Parker-Rees saw
action against a flying bomb that was crossing the coast at 400 mph
at 1,000 feet at 2030 hrs. Vectored onto it by Trimley Control, he
saw the glow from the jet engine and attacked it with three two-
second bursts but saw no results. Closing the range he attacked
it again, firing another burst from his cannon. This time the jet
propulsion unit went out; the V1 lost height and crashed into the
ground exploding near Chipping Ongar.

Warrant Officer SH Balam had an interesting experience with a
V1 on the night of the 17/18 December 1944. He was flying at 5,000
feet on patrol when Trimley Control directed him onto a V1 coming
in at 300 mph at 6,000 feet, climbing steadily.

Seeing the V1 in the searchlights from the ground AA batteries,
Balam immediately pulled the control column back putting on
more speed. He recorded the incident in his combat report.

*I climbed to position myself behind and I fired three medium bursts
from extreme range. After the third burst the Diver dived steeply
and the light became brighter. I was unable to follow it down but one
minute later I saw a fire appear on the ground some 10 miles south
west of Chelmsford at 0410 hrs.*

Around the same time that night, Flying Officer Deleuse engaged
a V1 coming in from Felixstowe at 340 mph between 4,000 and
5,000 feet. Firing a long burst from 100 yards away he saw pieces
fly off the flying bomb and it crashed, bursting into flames on
impact 2 miles south of Great Totham at 0432 hrs.

About an hour later, Warrant Officer Wojczynski patrolling at
3,000 feet saw the glow of a V1 coming in fast from the direction of

Colchester at 340 mph at 1,800 feet. He recorded the incident in his report.

> To ascertain the speed I made a three quarter attack from the rear and followed with three short bursts from dead astern without result. I closed to 200 yards and fired one long burst. The light went out and the Diver started losing height. One and a half minutes later there was a flash on the ground near Chelmsford at 0544 hrs.

That same early morning Flight Lieutenant Lillwall took off from Bradwell Bay with Flying Officer J Maday. The two Tempests climbed rapidly away from base into the early morning gloom. Directed by Trimley Control, based near Felixstowe, they saw the glow from a V1, like a horizontal shooting star, coming in from the Clacton area at 380 mph at 1,500 feet. Lillwall reported:

> As Flying Officer Maday chased this Diver I backed up behind him remaining at 4,000 feet and above the Diver. As Husky 25 (Flying Officer Maday) was put out of range I took over and attacked from 10 degrees to port and above. I gave one short burst and observed strikes and petrol vapour leaked out. About 30 seconds later I observed a flash below me. This was at 0640 hrs near Chelmsford.

In the squadron histories and combat reports there are fewer and fewer reports of combat with V1s and 501 Squadron was reassigned to other duties.

One thing these combat reports show is the difficulty pilots had in bringing these robot aircraft down. If we could imagine today a car chase 100 feet above the ground at 400 mph we would only get an inkling of how ferocious and dangerous the battle against the V1s really was.

Chapter Seven

A New Enemy:
No. 3 Tempest Squadron

Prior to 13 June when the flying bomb campaign began, No. 3 Squadron Tempests were flying in support of the land forces fighting on the beaches of Normandy, as well as attacking key ground targets in the run up to the D-Day invasion. The Squadron was flying out of Newchurch at the time.

At 0400 hrs on 13 June 1944 the flying bomb odyssey for No. 3 Squadron began in earnest. The entry in the Squadron history tells the story of the first sighting.

An aircraft identified by a fluctuating jet of flame as either a rocket or jet propelled aircraft flew across the airfield at a height of 1,500 to 2,000 feet steering a steady course of 330 degrees at an estimated airspeed of 350 to 400 mph.

Clearly visible from the ground, Squadron personnel watched it roar away from the airfield coned by searchlights. But no gun fired. Presumably it had taken the AA crews and Squadron by complete surprise.

Shortly after this sighting another doodlebug shot overhead and this time the guns opened up but without result and the pilotless aircraft continued on its way.

At 0510 hrs that morning, Squadron Leader AS Dredge, leading Pilot Officer GA Whitman, Flight Sergeant R Pottinger and Flight Sergeant CW Orwin, lifted off from Newchurch roaring into the dawn sky. Climbing, they wheeled around, heading out across the

Channel towards the Pas de Calais area to search for V1 launching sites. Turning south over Cap Gris Nez they spotted a bright light in the sky at 2,000 feet heading in a south-easterly direction.

Identified as either a flare from a flying bomb or the exhaust glow of an aircraft, the Tempests gave chase heading east when the light eventually disappeared out of sight.

Turning back towards their patrol area near Pas de Calais they suddenly encountered a barrage of intense and accurate flak. The AA shells burst around the Tempests as they searched for its source. Taking evasive action Squadron Leader Dredge spotted an E-boat 3 miles off Boulougne that was pumping flak into the air, trying to bring them down.

Dredge rolled into a dive, followed by the other Tempest pilots, firing short bursts of cannon fire at the enemy vessel. He could see shells striking the E-boat as he levelled out and climbed away, still taking evasive action against the flak.

But as the other Tempests attacked, all seeing hits of their cannon shells on the boat, the flak was suddenly silenced. Dredge came round again for another attack, raking the vessel with cannon shells that exploded all around the deck. The rest of the Tempests followed suit firing as they dived on the ship, causing a large fire in the stern.

Climbing away they formed up and Squadron Leader Dredge could see the E-boat was burning and drifting.[21]

On 16 June the Germans sent waves of flying bombs across the Channel heading towards London.

It's worth reiterating here just how difficult it was for the pilots to attack and destroy the V1s, especially at night. Though they were night-fighter trained they flew on instruments in constant contact with ground controllers who would direct them onto coordinates in the sectors where the V1s were approaching. They would scan the dark skies for identification rockets fired by the Observer Corps or for the telltale jet exhaust of the V1. If they were lucky the sky would be moonlit, giving them relatively good visibility. But the Tempest, Spitfire and Mustang pilots didn't have the sophisticated all-weather technology for flying at night or in low visibility. Only the Mosquitoes had onboard radar, which allowed them to get a fix on the targets they were chasing. In the words of the pilots, their best piece of equipment was the Mark 1 eyeball.

At 0750 hrs on 16 June 1944 when Flight Sergeant MJ Rose shot down the Squadron's first flying bomb. Rose climbed his Tempest to 3,000 feet as dawn filled the sky while Control vectored him onto the course of the V1. Rose could see the flame from the flying bomb's jet in the distance. From 5 miles he closed to 300 yards then fired one long burst of his cannon. The V1 burst into flames, rolled over and spun into an orchard south of Maidstone.

Later that morning, Wing Commander Beamont leading a section of Tempests, roared away from Newchurch at 1010 hrs. They were vectored onto more flying bombs and with Flight Sergeant RW Cole, Beamont closed on one of the V1s from 10 miles south of Dover. The V1 was flying at 3,000 feet so Cole and Beamont climbed above it, closing rapidly. At 600 yards they both opened fire, with several short bursts sending the flying bomb down out of control exploding near Faversham.

On that same sortie Pilot Officer SB Feldman was chasing a flying bomb heading south of Ashford when another V1 shot past heading north. Wheeling around, Feldman gave chase closing rapidly. He fired several short bursts from 700 yards, the cannon shells ripping into the tail unit. 'The V1 slowed to 280 mph,' Feldman wrote in his combat report. 'I fired a long burst at 250 yards and the Diver exploded in mid-air.'

Flight Sergeant S Domanski (Polish) rolled into a shallow dive as he was vectored onto another flying bomb near Dover flying at 3,000 feet. Checking his airspeed he saw the needle reading 450 mph. With his Tempest at near full throttle, Domanski closed on the V1 and from 450 yards away he fired a short burst, then again from a distance of 200 yards.

Suddenly, his reflector gunsight failed, so while flying at high speed above and behind the V1 he replaced the sight and drew closer to the flying bomb until he was 200 yards away. He made a quick 20-degree turn and fired again and this time the flying bomb went down, exploding near Ashford.

Flight Sergeant Pottinger was scrambled at 1000 hrs. Roaring into the morning sky, he raised his undercarriage, pushed his throttle forward and headed for the coordinates given to him by Control. 'I saw a Diver near Dover being chased by another Tempest,' he reported, 'It fired and broke away and no strikes were seen.' Closing, he fired a three-second burst and saw his shells hit the port wing of the V1, which burst into flames, sending it spinning into the ground near Ashford at 1025 hrs.

Flight Lieutenant AE Umbers picked up a flying bomb near Dover, passing below him. Turning to port, he dropped into a shallow dive coming in above and astern and fired two short bursts from 600 yards away, which were ineffective. Closing to 250 yards, he fired again hitting the V1, which careened out of control and exploded north of Dover at 1035 hrs.

Belgian Flight Lieutenant Van Lierde chased a flying bomb from Dungeness with his No. 2, Flight Sergeant DJ MacKerras. Flying at 400 mph, they gained on the flying bomb as it appeared and disappeared in and out of cloud. Van Lierde fired a burst, shooting off the starboard wing tip, which slowed the flying bomb a little. He was easily able to shorten the distance so he fired again, seeing his shells pound the fuselage and wings. Breaking off, Van Lierde watched MacKerras have a go as the V1's jet engine stopped. Van Lierde came back in again and at 200 yards fired another burst, which sent the flying bomb spinning into a quarry south of Chatham.

Flight Sergeant LG Everson got his first flying bomb at 1355 hrs that same day. 'I saw a Diver over Hastings,' he reported, 'and chased it for 2 to 3 minutes at 390 indicated air speed.' At 600 yards he opened fire and at 300 yards he saw strikes hit the starboard wing and flashes from the jet engine. The Diver rolled to starboard, dived down and crashed into the ground, exploding in flames 10 miles north of Hastings.

The last flying bomb No. 3 Squadron pilots shot down that day hit the ground at 1420 hrs. Flying Officer GA Whitman, an American, and Flight Sergeant HJ Foster picked up the V1's trail at Beachy Head. Flying at 410 mph they closed on the flying bomb, firing short bursts from 800 yards away. Hit, the flying bomb began to weave and porpoise, slowing down to 300 mph when Flight Sergeant Foster came in and fired a short burst from 300 yards away. Shells smashed into the V1, sending pieces flying off the tail. It spun into the ground, exploding west of Lewes.

Although standing anti-Diver patrols[22] were conducted over the next few days, the next busiest day came on 17 June 1944 when Flying Officer MF Edwards and his No. 2, Flight Sergeant CW Orwin, spotted a V1 off Boulogne, travelling at 400 mph towards London. Both Tempests dived on the V1, trying to close the gap. After a few minutes, Edwards, now south of Dover, only 600 yards from the flying bomb, fired three long bursts of his cannon that slowed the V1 down to 300 mph. Flight Sergeant Orwin dropped down behind it and fired a two-second burst. Both Tempests then fired again and a puff of black smoke erupted from the jet engine and the V1 crashed into the ground and exploded between Folkestone and Hawkinge.

Later that afternoon Tempests and Spitfires worked together to bring down a flying bomb. Wing Commander Beamont, flying with Flight Lieutenant Van Lierde, was vectored to Tenterden where both pilots saw a V1 being chased by two Spitfire XIVs. The Tempests, flying above and behind the flying bomb, dived on the target, sweeping in. Each fired a short burst before climbing away. Turning hard, the Tempests roared in again, each firing bursts of cannon fire at it. As they climbed away, they saw the Spitfires attack the same flying bomb, which finally went down north of Tenterden, exploding on the ground. Beamont and Van Lierde claimed the V1 as destroyed, sharing it with a Spitfire XIV.

At 1950 hrs Pilot Officer Feldman and Flight Sergeant MacKerras were vectored onto a V1 off Cap Gris Nez, flying at 320 degrees at 380 mph. Both Tempests gave chase, pushing their throttles open. Five miles north of Dungeness, they closed to 500 yards when Flight Sergeant MacKerras opened fire and the V1 slowed to 300 mph.

Pilot Officer Feldman closed to within 150 yards of the V1 and opened fire, seeing strikes on the port side of the jet engine. Black smoke erupted from it as pieces flew off and the V1 slowed to 200 mph, rapidly losing height in a gentle dive. However, both Feldman and MacKerras had exhausted their ammunition just to get this result and they saw four Spitfires pick up the chase. As they climbed away the two Tempest pilots saw the Spitfires orbiting the target area. 'If Spits destroyed this Diver it's claimed as half-shared destroyed!' Feldman reported.

That same night Wing Commander Beamont patrolling in his Tempest saw a V1 flying over his base at Newchurch at 380 mph that was fully illuminated by AA searchlights. Rolling his Tempest into a dive, he chased the V1 calling for the searchlight to be doused. As he closed within range he fired several short bursts. Despite his order to douse the searchlights they remained on and as the flying bomb began to slow down Beamont overshot the target. Turning hard he closed the range to 300 yards, firing more short bursts. 'After more strikes the Diver turned to port when intense flak of all varieties came up,' Beamont reported. 'I couldn't see the target and had to break.' He claimed this V1 as damaged and the time of combat was 2320 hrs.

The following day was even busier for the Squadron. 'The Tempests being the chief defensive weapons at present in use,' wrote the Squadron's historian. This day, there were twenty-one actions involving Tempests and flying bombs and the first took place in the early hours of the morning.

Flight Lieutenant Umbers, flying with Pilot Officer KG Slade-Betts as his No. 2, was vectored onto a V1 south-west of Dungeness flying at 1,000 feet at an indicated airspeed of 390 mph.[23] Pushing the throttle forwards to increase speed, Umbers chased the V1 with Slade-Betts in formation with him.

At what he thought was 400 yards, Umbers fired but saw no results. Suddenly, he realised the glare from the jet had confused his estimation of the range and it was nearer to 1,000 yards. No wonder he had no results. Pressing home their attack, both Tempests gradually closed on the target. They fired short bursts until they were at point-blank range when they saw pieces fly off the V1's port wing and fuselage slowing it to 250 mph. 'We fired further bursts when we were told by Control of obstructions ahead,' Umbers reported. Breaking away, the last the two Tempest pilots saw of the V1 was it flying at 900 feet at 200 mph. It later crashed at 0442 hrs.

Less than an hour later, Flight Lieutenant Van Lierde and Australian Flight Sergeant HJ Bailey climbed rapidly away from Newchurch just before dawn. They were vectored onto a V1 crossing over Dungeness travelling at 360 mph at 1,500 feet. The two Tempests headed towards the target, but AA fire from Newchurch forced them to break away. Returning to Dungeness they spotted another flying bomb heading towards London at the same height and speed as the first one, 4 miles east of Dungeness. They gave chase again, closing gradually on the V1. At 500 yards, Van Lierde fired a one-second burst of his cannon but saw no results as the flying bomb turned 30 degrees to port. This time, Bailey went in firing two bursts but from the glow of the jet he didn't see any of his shells hit the target. Suddenly the air was filled with AA fire from the gunners on the ground and the two Tempests had to break sharply away to avoid being blown out of the sky. As they turned, they saw the flying bomb hit the ground and explode at 0520 hrs.

Flight Sergeant MacKerras spotted a flying bomb through breaks in the cloud at 2,000 feet, travelling at 420 mph. Diving on it, he gradually closed on the V1 and over Biggin Hill fired two bursts from 400 yards away. Closing the gap, he fired another two bursts of his cannon from 250 yards away, this time seeing his shells rip into the V1 causing the starboard wing to fall off. The V1 spun into the ground, exploding on impact near the Biggin Hill Ops Room at 0815 hrs. 'This was confirmed by the Duty Information Officer who was blown down while temporarily outside his post of duty,' MacKerras wrote.

At 0900 hrs Flight Lieutenant AE Umbers shot down another V1 after chasing it from Dungeness. Flying at 2,000 feet, the V1 was travelling at 380 mph when Umbers closed in. From 250 yards away, he fired several short bursts of his cannon watching as his shells hit home. But the flying bomb disappeared into cloud. As it came out of the clouds, Umbers closed in again and fired, plastering the wings and fuselage of the V1. It staggered and rolled onto its back. Then suddenly it dived into the ground near a castle, exploding on impact near the Cranbrook area.

With the day barely started it was Flight Lieutenant AR Moore's turn next to destroy a flying bomb only 55 minutes after Flight Lieutenant Umbers had shot his down. Vectored onto a flying bomb at 2,000 feet, Moore clocked this one at 380 mph. Rolling into a steep dive, he overhauled the V1. Thumbing the firing button he blasted the flying bomb with a long burst of cannon fire that sent shells tearing into the jet engine. The V1 pulled up sharply, turned to port and spiralled into the ground, bursting into flames 5 miles west of Rye.

Flying Officer Whitman claimed a shared victory over a V1 when he spotted one crossing the coast off Dungeness at 2,500 feet, travelling at 400 mph plus. 'There were several other aircraft chasing it,' he recorded in his report. 'Another Tempest pulled ahead then broke away.' Closing on the V1, Whitman fired several short bursts and saw his shells striking the flying bomb's jet engine.

'A Tempest came down from above and fired and the Diver went down with the jet still operating.' The V1 slammed into a greenhouse in the Bexley area, exploding on impact at 1145 hrs.

At 1300 hrs that afternoon, Flight Sergeant RW Cole made a determined attack on a V1 flying at 3,000 feet over Dymchurch at 390 mph. Cole pushed the stick forward, diving on the target. Above and behind the V1, he closed to within 1,000 yards and fired a burst from his four cannon but saw no results. Closing the gap to 600 yards, he thumbed the firing button again and this time he saw his tracer hit the V1 but it remained on course and at speed. Determined to bring it down, he kept his speed up, and at 200 yards from the target he fired a long burst of cannon shells that tore into the V1. It exploded in mid-air 3 miles north of Dymchurch and the debris flew back into the Tempest causing damage. He managed to land safely back at base.

Flight Lieutenant Van Lierde narrowly avoided collision with another Tempest. He saw a V1 crossing the coast north of Dungeness. Diving on the target, he fired a beam burst from 600 yards away and completely missed. Turning tightly, he came around behind the V1, lining it up in his sights, when suddenly another Tempest from 486 Squadron skidded right across in front of him. Van Lierde takes up the story in his report.

This unseemly performance was repeated again. The Diver blew up on the ground near Ivychurch damaging a farmhouse and firing a haystack. I claimed that one shared destroyed with Flight Lieutenant Cook of 486 Squadron.

Over Biggin Hill, Tempest and AA fire destroyed another V1. Pilot Officer HS Wingate had picked up a V1 crossing the coast at Hastings, travelling at 410 mph at 2,500 feet. Rolling his Tempest into a dive, he fired from extreme range to no avail. Swooping down on the target, he closed the gap between them and fired his cannon again from 400 yards away as the V1 came in over Biggin Hill. Cannon shells smashed into the V1, which shuddered and slowed down 200 mph. It began to lose height when the sky was filled with flak, forcing Wingate to climb rapidly out of danger. He was later told by Biggin Hill that the target had crashed and exploded at 1630 hrs.

Wartling Control vectored Flight Sergeant MacKerras onto a V1 flying 2 miles south of Eastbourne at 2,500 feet at 340 mph. MacKerras gave chase, pushing his throttle forwards to increase his speed. He closed his Tempest to within 500 yards of the flying bomb when he thumbed the firing button, spurting cannon shells at the target. But his shells missed the V1. MacKerras closed to 200 yards and fired.

> I saw strikes on the port wing and the jet apparatus. The Diver lost height and I fired again and the target went down steeply and exploded on the ground near Gatwick at 1735 hrs.

A little later Flight Sergeant GE Kosh was vectored onto a flying bomb over Hastings at 3,000 feet travelling at 340 mph. Giving chase, he closed to 200 yards and fired, seeing pieces fly off the jet engine from which thick grey smoke erupted. Firing again, he saw the V1 lose height then glide over a small town, exploding in an orchard at 1800 hrs.

At 2100 hrs Flight Sergeant HJ Bailey chased a V1 from Eastbourne travelling at 410 mph at 3,000 feet. Diving on the V1, he levelled off behind the flying bomb and at 700 yards he fired three short bursts but saw no results. 'At 200 yards I fired one long burst and the starboard wing came off,' he reported. The target then rolled over and went straight down, exploding 4 miles north of Eastbourne.

While Bailey was destroying his flying bomb, Pilot Officer Wingate and Warrant Officer RS Adcock picked up a V1 at 4,000 feet over Dungeness that was being chased by Mustangs blazing away but with no results. The doodlebug was doing 350 mph when Wingate dived on it, coming in above and behind firing a burst at 200 yards. The Diver went straight into the ground and exploded near Appledore at 2115 hrs.

Wing Commander Beamont who was on patrol as well saw a Diver over Beachy Head at 3,400 feet, flying at 350 mph. A Spitfire attacked it, firing a burst, but obtained no results and the target continued. Beamont rolled into a dive, closing the gap until he was 150 yards away, when he fired a long burst of his cannon. Shells struck the V1, which suddenly exploded in blue and red flashes, blowing Beamont's Tempest over onto its back. Momentarily, dazed, Beamont managed to right the Tempest, which was now damaged, and turned back to base when he saw another V1 being pursued by Tempests. Despite the damage to his aircraft he turned towards it, rapidly catching up and firing a three-second burst from 300 yards away, which slowed the flying bomb down to 300 mph. Firing another burst, his cannon shells smashed into the target, slowing it down even more. Another Spitfire came in firing its guns and Beamont watched the V1 explode into the ground north of Hastings at 2210 hrs. Beamont claimed one V1 destroyed and one destroyed shared.

That night, Pilot Officer Slade-Betts was vectored onto a V1 over Rye at 2,000 feet. Its airspeed was 320 mph, which made it easier for Slade-Betts to rapidly narrow the distance between his Tempest and the target. At 200 yards away he blew the tail off the V1 with a short burst from his cannon, sending the V1 crashing into a field north of Bexhill where it blew up at 2230 hrs.

At the same time, Flight Lieutenant Umbers was vectored onto a V1 at 3,000 feet coming in over Hastings. Rolling into a dive, he roared down on the flying bomb. Thumbing his firing button he unleashed his cannon, firing several short bursts from 500 yards away. He saw his shells hitting the wings and jet engine, causing it to work intermittently while flames licked the port wing root. It staggered and began losing height. But Umbers suddenly pulled up sharply, warned of barrage balloons in the Dunsford Biggin Hill area by ground controllers. He claimed this as destroyed based on the damage he had caused.

Flying Officer RH Clapperton was vectored onto a V1 coming in over Beachy Head at 2,500 feet. Turning, he climbed the Tempest fast to gain height and moments later caught sight of the flying bomb. Peeling off, he dived on the target narrowing the gap. He fired twice, sending his shells into the V1, which rolled over and went straight into the ground, exploding into a field west of Hallisham at 2315 hrs.

Flight Sergeant MJ Rose picked up the glow from a V1 over Beachy Head at 2,500 feet, flying at 370 mph. Unfortunately, he overshot the target. He turned and came around again firing from slightly below and it exploded in mid-air at 2325 hrs.

The fight against the V1 began early on 19 June 1944. Flying Officer MF Edwards was vectored onto a flying bomb travelling at 380 mph at 2,000 feet, above the cloud over Dungeness. He rolled into a dive, rapidly closing the range between his Tempest and the target. At 150 yards away he fired a short burst and saw his shells hit home on the starboard wing of the V1, which then began to slowly roll, diving through the cloud. It hit the ground and exploded 3 to 4 miles west-north-west of Dungeness at 0725 hrs.

At 1455 hrs Flying Officer RE Barckley was vectored onto a V1 1,000 feet over Seaford, flying at 340 mph. Chasing it, Barckley waited until he was 600 yards away before he fired. The Tempest's cannon sent shells ripping into the flying bomb's jet engine. Getting closer, he fired another burst from 50 yards away and the Diver immediately rolled over and went into the ground, exploding west of Horley.

While Barckley was attacking his V1, Flight Lieutenant AR Moore was vectored onto the first of two flying bombs he destroyed that afternoon. He picked up a visual sighting after being vectored to the co-ordinates by ground controllers of the first one west of Rye, approaching at 2,000 feet. Moore pursued the V1 for several miles and finally, at only 250 yards away, he fired a long burst. He saw several strikes hammer the V1, slowing it down to 160 mph. Thumbing the firing button again he plastered the target with another burst from only 100 yards away, causing the flying bomb to explode in mid-air. Climbing quickly away, he was vectored onto another V1 west of Hastings. For 10 miles he chased the V1 in and out of cloud at 400 mph, closing the gap until he was able to fire a short burst from 150 yards out. Shells from his four cannon smashed into the tail unit, setting it on fire. Thick black smoke erupted from the engine unit and the V1 began losing height over a small village near Tonbridge. It smashed into the ground, exploding on impact.

At 2255 hrs Wing Commander Beamont, already on patrol, was warned of a V1 coming in over Pevensey, flying at 3,500 feet at 320 mph. Turning sharply, he picked up speed and caught sight of the glow from the V1's jet engine. He then saw that the flying bomb was also being chased by a Mustang[24] over Rotherfield, which was firing at the V1. Beamont could see the tracer going below the flying bomb, which continued on a steady course and speed. As the Mustang broke away Beamont went in to attack. 'I gave it a short burst from 250 yards and it went over on its back and dived into the wood 2 miles south west of Tunbridge Wells at 2210 hrs,' Beamont reported.

That same night Flying Officer Barckley picked up a V1 over Hastings flying at 2,000 feet at 360 mph. Turning hard, Barckley gave chase, when suddenly another Tempest came roaring in and fired from 400 yards then broke away. Determined, Barckley closed the gap between his Tempest and the flying bomb and opened fire. But again, the other Tempest came down and broke away the attack as Barckley fired again. Pieces flew off the V1 as it began to lose height, slowing down, diving towards Biggin Hill.[25]

While this was taking place, Flight Lieutenant AR Moore, his face reflected from the glow of his instruments in the cockpit, headed for the coordinates given to him by Newchurch Control, warning him of an approaching V1 coming in from the Channel north of Rye, travelling at 2,500 feet. Seeing the glow of the flame from the jet engine, he rolled the Tempest into a dive, manoeuvring behind the target, and fired a four-second burst. In the darkness, he couldn't be sure of the range. 'The Diver exploded and my Tempest was turned on its back,' he wrote in his combat report. This action took place approximately 6 miles north-north-west of Rye at 2310 hrs.

That night, Flying Officer Whitman and Pilot Officer Feldman were patrolling their sector when Feldman spotted the flames from the jet of a flying bomb at great distance. The two Tempests were well above the target, which was travelling at approximately 350 mph. Feldman gave chase, diving at full speed on the Diver. He fired a short burst from 500 yards away, then fired a long burst of his cannon at only 200 yards away. He saw his shells hitting the jet engine, which suddenly went out, the bright glow from its flame gone. 'The Diver spiralled gently on the same course and exploded in a park at Bexhill at 2300 hrs,' Feldman reported.

Feldman's radio suddenly stopped working and he returned to base, while Pilot Officer Whitman was vectored onto another flying bomb by Newchurch Control. He spotted this one approaching at 3,000 feet, crossing in at high speed. Giving chase, Whitman closed the range and fired a long burst from 800 yards away. He could see strikes on the V1 but it continued on its course. Whitman broke off his attack, climbed rapidly, turning hard to come around again. This time he waited until he was 300 yards away when he fired a short burst, which sent the Diver smashing into the ground near Cranbrook at 2320 hrs.

In the early morning of 20 June 1944 Flight Lieutenant AE Umbers was vectored onto a flying bomb flying at 1,000 feet, crossing in over Bexhill. Diving into line astern at 450 mph, Umbers closed on the V1. 'I opened up with a burst from 500 yards,' Umbers reported.

'I closed to 150 yards firing short bursts and saw strikes on the fuselage.'

The flying bomb slowed to 250 mph and began losing height. 'I fired another burst from 150 yards which stopped the jet and the Diver went down emitting grey smoke and exploding in the Redhill area at 0545 hrs.'

Later that morning, Pilot Officer Feldman destroyed another Diver after being vectored into the Bexhill area. The target was flying at 2,300 feet at 360 mph. Pushing his throttle forward he dived on the doodlebug and came down parallel with it, over-shooting. Levelling out, he turned the Tempest sharply, coming in behind the V1 again and opened fire at 700 yards, firing short bursts to 300 yards but had no results. Feldman reported:

I fired again at 300 yards and a piece of the starboard wing flew off. The Diver weaved violently and went down exploding on the ground south west of Tonbridge.

This took place at 0840 hrs.

Pilot Officer Slade-Betts chased a V1 that crossed the coast approaching London east of Eastbourne at 2,000 feet. He shot it down from 500 yards away, sending it straight into a field where it exploded on impact some 6 miles north of Eastbourne at 0940 hrs.

In the afternoon, Pilot Officer HS Wingate was given the coordinates of a V1 coming in from the Channel south of Hastings on a course for London, at 2,500 feet at 330 mph. Turning, he rolled his Tempest into a dive, rapidly closing the range and fired a short burst. 'I pulled to one side and the Diver went into the ground and exploded south west of Hastings.' This was at 1335 hrs.

Pilot Officer SB Feldman took off from Newchurch at 1815 hrs, vectored onto a V1 crossing the coast near Eastbourne at 1,000 feet, flying at 340 mph. From 500 yards away, he fired two short bursts at it and missed. Increasing his speed, he closed to 200 yards and fired another burst. The V1 dropped into a shallow dive and started weaving. Feldman came in again, firing another burst, which blew the V1's wing off. It spun into the ground, exploding on impact north of Eastbourne.

As night fell, Flight Sergeant DM Smith climbed into the air from Newchurch at 2140 hrs. The Tempest's huge Napier Sabre engine purred as he pushed the throttle forward, heading to the Hastings area, directed to the coordinates of a V1 approaching at 3,000 feet flying at 320 mph. In the gloom he could see the glow of the jet engine as it shot past and underneath him not less than 200 yards away. Turning tightly, he increased his speed, chasing the V1. He fired at it from 600 to 200 yards with several short bursts of cannon fire. Breaking to port he turned again, firing another burst, which shot off the port wingtip. 'The target rolled on its back and went down and exploded on the ground 6 miles north of Hastings at 2200 hrs,' Smith reported.

Only fifteen minutes after Smith had taken off, Flying Officer, RH Clapperton lifted his Tempest off the runway, soaring away from Newchurch at high speed into the night sky. He caught sight of a flying bomb north of Dungeness being attacked by AA fire from the coastal guns. Above the flying bomb, Clapperton heading inland, following its trajectory at 390 mph. He then dived his Tempest, dropping in behind the V1, and fired a long burst, seeing his shells smash into the port wing. Suddenly, the V1 heeled over and spun into the ground, exploding south-west of Ashford.

On 21 June, the first V1 was destroyed by pilots of No. 3 Squadron at 0600 hrs. Flight Sergeant RW Cole climbed into the dawn sky at 0535 hrs from Newchurch and was vectored onto a V1 flying at 4,000 feet at 370 mph. Putting the Tempest into a shallow dive he chased the flying bomb at high speed, coming in above and behind the target. He closed range and fired from 80 yards away. The target climbed slightly, turned over and fell into open ground, exploding on impact north-east of Hastings.

Cole was then vectored onto another flying bomb coming in 7 miles south of Rye at 270 mph, flying at 4,000 feet. Turning tightly, he climbed the Tempest at full power until he was able to dive on the flying bomb. Levelling off, he fired a half-second burst from 100 yards away. The V1, hit by shells, suddenly turned to port, flew along the coast, then quickly dropped into the sea and exploded off Bexhill at 0600 hrs.

On 23 June two pilots, Pilot Officer Slade-Betts and Flight Sergeant Rose, both had engine trouble and were forced to land in difficult circumstances. Slade-Betts managed a wheels-down landing at Woodchurch, the cause of his engine trouble a cannon shell in the radiator, while Rose did not fair as well. Over the airfield at Newchurch, Rose put his wheels down as his engine spluttered, hoping he could get down in one piece. But he overshot the runway, bouncing over the grass. Then suddenly his aircraft hit a ditch, sheering off his undercarriage and bringing him to a sudden, jolting halt at the end of the runway.

25 June was a busy day for the Squadron with most of the action taking place in the late afternoon, early evening and night. The first flying bomb to fall was at the hands of Flight Sergeant RW Cole, airborne from Newchurch at 2030 hrs. He was vectored onto a V1 coming in 4 miles north of Rye at 3,000 feet. At patrol height, he gave chase, rolling the Tempest into a dive and closing the range between his Tempest and the target. He opened up with his four Hispano 20-mm cannon at 400 yards, then at 300 yards he fired another burst. Checking his horizon indicator to make sure he was straight and level, he lined up the V1 and fired another burst from 250 yards away, sending it straight into the ground where it exploded on impact 7 miles north of Hastings.

At 2140 hrs, Squadron Leader AS Dredge took off from Newchurch, climbing quickly into the night sky. Given the coordinates of a V1 crossing in between Fairlight Cove and Hastings by Control, he turned hard and headed for the target. Spotting the bright glow from the jet engine, he checked his airspeed indicator and altimeter and realised the V1 was flying at 2,000 feet at 350 mph. He dropped the Tempest into a shallow dive, closing on the target, and at 300 yards he fired a short burst but saw no results. Getting closer, he fired again and this time he could see the shells pounding the starboard wing of the V1. At a distance of 150 yards he fired a third burst. The V1 pulled up sharply as the starboard wing came off. It hit the ground, exploding in a field 2 miles east-south-east of Hawkhurst. The time of impact was 2150 hrs.

Flight Sergeant MJ Rose was already in the air when Squadron Leader Dredge took off, patrolling the Beachy Head area.[26] Beachy Head Control then vectored Rose onto a V1 between Hastings and Rye at 2,000 feet at 350 mph. Rose rolled his Tempest into a dive bearing down on the target and fired two shorts bursts from 100 yards away, ripping both wingtips off the V1. 'The Diver flicked over and dived into the outskirts of a small village in Goudshurst area at 2136 hrs,' Rose recorded in his combat report.

Flight Lieutenant Van Lierde with Flying Officer Whitman as his No. 2 roared into the night sky from Newchurch at 2250 hrs. Directed to their patrol sector by ground control, they picked up a visual sighting of a V1 coming in over Lydd with the aid of identification rockets fired from the ground. Both Tempests flew towards the target at high speed and at 200 yards took turns firing several bursts of cannon fire at it. The jet engine went out and the V1 hit the ground, exploding south-west of Ashford. At 2310 hrs they picked up the glow of the exhaust flame from the jet engine of another incoming V1 over Dungeness, travelling at 2,000 feet 4 miles inland. Van Lierde roared down on the target, lining it up in his gunsight as he closed the gap between them. Finally, he fired a long burst that sent the V1 smashing into the ground, where it blew up in an unknown position at 2319 hrs.

While this was taking place, Flight Sergeant MacKerras and Flight Sergeant Bailey were vectored onto a V1 over Beachy Head at 2,500 feet by Beachy Head Control. Levelling off from a dive, MacKerras lined up his Tempest behind the target and fired a two-second burst from 300 yards away. His four cannon send a torrent of shells into the V1's jet engine that exploded, sending the remains of the V1 into the ground where it disintegrated.

Climbing back up to patrol height, MacKerras caught sight of a glow from another V1's engine. He turned and dived on the target, firing several short bursts. He saw his tracer shells strike the V1 and it began losing height but disappeared into cloud. MacKerras didn't get confirmation that this V1 was destroyed.

Flight Sergeant HJ Bailey was vectored towards a sector where V1s were approaching. He sighted a Diver coming in west of Dungeness at 3,000 feet and immediately gave chase, keeping the glow from its jet engine in sight. As he closed range the night sky was suddenly filled with exploding AA shells as the gunners below tried to bring the V1 down. Bumped and jolted from the exploding shells around him, Bailey managed to fire a couple of two-second bursts at the flying bomb before breaking away to avoid getting shot down by British AA guns! As he climbed away he saw the V1 fall to earth and explode at 2330 hrs.

Pilot Officer SB Feldman, already airborne from Newchurch, was vectored onto a V1 20 miles south-east of Hastings at 2,500 feet. Acknowledging Beachy Head Control he peeled off, diving onto the target. At 400 yards he fired several short bursts that sent the V1 crashing into the sea, approximately 15 miles south-east of Hastings.

On 28 June Flying Officer Clapperton shot down three Divers in one sortie, bringing the total Squadron score to 100 flying bombs destroyed in just thirteen days.

Another very busy day was 30 June. Beachy Control vectored Flight Sergeant HJ Foster onto a V1 crossing in 2 miles south of Dungeness at 0630 hrs at 4,500 feet and flying at 350 mph. Acknowledging, Foster rolled into a dive, attacking the flying bomb with bursts from his cannon and shooting off the V1's wing. The flying bomb went straight into the ground and exploded in a cloud of smoke and flames.

At 1030 hrs, Flying Officer KG Slade-Betts took off from Newchurch, climbing his Tempest rapidly into the morning sky. Picked up by Beachy Head Control, they vectored him onto a V1 coming in at 340 mph at 5,500 feet, 3 miles east of Dungeness. Picking up the exhaust flame from the flying bomb, Slade-Betts put his Tempest into a shallow dive, chasing the V1 and firing from long range. He said of the attack:

I closed to 150 yards. The Diver's tail was shot away. The jet apparatus was damaged and the flames ceased and then the Diver went through the cloud, followed by me, and exploded on the ground 4 miles south of Maidstone at 1117 hrs.

Of all the action that day, Flight Sergeant Cole had the most interesting time. Lifting off from Newchurch at 1030 hrs, he climbed the Tempest rapidly away from the airfield. He picked up Beachy Head Control once airborne and headed for the coordinates of a V1 crossing in 4 miles south-east of Rye flying at 350 mph at 4,500 feet. Seeing the flying bomb, Cole immediately put on more speed, dropping into a shallow dive, bringing his Tempest above and behind the V1. From a distance of 600 yards he opened fire but missed. A few minutes later, with his Tempest flying at 400 mph, he fired again from 300 yards and this time his shells struck the flying bomb, which turned to starboard and plummeted in the ground and blew up 1½ miles from Rye. This was at 1045 hrs. Vectored onto another set of coordinates, he climbed the Tempest and picked up a visual sighting of another flying bomb coming in 6 miles north of Hastings, at 350 mph around 4,500 feet. As he headed towards it he saw another Tempest chasing it but not attacking it.

Peeling off into a dive, Cole roared down on the V1, fired several short bursts and saw his cannon shells rip into the flying bomb's fuselage and wings causing it to waver. Flying ahead of it, he tried to force it down in the Tempest's slip-stream but this didn't work and he left the V1 losing height north-west of Tonbridge at 1115 hrs.

He was then put onto another V1 coming in over Newchurch at 360 mph at 4,000 feet. Chasing it, he rapidly closed the range then fired several short bursts of cannon fire at the German flying bomb, seeing his shells hammer the starboard wing. Immediately, the V1 began executing a number of slow rolls, rapidly losing height until it exploded in flames in the Tonbridge area at 1140 hrs.

Beachy Control vectored another Tempest pilot from No. 3 Squadron onto a V1 that morning at 1130 hrs, which was 10 miles north-west of Le Treport travelling at 380 mph at 4,500 feet. Flight Sergeant S Domanski spotted the enemy flying bomb and fired at it from 800 yards but overshot as the V1 slowed. Turning tightly, he came back around behind the V1 and fired, this time from only 100 yards. He saw his shells striking the starboard side of the V1's fuselage, which burst into flames and crashed into the sea 10 miles south of Dungeness at 1150 hrs.

Flying Officer DJ Butcher had one of the oddest reactions of a flying bomb to cannon fire in the Squadron. Lifting his Tempest off the runway at Newchurch he roared into the night sky at 2130 hrs, climbing rapidly away. Once airborne he picked up Beachy Control. Here he takes up the story in his own words.

I saw a Diver with the aid of ROC rockets north of Eastbourne at 2,000 feet at 320 indicated airspeed. I closed to 150 yards dead astern and fired a 2-second burst seeing strikes. I fired a second burst from 250 yards that caused the Diver to stall and dive to near ground level. It then climbed to nearly 1,000 feet and then dived in exploding on the ground at 2205 hrs.

July 1944 proved to be even busier than June had been for No. 3 Squadron.

The first day of July saw Flight Sergeant Domanski take off from Newchurch at 0455 hrs and as he climbed rapidly into the fresh, early morning sky he was picked up by Wartling Control. He was vectored onto two flying bombs coming in a mile apart from each other midway over the Channel, flying at 4,000 feet at 380 mph. Giving chase, he closed to 200 yards on the first V1 and fired two short bursts, sending the flying bomb crashing into the sea, where it exploded on impact at 0515 hrs. Heading for the second V1, he pushed his throttle forward, building up the Tempest's speed and closing the gap. Coming in dead astern of the V1 he fired another burst and saw his shells strike the target, but it began to lose height and was lost in cloud.

Flying Officer R Dryland had taken off from Newchurch at 0455 hrs along with Flight Sergeant S Domanski and was vectored onto a V1 over Rye by Wartling Control. Spotting the glow of the exhaust flame, he brought his Tempest in right behind the flying bomb in a dive and fired a three-second burst, but the V1 disappeared into cloud and Dryland couldn't tell if it crashed. However, Biggin Hill Control reported a flying bomb had gone down in the same area in the relevant time so this was credited to Dryland as destroyed.

Two days later, Flight Lieutenant Van Lierde opened the scoring for the day after taking off from Newchurch to begin another anti-Diver patrol. Climbing rapidly away from the airfield into the morning sky at 0745 hrs, he was picked up by Beachy Control and vectored onto a flying bomb coming in 25 miles south of Dungeness, flying at 2,500 feet at 360 mph. Picking up a visual sighting of the V1, he manoeuvred the Tempest in behind the target, increasing the fighter's speed and closing the gap. The huge Napier Sabre engine roared as the Tempest tore after the V1. Within a few minutes he was 600 yards away and he fired his first burst but saw no strikes. Moments later, he thumbed the firing button again, sending a hail of cannon shells into the Diver jet engine from 400 yards away. The jet failed and the V1 began weaving an erratic course. From 200 yards he fired another burst accurately aimed from dead astern of the V1, which suddenly slowed down appreciably and disappeared into cloud 15 to 20 miles between Beachy Head and Bexhill at 0755 hrs. Later that day, reports came in from the Observer Corps of a V1 seen flying on an erratic course and crashing 4 miles north of Horsham at approximately the same time.

Just before Van Lierde landed back at Newchurch at 0810 hrs, Flight Sergeant DJ MacKerras was airborne at 0805 hrs from

Newchurch on an anti-Diver patrol when he was directed by Beachy Head Control onto a V1 coming in towards Britain from 10 miles off Boulogne in France. He immediately poured on the power, heading out across the Channel. He caught sight of the flying bomb travelling at 2,000 feet at 300 mph. Rapidly closing, he fired a short burst from 400 yards away but saw no strikes. At 200 yards he fired again, his shells striking the wings and pulse-jet apparatus. The V1 broke up and the warhead crashed into the water, exploding on impact 10 miles south-east of Dungeness at 0837 hrs.

The next flying bomb was destroyed by pilots of No. 3 Squadron in the late afternoon. Pilot Officer HS Wingate roared off the runway, climbing his Tempest rapidly away from Newchurch at 1700 hrs in company with Flight Sergeant HJ Bailey. They climbed up to patrol height while in communication with Wartling Control who gave them the coordinates of a V1 approaching Hastings, flying at 2,500 feet at 350 mph. Rolling into a dive, Wingate brought the Tempest in behind the V1 and, levelling off, he fired three short bursts from 400 yards away. Pounded by cannon shells from Wingate's guns, the V1 exploded in mid-air.

Vectored onto another flying bomb coming in over Hastings at 2,500 feet, Wingate and Flight Sergeant HJ Bailey flew off in hot pursuit. As they closed in, they could see another Tempest from 486 Squadron chasing the same V1. This aircraft dived on the target firing its guns but no strikes were seen on the flying bomb. Wingate then closed on the target and from 50 yards away fired a two-second burst from his cannon that blew the V1 apart. Wingate reported:

The third and last Diver of this sortie was seen coming over the Hastings gasworks at 2,500 feet at 350 indicated. Red Two (Bailey) fired a short burst without success and then I closed in to 50 yards dead astern and loosed a short burst and the Diver exploded in mid-air at 1755 hrs.

Both pilots landed back at Newchurch at 1810 hrs.

Pilot Officer KG Slade-Betts and Flight Sergeant MJ Rose lifted off from Newchurch at 1800 hrs, soaring into the early summer evening sky. Attaining their patrol height, they were directed by Wartling Control towards a V1 crossing in 2 miles north of Hastings at 2,000 feet, flying at 320 mph. Increasing speed, Slade-Betts gave chase. He rolled his Tempest into a steep dive on the target, coming in dead astern and levelling off at 150 yards. Then he fired five two-second bursts. The flying bomb blew up in mid-air 15 miles north of Hastings at 1900 hrs. Debris shot back at Slade-Betts and a piece tore through his starboard wing, forcing him to head back to base. As he was landing back at Newchurch, Flight Sergeant Rose returned towards the patrol line when he sighted another V1 with the aid of identification rockets fired by the Royal Observer Corps. He could see the glow from its jet and quickly checked his instruments to see the indicated airspeed and altitude, knowing it was flying at roughly 3,000 feet at 350 mph. Bursts of heavy flak chased the V1 but as Rose engaged the AA fire died away. Closing dead astern at 300 yards he pressed the firing button, sending a storm of cannon shells towards the V1, but saw no hits. Increasing his speed, Rose narrowed the range to 250 yards, lining the V1 up in his sights. He then fired a one-second burst, raking the V1. Smoke and flames poured from the flying bomb, which dropped vertically down through the cloud, exploding beside a main road in the Ashford/Maidstone area.

On 4 July 1944 the Squadron was in action again. The first flying bomb to go down was in the afternoon. At 1510 hrs Flying Officer RH Clapperton lifted off from Newchurch, climbing rapidly up to his patrol height. Under Wartling Control he was directed onto a V1 crossing in 4 miles south of Pevensey Bay, flying at 360 mph at 2,500 feet. Turning, he dived on the target, manoeuvring his Tempest dead astern of the V1 and closing rapidly. He fired three bursts from his cannon and saw shells strike both wings. The V1 went straight down and exploded on the ground at Hellingly, 2 miles north of Hailsham at 1545 hrs.

Ten minutes earlier, Flight Lieutenant Van Lierde roared down the runway with Flight Sergeant CW Orwin. Their Tempests leapt into the air. Reaching their patrol height of around 6,000 feet Beachy Control vectored the section onto a V1 coming in 10 miles south of Beachy Head at 3,000 feet, flying at 340 mph. Van Lierde saw the V1 and rolled his Tempest into a dive, tearing down on the target. He levelled off behind the target, rapidly closing the range between them. From 400 yards he fired the first burst and fired his last from 150 yards. Van Lierde reported:

This caused the jet apparatus to vomit further flames and black
smoke. The Diver then went in and crashed and exploded on the
ground 3 miles northeast of Pevensey at 1620 hrs.

In his report, Van Lierde made a strange entry that has no
explanation.

As the Diver was going down at about 100 mph I saw black and
white stripes on the upper surfaces of the wings and what were
believed to be USA markings (stars) also on the wing surfaces.

One can only wonder if this observation was accurate and if
it was why were the Americans testing a captured version of the
flying bomb, or their own version of it, over English skies at the
height of the flying bomb menace? Or had the Germans decided
to try to confuse the Allies by using American markings on their
V1s? We may never know the truth.

Later that afternoon, Beachy Head Control vectored Warrant
Officer RS Adcock and Flight Sergeant LG Everson, patrolling over
the Channel, onto a flying bomb, which was travelling 25 miles
north-west of Le Touquet at 2,000 feet at 300 mph. Both Tempests
turned towards the coordinates, increasing their speed. Closing in
on the target, the two Tempests chased it across the Channel with
Adcock leading. Diving on the doodlebug, he levelled off dead
astern and fired two bursts from 150 to 200 yards away and saw
his shells smash into the starboard wing, which started smoking
as pieces flew off. The V1 slowed down to 250 mph and Adcock
thumbed the firing button again but nothing happened. Out of
ammunition, he radioed for Flight Sergeant Everson to continue
the attack.

Peeling off, Everson dived his Tempest on the target, levelling
off behind the V1. Then he fired a burst of cannon fire from 300
yards. Climbing, he opened his throttle, turned and dived down
on the doodlebug again, coming in across the starboard quarter
and firing his cannon. His shells hit the jet engine, which
exploded, sending the remains of the V1 into the sea. The V1 blew
up on impact 15 miles south of Dungeness at 1730 hrs.

That same day Pilot Officer Slade-Betts, under the control of
Beachy Head, was vectored onto a V1 15 miles south of Bexhill,
which he shot down with five bursts of his cannon at 1815 hrs.

Flight Lieutenant AR Moore, also in touch with Beachy Head Control, was vectored onto a V1 south of Eastbourne. He hit it with two short bursts fired from dead astern from 100 yards, sending the Diver into the sea 20 yards off shore in Pevensey Bay at 2030 hrs.

Flight Lieutenant Van Lierde was involved in another remarkable action. Taking off from Newchurch with Pilot Officer SR Feldman as his No. 2, the Tempests roared into the night sky to begin their anti-Diver patrol. As they climbed into the gloom they were picked up by Beachy Head Control and vectored onto a flying bomb crossing in 10 miles south of Bexhill, travelling at 2,500 feet at 400 mph.

As Van Lierde was leading he saw the glow of the exhaust flame from the jet engine and dived on the V1. Lining the V1 up in his gunsight, he manoeuvred his Tempest in behind the flying bomb, his throttle open wide. He fired two one-second bursts of his cannon from 300 yards away, the tracer ripping into the target. The V1 fell and exploded into the ground 12 miles north of Beachy Head at 2108 hrs.

Beachy Head Control vectored the Tempests onto another flying bomb south of Hastings flying at 2,000 feet at 300 mph. Concentrating on the exhaust glow Van Lierde lined up his gunsight and fired several bursts, seeing his tracer shells hitting the V1. It went straight down and exploded into the sea 4 miles south of Hastings at 2130 hrs. The next flying bomb to fall to Van Lierde's guns he picked up from the exhaust flame flying over the sea at 1,500 feet at 320 mph. Using his superior speed, he brought the Tempest in behind the target and fired a two-second burst from 150 yards away.

Smoke and flames gushed from the stricken flying bomb. Van Lierde recorded:

> It pulled up in front of the Tempest, looped and went into the sea without exploding. It skated off the surface, rose to 150 feet then went straight down and exploded on the water about 4 miles south of Hastings at 2145 hrs.

Flares fired from the Royal Observer Corps helped him identify a fourth V1 between Hastings and Bexhill at 3,000 feet, flying at

340 mph. Giving chase, Van Lierde and Feldman closed rapidly on the V1. From 150 yards Flight Lieutenant Van Lierde fired a two-second burst but overshot the target. He saw flames pouring from the port side of the fuselage, the V1 slowing down. His ammunition gone, he called his No. 2 Pilot Officer Feldman to finish it off.

Before Feldman could open fire another Tempest came in and attacked. The flying bomb heeled over, plummeting straight into the ground and exploding 15 miles north of Hastings. Feldman then caught sight of a flying bomb crossing in 20 miles south of Rye at 2,000 feet, at 320 mph. Turning, he roared down on the target, firing two short bursts from 400 yards directly behind the V1 and saw his shells pepper the target. But it continued on its course and speed. Remaining dead astern of the V1 he closed to 200 yards and fired a further two short bursts, his cannon shells smashing into the jet engine, which flickered. The stricken flying bomb dropped its nose and went straight down, exploding in the sea 10 miles south of Rye at 2155 hrs.

The two Tempests were vectored onto another flying bomb south of Hastings, flying at 2,500 feet at 300 mph. Feldman, now leading, rapidly overtook the V1, closing the gap between them. From 300 yards he fired a short burst of cannon fire. Shells from his guns smashed into the jet engine, spewing smoke and flames, slowing the V1. Feldman continued the attack, closing to 100 yards, where he gave it a three-second burst. He saw strikes on the wings and fuselage. Pieces flew off the Diver, which exploded in mid-air, while the warhead went straight into the ground and blew up 3–5 miles south of Hastings at 2157 hrs. Both pilots landed back at Newchurch at 2208 hrs, exhausted. They had taken off at 2100 hrs and in just over one hour destroyed five doodlebugs.

At 2205 hrs Flying Officer RH Clapperton and Flight Sergeant LG Everson climbed into the night sky from Newchurch. In the darkness, they could see the navigation lights on their wingtips as they formed up in a line astern, two Tempests on anti-Diver patrols looking for 'trade'.[27]

Directed by Beachy Head Control they picked up a V1 15 miles south of Hastings, flying at 2,500 feet at 380 mph. Flying Officer Clapperton gave chase, coming in directly behind the target. Firing two one-second bursts, his shells hammered the V1 and sent it crashing into the ground 2 miles north of Hastings where it exploded at 2215 hrs.

In the darkness of night, Clapperton picked up the trail of the exhaust flame of another V1 approximately 10 miles south of Hastings, flying at 2,500 feet at 360 mph. Clapperton dived on the target, closing to 300 yards. Then he fired a burst of cannon fire at it, hitting the jet engine. The flying bomb went down and exploded when it hit the sea 3 miles south of Hastings at 2245 hrs.

A third V1 was seen approximately 10 miles south of Hastings crossing in at 2,000 feet, flying at 380 mph. Turning tightly, Clapperton peeled off, diving on the target and firing a long burst from his cannon from 150 yards. 'The petrol exploded in the air,' he wrote in his combat report. 'And the warhead exploded in the sea three miles south of Bexhill at 2300 hrs.'

Flight Sergeant Everson was vectored onto a V1 15 miles south of Hastings, crossing in at 3,000 feet at 320 mph. Manoeuvring his Tempest behind the flying bomb, he quickly narrowed the range. Then from a distance of 150 yards he pressed the firing button, sending a storm of cannon shells into the jet engine. It exploded, erupting into flames and smoke. The V1 turned suddenly to port then crashed into the sea 10 miles south of Hastings at 2255 hrs, exploding on impact.

More work came the Squadron's way on 5 July when Flying Officer MF Edwards and Flight Sergeant HJ Bailey took off from Newchurch at 1632 hrs. Climbing rapidly up to their patrol height, they were vectored onto a flying bomb 40 miles south of Dungeness, travelling at 3,000 feet at 400 mph. Diving on the target, Edwards closed in directly behind the V1 and fired at it from 700 yards away, seeing some of his shells hit the target. Pressing his attack home he fired again from 300 yards, the shells ripping into the V1's port wing. It staggered and slowed. Then from 100 yards he fired again, sending the flying bomb into a straight dive. It hit the ground and exploded on impact near Edenbridge at 1720 hrs.

On the same sortie, Flight Sergeant Bailey picked up another V1 coming in 15 miles south of Beachy, flying at 2,500 feet at 300 mph. He rolled the Tempest into a dive, roaring on the target, firing at it from 50 yards. His cannon shells snuffed out the jet engine and the V1 went straight into the sea, exploding on impact at 1741 hrs.

On the same day, Flying Officer R Dryland knocked down three flying bombs in one patrol. Lifting off from Newchurch at 1730 hrs, he climbed his Tempest rapidly up to his patrol altitude and was vectored onto his first V1 by Beachy Head Control. It was coming in fast at 3,000 feet at 350 mph. Diving on it, he blew the port wing off with a storm of cannon shells from 150 yards away and the V1 went straight into the ground, exploding 1 mile north of Rye at 1755 hrs. He caught sight of his next victim 8 miles north of Dungeness at 3,500 feet, travelling at 350 mph. Manoeuvring his Tempest directly astern of the V1, he closed rapidly to 100 yards. He let loose a burst of shells that smashed into the jet and wing, putting out the jet. Immediately, the V1 went straight into the ground and blew up at 1855 hrs.

In continuous touch with ground control he picked up the third V1 some 5 miles south of Beachy Head, crossing in at 2,000 feet at 350 mph, heading inland towards the London area. Pressing his rudder and the control column, he brought the Tempest in behind and slightly above the flying bomb, then fired from 150 yards away. The doodlebug went straight down and exploded on the ground east of Falmer.

Flying Officer Edwards and Flight Sergeant Bailey were up again at 1825 hrs. They were vectored onto a flying bomb travelling 15 miles south of Dungeness at 3,200 feet at 370 mph, heading inland. Chasing it, Edwards brought his Tempest in behind the V1 and fired from 500 yards. Closing the gap to 300 yards he fired again and this time the V1 rolled over and dived straight in, exploding on the ground near Tenterden at 1845 hrs. He saw the glow from another flying bomb's engine over Hastings coming in fast at 3,000 feet at 380 mph. He saw other fighters chasing the V1. Using his speed, he rolled his Tempest into a dive, bringing it round behind the target, overtaking the other aircraft and firing bursts from his cannon from 300 to 200 yards away. Under a storm of cannon shells the Diver blew up in mid-air over Tenterden at 1930 hrs.

Vectored by Wartling Control, Flight Sergeant Bailey attacked a flying bomb coming in at 3,000 feet at 350 mph, 10 miles south of Pevensey. From 150 yards he fired a two-second burst, hitting the target. It rolled over and smashed into the sea, disintegrating in a cloud of flames and smoke about 3 miles south of Pevensey.

Flight Lieutenant Umbers was airborne on his patrol at the same time as Flight Sergeant Bailey. Beachy Head Control directed him towards the coordinates of another V1 crossing the coast 3 miles north of Beachy Head at 3,000 feet, travelling at 380 mph. Coming in at an angle on the V1, he fired a deflection burst but saw no results. Bringing his Tempest in behind the target, he closed to

400 yards and fired again. No strikes were seen so he followed the V1 through cloud over Redhill, dropping his height and firing another short burst. This time he saw the cannon shells smash into the wings and fuselage. The flying bomb slowed and disappeared into cloud over Redhill.

On 6 July Flight Lieutenant Van Lierde opened the day's scoring early in the morning.

> *I saw a Diver 6 miles off Hastings. I dived from 6,000 feet and gave 3 two second bursts from 200 yards observing strikes. The jet went out and then came on again with a brighter and longer flame.*

Van Lierde overshot the V1 as it slowed suddenly to 120 mph then he turned the Tempest tightly, diving on the V1 that had already dropped to 1,500 feet. Orbiting the target, he could see flames pouring out of the port side of the fuselage. As he turned above the flying bomb, four other aircraft came in attacking the V1, which went down and exploded near Tonbridge at 0455 hrs. Van Lierde claimed one flying bomb destroyed.

While Van Lierde was airborne and attacking his V1, Squadron Leader Dredge was scrambled from Newchurch. He roared into the early morning air, climbing rapidly to 6,000 feet. Directed by Beachy Head Control onto a flying bomb approaching the coast 5 miles north of Dover at 2,500 feet at 350 mph, Dredge turned his Tempest towards the coordinates. Spotting the glow from the V1's jet exhaust, he rolled the Tempest into a dive and bore down on the target south of Canterbury. From 100 yards he fired a 1½-second burst in a deflection shot. Manoeuvring the Tempest in behind the flying bomb he fired again from 100 yards, seeing his shells hammer the jet engine, which slowed down the V1 to 100 mph. It turned to the north, losing height and exploding on the ground in the Faversham/Sittingbourne area at 0450 hrs.

At 0425 hrs Flight Lieutenant Umbers and Flying Officer Clapperton rose into the morning sky, climbing up to their patrol height. Vectored onto a flying bomb crossing the coast at 2,500 feet at 360 mph by Beachy Head Control, Umbers peeled off, diving on the V1. He fired a burst from 400 yards away, his shells hitting the target and forcing it to slow down. As it did, Umbers had to break off the attack to avoid ramming the target. The V1 plummeted into the ground and exploded at 0455 hrs.

Flying Officer Clapperton picked up a V1 6 miles north of Ashford, flying at 3,000 feet at 360 mph. Diving down, he brought his Tempest in behind the flying bomb and fired a burst of cannon fire at it from 300 yards directly behind it. Cannon shells hammered the jet engine, which went out in a shower of sparks, while the port wing also received several hits that sent the Diver straight into the ground, where it exploded near Tonbridge at 0452 hrs.

The early morning of 6 July was very busy. While Clapperton and Umbers were grappling with their V1s, Flying Officer Edwards and Flight Sergeant Bailey were airborne from Newchurch, roaring into the crisp early morning air. They were directed by Beachy Head Control onto a flying bomb. Climbing, they spotted the V1 coming in south of Dungeness at 4,000 feet, travelling at 400 mph.

At 7,000 feet, Edwards rolled into a dive, followed by Bailey. The two Tempests roared down on the target with Edwards leading. Pulling back on the stick, he levelled out, coming in dead astern of the flying bomb. He fired from 300 yards. Watching his shells pound the V1, he saw it suddenly explode in mid-air 10 to 15 miles south of Dungeness and both Tempests took evasive action to avoid being hit by the debris.

On the same patrol Flight Sergeant Bailey picked up a Diver 15 miles south of Bexhill, flying at 3,500 feet at 350 mph. Before he could dive down for the attack he saw a Mosquito fire from 1,000 yards away with no results. Bailey turned hard, diving rapidly and bringing the Tempest in behind the V1 at top speed. He fired his cannon from 400 yards away. After crossing the coast other aircraft came in and attacked the V1. Bailey turned tightly, coming back in for a second time and firing a two-second burst from 5 degrees off the stern. His cannon shells struck the jet engine, slowing the V1, which turned, losing height and hitting the ground where it blew up at 0450 hrs.

Pilot Officer Wingate shot down another V1 that morning at 0640 hrs near Tonbridge.

In the afternoon, Wing Commander Beamont attacked a V1 over Pevensey when a strange thing happened.

I was closing to 300 yards and I fired. The Diver slowed and I was firing again when another Diver came down and went through the line of fire.

Though he never saw the one he was attacking go down he assumed it crashed and exploded near Pevenesey at 1415 hrs.

The last score of the day was credited to Pilot Officer HR Wingate who shared in the destruction of a V1 with 486 Squadron pilot WO Hooper.

At 0402 hrs on 7 July 1944 Flight Lieutenant Moore was scrambled to intercept a flying bomb. It was coming in 25 miles south of Dungeness, travelling at 2,500 feet at 385 mph. Climbing rapidly away from Newchurch, he turned and dived on the target, firing a burst at it from 600 yards out but seeing no results. Pulling up, he turned again, coming back in behind the V1, then fired a two- to three-second burst from 400 yards away. This time his cannon shells hammered the flying bomb and it went down, crashing into the ground 8 miles north of Hastings at 0510 hrs.

Just twenty minutes later, Flight Lieutenant Van Lierde took off from Newchurch. He climbed his Tempest rapidly up to patrol altitude, with Warrant Officer RS Adcock right beside and slightly behind him. Vectored onto a V1 by Beachy Head Control, he saw the Diver 10 miles south of Hastings, crossing in at 3,200 feet at 340 mph. Turning, he rolled his Tempest into a dive, coming around behind the V1. He rapidly closed the gap until at 400 yards he fired a burst of cannon at it, seeing his shells pepper the V1. Van Lierde reported:

> When we were over the coast I attacked again from 250 yards and a large piece came off the Diver. It slowed to 120 mph and when at 300 feet from the ground it was attacked by a Spitfire with 'W' squadron letters believed to be DL who attacked with a short burst.

The flying bomb crashed and exploded in a wood in the Cranbrook area at 0546 hrs. Van Lierde continued:

> The Diver was already going down in flames when attacked unnecessarily by the Spitfire whose attack produced no result and did not hasten the end of the Diver by one second.

In the same sortie he spotted another flying bomb and together with Adcock attacked it and sent it exploding into the sea 15 miles south of Dungeness.

That day, both Flying Officer Barckley and Pilot Officer Wingate attacked and destroyed a flying bomb each. In total, seven flying bombs were destroyed that day.

But 8 July saw the Squadron shoot down six V1s and share one while on 9 July another six were destroyed. Over the next few days it went quiet with very few flying bombs coming across from France. Only seven were destroyed by pilots of No. 3 Squadron and one shared during this period.

It was a different story, though, on 12 July, with seventeen flying bombs falling to the guns of No. 3 Squadron Tempests with Squadron Leader Dredge, Flight Lieutenant Van Lierde and Flight Lieutenant Moore each destroying three.

Poor weather and a lack of flying bombs meant that although the pilots were flying standing anti-Diver patrols they engaged very few between 13 July and 17 July.

However, on 18 July activity began to pick up as the weather cleared. First to attack and destroy a V1 was Flying Officer R Dryland who roared away from Newchurch at 1430 hrs. He was vectored by Beachy Head Control onto a V1 coming in 2 miles west of Hastings. The Diver was travelling at 2,000 feet at 300 mph as Dryland rolled into a dive, tearing down on the target. But before he was in range he saw a Spitfire come barrelling in out of a dive, overshooting the V1 and climbing away without firing.

Dryland then manoeuvred his Tempest behind the V1 and from 100 yards thumbed the firing button, hitting the V1 with a four-second burst of cannon fire, which knocked the jet out. The V1 rolled over and went straight down, exploding on impact. Later that night, Dryland bagged another one, which crashed and burned 20 miles north of Hastings at 2245 hrs.

At 1935 hrs Flight Sergeant MJ Rose took off from Newchurch with his No. 2 and was vectored onto a new target by Beachy Head Control. Picking up a visual sighting of the V1 crossing in west of Hastings at 2,500 feet at 350 mph, the two Tempests wheeled around, rolling into their dives and pulling out astern of the target at 500 yards. Rose fired a burst from his cannon and the V1 climbed to 3,000 feet. Determined to finish it off, he closed rapidly and fired again several times until he was 200 yards away. Shells struck the V1 several times and thick black smoke poured out and it went down. The pilots did not actually see the crash but they suspected it hit the ground 3 or 4 miles south of Mayfield.

Later that evening Flight Lieutenant Moore and Flight Sergeant Bailey scrambled from Newchurch, climbing rapidly to 5,000 feet. Once airborne they were picked up by Beachy Head Control and vectored onto an incoming V1 north of Rye. Both Tempests attacked and it was Flight Sergeant Bailey who scored several hits from only 150 yards away as they flew north. After several bursts of cannon fire, this V1 blew up in mid-air, forcing the Tempests to take rapid evasive action to avoid flying into the debris and causing damage to their aircraft.

On 19 July Flight Sergeant RW Cole took off from Newchurch at 0855 hrs with Warrant Officer R Hassall. The two Tempests were vectored by Beachy Head Control onto a V1 coming in 2 miles north of Lydd at 3,000 feet at 380 mph. Cole turned and dived on the target, attacking it from 600 yards, firing short bursts from his cannon to 200 yards. He saw his shells strike the wing and tails. The V1 rolled over and went straight down, exploding near Appledore at 1004 hrs.

Warrant Officer Hassel attacked a Diver over Rye and saw it go down and explode at 0915 hrs.

Later that morning at 0950 hrs, Pilot Officer Wingate was vectored onto a V1 by Beachy Head Control. He saw the flying bomb 8 miles north-west of Dungeness, flying at 2,000 feet at 320 mph. Pushing the throttle open, he dived his Tempest down on the target, coming in directly behind it. Closing rapidly to 100 yards he fired a burst, seeing his cannon shells hammer the flying bomb's port wing. He then fired again and the V1 went down, exploding on the ground near Tenterden at 0958 hrs.

Beachy Head Control vectored Flight Lieutenant Moore and Flight Sergeant Rose onto a V1 coming in 2 miles north of Rye, flying at 3,000 feet at 380 mph. 'I closed to 250 yards astern and gave two short bursts,' Moore reported. 'The Diver went down and exploded on the ground 8 miles north of Rye at 1120 hrs.'

Moore then picked up another V1 3 miles north of Dungeness. 'We closed to 200 yards and I gave two short bursts. The jet exploded and the Diver went down exploding on the ground at 10 miles north of Dungeness at 1155 hrs.'

At noon that day, Flying Officer Dryland shot down a V1 crossing in over the coast 2 miles west of Newchurch at 2,000 feet. It went down and blew up near Biddenden at 1210 hrs.

Later that evening, Flying Officer Clapperton was directed by Beachy Head Control onto a flying bomb coming in 3 miles east of Hastings at 2220 hrs. The V1 was flying at 2,000 feet at 360 mph as he brought his Tempest in behind the V1 and closed to 50 yards 'when another aircraft, which I couldn't identify attacked from 500 yards away then broke off.' Clapperton now brought his Tempest in again at near point-blank range and fired. 'The petrol blew up and the Diver went down exploding on the ground 10 miles north north east of Hastings at 22.31 hrs,' Clapperton reported.

On 20 July Flying Officer Barckley opened the scoring by dispatching a flying bomb using a deflection shot from 250 yards away. This sent it down and it exploded on impact 5 miles west of Rye at 0542 hrs.

Flight Lieutenant BC McKenzie attacked a flying bomb while under Hythe Control over New Romsey from 200 yards away. Flying at 2,000 feet and at 330 mph, the V1 lost pieces from its fuselage from the hail of cannon fire from McKenzie's guns. It exploded north of Paddock wood at 0550 hrs.

The last success of the day was from Flight Lieutenant MacKerras who shot the port wing off a V1 flying between Hastings and Bexhill at 2,000 feet at 320 mph. It exploded on the ground near Battle at 0630 hrs.

The following day, Pilot Officer KG Slade-Betts was vectored onto a V1 by Beachy Head Control that was flying at 3,000 feet at 350 mph. Peeling off, he rolled his Tempest into a dive, levelling off behind the V1. Closing to 250 yards he fired several short bursts, destroying the flying bomb in mid-air. He then picked up another V1 coming in 10 miles north of Eastbourne at 3,000 feet, travelling at 300 mph. Closing rapidly to 200 yards, he fired one long burst of cannon fire. He saw his shells hammer the flying bomb, which blew up when it hit the ground 14 miles north of Beachy Head at 0630 hrs.

Five minutes later Flight Sergeant Rose lifted into the early morning air, on an anti-Diver patrol. Climbing to patrol height, he picked up Fairlight Control and was vectored onto a V1 at 3,500 feet travelling at 300 mph, heading for London. Closing to 150 yards he fired a long burst and shot the left wing off, sending the Diver spinning into the sea 30 miles south of Hastings where it blew up at 0730 hrs.

The last attack of the day was by Pilot Officer Slade-Betts who shot down a flying bomb 30 miles south of Hastings at 1007 hrs with five bursts of his cannon.

The Squadron had a busy day on 22 July. The first flying bomb to go down that day fell to Flight Lieutenant Moore's cannon when he shot down a V1 north of Rye at 1520 hrs. He picked up a second Diver coming in over Rye at 2,000 feet at 340 mph. Diving on it, he closed rapidly, coming in behind the V1, and fired a short burst from 200 yards away. He sent it crashing into the ground where it blew up near Biddenden at 1535 hrs.

Flight Sergeant Cole was vectored onto a V1 6 miles north of Dungeness by Beachy Head Control, coming in at 3,000 feet at 340 mph. It took him eight short bursts from his cannon to send the flying bomb spinning into the ground south-east of Kingsworth at 1705 hrs.

At 1745 hrs Squadron Leader Dredge was airborne from New-church, on a standard anti-Diver patrol without being vectored onto any coordinates. Dredge caught sight of a flying bomb coming in over Dungeness at 3,000 feet, travelling at 380 mph. Dredge reported:

> I closed to 250 yards 15 degrees off below and to starboard and gave a 2 second burst. I saw strikes on the jet unit and the Diver climbed slightly into the fringe of cloud and slowed to 340. I closed to 300 yards dead astern and gave two 1½ second bursts and the port wing broke off and the Diver spun in exploding on the edge of a farmyard 1 mile south east of Biddenden.

The time Dredge entered in his report was 1807 hrs. He was back on the ground at Newchurch twelve minutes later.

There is some confusion over Flight Sergeant Rose's account of his engagement with a V1 that ended with two Spitfires getting involved. He took off from Newchurch with Warrant Officer Hassall at 1725 hrs, climbed to patrol height and was directed by Beachy Head Control onto a V1 crossing in 4 miles east of Hastings at 2,000 feet and travelling at 330 mph. Turning, Rose dived on the V1, coming in behind it. He fired two long bursts from 200 yards away, sending the flying bomb crashing into the ground at Newenden. Climbing back up to patrol height both Tempests were vectored onto another V1 approaching the coast heading inland for London. It is this second Diver that is controversial. The two Tempests picked up the second V1 over Bexhill. Flying at 2,500 feet the flying bomb's indicated airspeed was 350 mph. Manoeuvring his Tempest in behind the V1, Rose chased it for 8 miles when two Spitfires dived down in front of his Tempest. Rose reported:

> They closed to 500 yards firing long bursts without strikes. The Spits pulled away and we closed to 300 yards and gave two medium bursts with strikes and the Diver stalled and dived to below 500 yards and carried on in a shallow dive.

One of the Spitfires came back again and attacked the V1 but it exploded on the ground roughly 6 miles south–south-east of Tunbridge Wells at 1909 hrs. 'No strikes were seen from any of the Spitfire attacks,' Rose continued. So he claims that although the Spitfires fired they didn't hit the target but he did.

Mustangs were involved in the next engagements. At 1900 hrs Flight Lieutenant Moore rocketed off the runway at Newchurch, sending his Tempest roaring into the sky. Picking up Beachy Head Control as he climbed he was vectored onto a flying bomb 3 miles inland from Hastings at 3,000 feet flying at 380 mph. 'Mustangs were firing at it from 500 yards away. With one strike only,' Moore wrote. 'But the Diver was still drawing away unaffected.'

Moore pushed the throttle forward, increasing his speed and brought the Tempest above and behind the V1. Then in a shallow dive he closed on the target. From 350 yards he thumbed the firing button, sending a hail of cannon shells into the target from dead astern of it. This battering from the Tempest roaring in behind the V1 slowed the flying bomb and sent it straight into the ground where it exploded 8 miles north-west of Hastings at 1917 hrs.

Vectored onto another flying bomb coming inland, Moore saw the long flame from the jet engine in the twilight gloom and wheeled around, with Warrant Officer FM Reid, his No. 2, with him in line astern formation. He tore down on the target 3 miles north of Bexhill, crossing in at 2,500 feet at 320 mph. Coming directly astern of the V1, he closed to 100 yards and fired a short burst that sent it exploding on the ground at 1927 hrs.

Flying Officer DJ Butcher was chasing a V1 under Beachy Head Control north of Hastings. Flying dead astern of the Diver he fired short bursts between 250 to 50 yards away when suddenly his engine cut. As it did, the V1 slowed considerably and two Mustangs came in finishing it off. It crashed 8 miles north of Bexhill at 2110 hrs, while Butcher was able to get his stricken Tempest back on the ground at 2125 hrs.

Beachy Head Control vectored Flying Officer MF Edwards and Flight Sergeant RW Cole onto a V1 crossing the coast at 2,500 feet over Dungeness travelling at 360 mph. Peeling off, Edwards dived on the target, closing rapidly to 600 yards and firing three long bursts as he came in directly behind it. Cannon shells ripped into the V1. Just as he was about to fire again, a Mustang came in from his port side just as the flying bomb crashed, bursting into flames 4 miles north of Rye at 2147 hrs.

Cole, Squadron Leader Dredge and Pilot Officer Wingate destroyed V1s in different actions up until 2320 hrs that night.

The Squadron had another busy day for destroying flying bombs on 23 July. Flight Lieutenant Van Lierde took off from Newchurch with his No. 2 at 0438 hrs on an anti-Diver patrol. Vectored by Beachy Head Control, Van Leirde picked up a Diver over Bexhill travelling at 2,000 feet at 360 mph. As he came in over the coast flak suddenly lit up the sky, forcing Van Lierde to break off his chase. He came back in again 4 miles north of Beachy Head where he picked up another V1 approaching Hastings chased by a pilot from 486 Tempest Squadron firing at it from long range. 'As the other Tempest pilot broke to port I fired two bursts and saw strikes on the port side of the target,' Van Lierde reported. The V1 dived steeply into the ground where it exploded at 0459 hrs. He claimed that one as destroyed shared.

Control vectored him onto another V1 coming in at Beachy Head at 2,000 feet flying at 340 mph. 'I was about to open fire when a Spitfire popped up in front and engaged the target until all its ammunition was exhausted,' Van Lierde reported. The V1 con-tinued on its course completely unaffected so Van Lierde had a go, firing several short bursts from dead astern and seeing several strikes all over it. The V1 exploded on impact with the ground at 0509 hrs. He claimed that one as destroyed. Climbing away, he turned the Tempest back towards Hastings and a few minutes later saw another V1 coming in off shore. Diving, he fired a deflection shot first but missed then wheeled around. He came in behind it and fired two bursts, seeing his shells striking the flying bomb.

Flak from a convoy in the Channel opened up and the anti-aircraft shells burst around him, forcing him to break away. A few minutes later, away from the flak he re-engaged the V1 and sent it crashing into the sea between the convoy and Hastings at 0545 hrs.

At 0630 hrs, Flight Sergeant R Pottinger was airborne from Newchurch on patrol. He was vectored by Beachy Head Control onto a flying bomb 1 mile south of Hastings, which he attacked from 400 yards away, firing several short bursts from long range and shooting off the port wing. The V1's fuel caught fire as it turned over and went in but Pottinger did not see it crash as he had to take evasive action in his Tempest to avoid the burning fuel. But his claim of a V1 destroyed coincides with a Royal Observer Corps report of a V1 exploding on the ground at 0645 hrs.

At 1600 hrs Pilot Officer Slade-Betts and Flight Sergeant Rose were vectored onto a Diver over Dungeness flying at 340 mph at 2,000 feet. Slade-Betts fired six short bursts from 150 yards away. His cannon shells smashed into the V1, causing it to catch fire and slow down. It was gliding down when it was attacked by another aircraft. The V1 crashed and exploded on a small house in a village near Appledore at 1630 hrs. But Slade-Betts' Tempest had developed a glycol lead forcing him to land at Woodchurch. Flight Sergeant Rose picked up a V1 west of Dungeness doing 350 mph at 2,000 feet, chased by three other aircraft. 'They were all out of range,' Rose reported. 'I pulled up from below and gave a long burst from 150 yards.' The V1 exploded in the air and the debris showered the Tempest, which suddenly developed engine trouble. Rose had to force land at Brenzett at 1655 hrs.

Beachy Head Control vectored Wing Commander Beamont onto a flying bomb 1 mile off Hastings travelling at 2,000 feet at 370 mph, chased by two Spitfires at 1655 hrs that same day. The first Spitfire opened fire but without success. Beamont then brought his Tempest in behind the V1 and fired a burst from 400 yards, which was also unsuccessful. Putting on more speed, he closed the gap to 100 yards and fired a short burst. His cannon shells smashed into the jet engine, which subsequently went out. The V1 spun into the ground and blew up in a wood west of Tonbridge at 1709 hrs. 'This ties in with a ROC report of a crash at the relevant time,' Beamont recorded in his report.

In the early evening, Flying Officer GA Whitman and Flight Sergeant HJ Foster attacked a V1 2 miles west of Rye, firing at it until their ammunition was exhausted. The V1 slowed down, flying an erratic course until it crashed 2 miles north of a balloon barrage, exploding on impact at 1845 hrs.

As night fell, Tempest pilots had to start identifying the V1s from the glow of their jet engines or from rockets fired by the Observer Corps used to identify an incoming V1. This was the case with Flight Sergeants Bailey and MacKerras. Bailey sighted some rockets and moments later saw the flame from a V1 flying at 380 mph at 1,500 feet. He fired from 700 yards away with no results. Another Tempest from 486 Squadron attacked without success so Bailey closed the range to 50 yards and blew the starboard wing off the flying bomb. It spun into the ground, exploding in an open field. This was confirmed by Beachy Head Control from a report from the Observer Corps.

MacKerras picked up the glow from a flying bomb's jet engine west of Dungeness, flying at 340 mph at 1,500 feet, after being vectored to the coordinates by ground control. The V1 was being chased by two Spitfires. Pushing the throttle forward, he overtook the Spitfires and fired a two-second burst from 250 yards away. Pieces flew off the V1 as white smoke poured out. It went straight into the ground and exploded east of Maidstone at 2104 hrs. Both Bailey and MacKerras claimed one flying bomb each destroyed, which was confirmed by ground reports.

At 2058 hrs Squadron Leader Dredge shot down a V1 with two one-second bursts from his cannon from 200 yards behind the flying bomb, ripping the starboard wing away and sending the target crashing into the ground north of Biddenden Green.

Roaring into the night sky at 2245 hrs, Wing Commander Beamont was vectored onto a flying bomb by Beachy Head Control, which was coming in over Hastings at 350 mph at 2,000 feet. Beamont manoeuvred his Tempest behind the V1, rapidly closing the gap. From 300 yards he opened fire with a two-second burst, seeing his shells strike the V1's belly. Beamont reported:

It wheeled over on its back and as I broke away two Spitfires attacked as the Diver was going down on its back. The V1 exploded on the ground just north of Hastings at 2315 hrs.

Flight Lieutenant Van Lierde picked up a V1 coming in fast over Beachy Head at 340 mph. Diving on it, he fired from 300 yards away, seeing strikes on the starboard wing. Breaking away, a Tempest from 486 Squadron attacked the same flying bomb then Van Lierde attacked again. His cannon shells slowed the V1, which began to lose height. The other Tempest came in again, firing his cannon. 'As it was going down two Spitfires screamed down and fired short bursts just before it crashed on top of Beachy Head at 2240 hrs,' Van Lierde reported.[28]

At 2250 hrs Flight Sergeants Cole and Bailey with Pilot Officer Feldman roared into the night sky from Newchurch on an anti-Diver patrol. Climbing to 9,000 feet, they were informed of a flying bomb by Beachy Head Control coming in at 3,000 feet, flying at 400 mph. Seeing the long exhaust flame below him in the distance Cole peeled off, diving on the target. Levelling off 250 yards behind the V1, he fired several short bursts. Momentarily, the jet engine cut out, slowing the flying bomb. Bailey and Feldman now came in to attack, diving on the stricken V1 and peppering it with cannon fire, which caused it to go straight down and crash 2 miles north of Newchurch. The explosion was seen from Newchurch airfield.

Flight Sergeant Cole attacked another V1 as it was approaching Hastings at 360 mph. Picking it up over the sea, he fired then stopped as it came in over the town. Closing to 150 yards he fired again, seeing strikes all over the target. 'Suddenly another Tempest came across in front of me, forcing me to turn tightly and climb to avoid collision,' he reported. Climbing his Tempest, he saw two other aircraft attack the same Diver, which exploded 2 miles north of Hastings.

At dawn on 24 July Flight Lieutenant McKenzie was vectored onto a V1 by Fairlight Control at 0510 hrs, flying south of Hastings at 2,000 feet at 340 mph. Diving on the target, he lined up the flame in his sights as he brought the Tempest directly behind the flying bomb. The flame from the jet was bright in the morning gloom as he fired a short burst from 200 yards away. He could see strikes from his tracer hitting the jet engine, which increased its flame. His second burst then sent the V1 crashing 2 miles south of Robertsbridge at 0530 hrs.

In the afternoon, Beachy Head Control vectored Flying Officer Edwards onto a Diver 3 miles east of Hastings. Turning, he peeled off giving chase. When he was 800 yards away and 4 miles inland, two Spitfires came down from port firing deflection shots at the flying bomb. 'This caused links and cartridge cases to fall all around the Tempest,' Edwards reported. 'No strikes were seen and the Spits dropped behind.'

Edwards closed his Tempest to 200 yards away, directly behind, and fired two long cannon bursts that sent the flying bomb straight into the ground, where it erupted into flames and smoke in the Benchley area at 1645 hrs. Climbing back to patrol height, he was vectored onto the coordinates of another V1 by ground control and picked it up visually approximately 5 miles east of Hastings, flying at 2,500 feet at 380 mph. It was being chased by two Mustangs, which were firing at it. 'Both Mustangs broke and the Diver continued apparently unaffected so I closed to 50 yards and gave a 2 second burst from dead astern and saw strikes all over the Diver.'

Edwards broke off the attack to avoid collision, turning tightly. He climbed away, watching the flying bomb go down with the Mustangs on its tail. 'The V1 blew up when it hit the ground near Tenterden at 1635 hrs.'

The pilots of No. 3 Squadron had another busy day on 26 July. Flight Sergeant MacKerras took off from Newchurch at 0600 hrs, climbing his Tempest rapidly up to patrol height around 6,000 feet. Picked up by Beachy Head Control, he was vectored onto a V1 coming in near Battle at 320 mph flying at 3,000 feet. Getting a visual sighting of his target he peeled off, attacking it from behind. He fired a two-second burst from 500 yards away then closed to within 150 yards, firing again and seeing his tracer hit the port wing. The flying bomb slow rolled and exploded on the ground near Tunbridge Wells at 0630 hrs.

Control vectored Flying Officer Whitman onto a V1 east of Hastings coming in at 2,000 feet at 380 mph. Whitman fired a deflection shot from 350 yards astern that knocked the jet engine out and sent the flying bomb crashing into the ground near Tunbridge Wells at 0755 hrs.

At the same time, Flight Lieutenant Moore attacked a Diver over Beachy Head, flying at 3,000 feet at 320 mph. Diving on it, he closed to 10 yards then dropped back to 100 yards away when he fired a short burst from his cannon. The shells ripped into the V1 and it went straight into the ground, exploding 5 miles north of Beachy Head at 0803 hrs.

At 1300 hrs Flight Sergeant MacKerras, airborne from New-church, contacted Beachy Head Control who vectored him onto a V1 coming in over Folkestone at 3,000 feet at 340 mph. He reported:

I dove on the target coming in behind and above it, firing from 400 yards away. [Shells hit the jet engine.] I closed to 200 yards and fired a short burst and blew the wing tip off. The Diver rolled on its back and went down to 500 feet. It levelled out for a moment and then went down exploding on the ground south of Ashford.

That evening Flight Lieutenant Van Lierde engaged another V1 under the direction of Beachy Head Control, south of Bexhill. The flying bomb was travelling at 380 mph at 3,000 feet when Van Lierde closed to 400 yards and let loose a burst of cannon fire. Closing to 200 yards, he pressed the firing button again, unleashing a torrent of shells that hammered the V1 and sent it crashing into the ground 6 miles north of Bexhill at 2208 hrs. Van Lierde and his No. 2 Flying Officer Edwards were directed towards another V1 coming in over Hastings at 360 mph. Seeing the orange glow from the jet engine, Edwards wheeled around, diving on the target attacking it from 200 yards away. He saw several strikes and broke off, climbing rapidly away. Van Lierde came in again, attacking it from 300 yards away. He sent it crashing into the ground at 2212 hrs. They then picked up a third V1 north of Bexhill and Van Lierde brought his Tempest in behind it firing a short burst. The V1 exploded on the ground 10 miles north of Bexhill at 2215 hrs.

The first flying bomb to go down on 27 July fell to the guns of Flying Officer RH Clapperton. Diving, he manoeuvred the mighty Tempest in behind the V1, which was roaring inland at 350 mph. 'I fired two short bursts from 200 yards away and saw strikes on the jet engine and starboard wing,' he reported. The flying bomb went down near Maidstone, exploding on the ground at 1515 hrs.

That afternoon, Flight Lieutenant Van Lierde roared off the runway at Newchurch, climbing rapidly up to his patrol altitude in constant contact with Beachy Head Control who vectored him towards approaching contacts over Dungeness. Visually spotting a flying bomb travelling at 320 mph at 3,000 feet, Van Lierde rolled his Tempest into a dive. Attacking it from 250 yards away he sent the V1 crashing into the ground near Rye at 1640 hrs. He was then directed towards another V1 near base, travelling at 380 mph at

2,500 feet. Diving on it he levelled off behind the V1, matching its speed, and opened fire from 400 yards and then closed the gap until he was 50 yards away then fired again. His cannon shells peppered the target, sending it down 3 miles south of Tonbridge at 1645 hrs. He attacked a third V1 south of Tonbridge. Van Lierde reported:

> *I attacked from astern with two one second bursts. The jet spluttered and went out and the Diver carried on at reduced speed losing height but had to be left owing to balloons.*

Van Lierde was up again at 1925 hrs when he attacked another V1 east of Eastbourne with four one-second bursts, shooting both wingtips off the V1. Closing to 200 yards, he fired a three-second burst of cannon fire at the target, ripping the port wing off as the flying bomb erupted in flames and crashed 5 miles south of Tunbridge Wells at 2002 hrs.

At 2140 hrs Flying Officer Clapperton, under Beachy Head Control, was vectored onto a V1 flying at 3,000 feet in the Tunbridge Wells area. Lining up the jet engine glow in his sights, he closed rapidly to 150 yards and fired a short burst from his cannon. Suddenly, the V1 exploded in mid-air, showering the Tempest in debris and damaging it. Clapperton managed to land safely at 2320 hrs.

Within a few days the flying bombs came over less and less and by early September No. 3 Squadron was reassigned back to attacking ground and air targets in Europe. The anti-Diver patrols would last only for the rest of August.

CHAPTER EIGHT

Grinding it Out:
486 Tempest Squadron

W hile many other aircraft were involved in the battle against the doodlebug, the Tempests played a significant part in stopping more than a third of the V1s that were launched against Britain. They were the aircraft most capable not only of destroying the flying bombs but out-flying them in speed.

It's worth stating here that these pilots, regardless of the aircraft they flew, and their ground crew weren't supermen or great heroes. They were young men, in their late teens and early twenties, fighting for their lives in a war most of them didn't quite understand.

Those young men should have been playing rugby, football or cricket, dating young girls, going through university or looking for work, starting families but they weren't. They were killing other young men because Hitler had to be stopped. Their lives were put on hold while the world was ruptured by war.

So let's have another look at the day-to-day grind of the battle against the flying bomb. As we have seen, this was a round-the-clock battle with most of it taking place at night.

No. 486 (NZ) Squadron was another Tempest squadron flying out of Newchurch that had great success against the V1 but it also suffered losses as well. This Squadron was made up entirely of pilots from New Zealand with the exception of the Commanding Officer. For them, the fight against the flying bomb began on 16 June 1944 when Flight Sergeant BJ O'Connor, flying No. 2 to Flight Lieutenant HN Sweetman, dived from patrol height onto a V1 that was coming in between Hythe and Dungeness at 320 mph at 3,000 feet. Roaring down, he attacked from dead astern, firing three short bursts of his cannon. The shells hammered the flying bomb and it disintegrated in the air around 1200 hrs.

The following morning at 0545 hrs Flying Officers SS Williams and TM Fenton roared away from Newchurch, climbing rapidly into the morning sky up to their patrol height.[29] Directed towards the Sevenoaks area by ground controllers, Fenton saw the glow from a V1 and dived on it, firing several bursts and shooting it down. They both landed back at Newchurch at 0645 hrs.

That evening it was Pilot Officer RJ Dansey's turn to shoot one down. He and Flight Sergeant JH Stafford took off from Newchurch at 2020 hrs. During the patrol they were directed by ground control onto the coordinates of a V1 crossing the coast. Spotting it, Dansey peeled off, diving on the V1. He fired, sending it crashing into the ground near Faversham.

On 18 June Flight Lieutenant HN Sweetman and Flying Officer WA Hart roared into the air, climbing rapidly away from Newchurch, heading towards the Channel at 0435 hrs on an anti-Diver patrol. Directed towards the French coast, Sweetman saw the glow of a V1's exhaust and attacked, shooting it down with several short bursts of cannon fire.

At 0835 hrs Flight Sergeant SJ Short with Warrant Officer OD Eagleson as his No. 2 took off. Climbing to their designated patrol height, they were directed towards approaching contacts by ground controllers. Spotting a V1 coming over the coast, Eagleson peeled off and dived on it, thumbing his firing button. 'I saw strikes all over the Diver and it exploded in the air over Tonbridge,' he reported.

A little later that morning, around 1020 hrs, it was Pilot Officer RJ Dansey again who attacked and destroyed another V1, sending it crashing into the ground where it exploded on impact north of Tonbridge.

Flying Officer JR Cullen, while on an anti-Diver patrol with Flying Officer RJ Cammock, was directed onto the coordinates of a flying bomb crossing the coast near Dartford. Diving on it, he destroyed it with several bursts of cannon fire. Both pilots then chased another Diver and attacked it but saw no results.

That evening Flight Sergeant OD Eagleson, with Flying Officer NJ Powell, climbed rapidly away from Newchurch at 1935 hrs up to their patrol height. Turning his Tempest, Eagleson headed out over the Channel as ground control gave him a steady stream of coordinates for flying bombs coming towards the coast. Within a few moments, Eagleson saw the glow from a V1's exhaust some 10 miles north of Newchurch and headed towards it. Above it, Eagleson peeled off, rolling into a dive, followed by Powell. Roaring down on the V1, he opened fire and destroyed the V1 5 miles north of their base.

Climbing back up to their patrol height, Eagleson and Powell turned towards a new set of coordinates and soon picked up another V1 approaching the coast near Rye. Both Tempests dived on the target, firing their cannon. 'The Diver's wings were riddled,' Eagleson reported. 'And it was losing height rapidly but I was unable to make a further attack.' Nevertheless, the kill was confirmed.

On 19 June, Pilot Officer RJ Dansey took off from Newchurch at 0435 hrs with his wingman Warrant Officer Kalka in line astern with him. Climbing to patrol height, they picked up their controller and began to patrol for V1s. Seeing the exhaust glow from a V1 below him, Dansey rolled his Tempest into a dive and attacked the target from dead astern. 'I fired on the Diver from 800 to 600 yards,' he reported. 'Black smoke emitted from it and it hit a balloon. I claimed that V1 as damaged.' However, Warrant Officer Kalka had to cut short his patrol due to technical problems and was back at Newchurch by 0600 hrs while Dansey landed twenty minutes later.

Next to destroy a V1 were Flying Officers SS Miller and RJ Cammock who had taken off from Newchurch at 0530 hrs on their anti-Diver patrol. Both pilots picked up a target and attacked a V1, sending each of them crashing into the ground where they exploded.

Less than an hour later Flight Sergeant WT Wright with Flying Officer TM Fenton climbed away from Newchurch, reaching their patrol height of around 6,000 feet within a few minutes. Directed by ground control onto coordinates of an approaching V1, Flight Sergeant Wright spotted it and peeled off, diving his Tempest onto the target and chasing it. Suddenly, the Tempest's engine began running rough then cut out. The Tempest crashed-landed at Pevensey Bay and was a write off but Wright himself was miraculously unhurt. He had taken off from Newchurch at 0730 hrs and crash-landed at 0745 hrs. Fenton continued the patrol and returned to base at 0835 hrs.

During the day Flight Lieutenant V Cooke was up flying a long-range tank test when he spotted a V1 crossing the coast 4 miles south-west of the airfield. 'The pilot attacked with ball ammunition and destroyed the Diver which exploded on the ground,' the Squadron diarist recorded in the Squadron history.

At 2030 hrs Pilot Officer RD Bremner and Flight Sergeant JH Stafford lifted off from Newchurch on their anti-Diver patrol. Reaching their patrol height, Stafford spotted a V1 and attacked, sending it crashing into the ground where it exploded after several bursts of cannon fire. During the rest of that evening two flying bombs were destroyed by Flight Lieutenant Sweetman and Squadron Leader JH Iremonger.

On 20 June the scoring was opened by Pilot Officer Dansey who was on patrol at 0930 hrs when he spotted a flying bomb and attacked it. He landed back at base at 1050 hrs.

The only other flying bomb destroyed that day was by Flight Sergeant JH Stafford, flying with Flight Sergeant J Steedman. They rose into the night sky at 2150 hrs climbing to their patrol height. They were directed by ground control onto the area where the radar stations had picked up flying bombs. Stafford spotted his V1 and dived on it, firing several bursts until it blew up.

The following day no flying bombs were destroyed, although the patrols were kept up throughout the day and evening. But on 22 June the first flying bomb of the day was destroyed in the early morning hours. Flight Lieutenant JH McCaw with Flying Officer WA Hart soared into the air at 0440 hrs. Climbing rapidly, they headed towards the Hastings area. Reaching their patrol height, they were directed by ground control towards approaching V1s. Spotting one, McCaw dived on it, chasing the V1 for a few minutes until he was in range when he opened fire destroying it between Hastings and Eastbourne. As he climbed away his engine suddenly began coughing and spluttering. The Squadron diarist recorded the incident:

Turning for home, he nursed the Tempest gently back towards base and landed safely. He switched aircraft and resumed the patrol at 0520 hrs and brought down another Diver in the Rye vicinity.

While Flight Lieutenant McCaw was in the air attacking his second flying bomb, Flying Officer JG Wilson with Pilot Officer

K McCarthy took off from Newchurch at 0525 hrs, their engines purring as they rocketed into the sky. The first to destroy a V1 was Wilson when he attacked one and shot it down in the Crowborough area. McCarthy spotted a V1 a few minutes later coming in near Hastings and gave chase. Diving on it, he attacked from dead astern, firing several bursts from his cannon, and shot it down. They were both back at base by 0640 hrs.

At 0600 hrs Flying Officers WL Miller and TM Fenton roared into the dawn sky, pushing their Tempests hard towards their patrol height. In constant contact with ground control as they flew on their patrol line, Miller spotted the tell-tale exhaust glow of a V1 in the morning gloom and rolled his Tempest into a dive, attacking the target. Peppering it with cannon fire, he saw the V1 crash into the ground 10 miles north of Hastings where it exploded on impact. Climbing rapidly he formed up with Miller and continuing the patrol they were directed towards another V1, coming in fast over the Redhill area. Both pilots peeled off, diving onto the target. 'They saw their shells strike the flying bomb but they had to break off the engagement as they were too near the gun belt,' the Squadron diarist recorded. They were unable to claim it as destroyed.

The Squadron diarist continues:

Flying Officer T.M. Fenton maintained his anti-Diver patrol too long. He returned to base with insufficient petrol to adopt emergency procedures when his wheels and flaps failed to react normally. He crashed landed at the base and was slightly injured.

Next to engage a V1 was Warrant Officer G Hooper on patrol as No. 2 to Squadron Leader JH Iremonger. Both Tempests took off at 0735 hrs on their anti-Diver patrol. Over the Channel, Hooper spotted a V1 below him and turned his Tempest towards it, rolling into a dive. 'As I came down behind it and opened fire, two Spitfires did the same,' he reported. All three aircraft attacked it at once, seeing strikes on the V1. Eventually it was destroyed, blowing up in the air, and each pilot was credited with a third of a kill.

At 0930 hrs Flight Lieutenant JH McCaw with Flight Sergeant OD Eagleson took off from Newchurch on another anti-Diver patrol. As they climbed rapidly away from base they were directed towards interception coordinates and reaching their patrol height McCraw spotted a flying bomb approaching at high speed. Diving, he chased the V1 as it headed inland. Then as the range decreased he fired his cannon at the target and destroyed it 4 miles north of Newchurch. Both pilots landed back at base at 1000 hrs.

Ten minutes later, Warrant Officer CJ Sheddon and Flight Sergeant BJ O'Connor took off from Newchurch, climbing fast towards the Hastings area, directed towards flying bombs that were approaching the coast. Reaching their patrol altitude, Sheddon spotted a V1 and attacked it, shooting it down 1 mile north of Hastings. O'Connor chased another V1, firing several bursts at it from dead astern. 'The Diver rolled onto its back and disappeared into some cloud but I didn't see what happened to it so I was unable to claim it as destroyed,' he reported. He landed back at base at 1135 hrs and five minutes later Sheddon touched down as well.

While this was taking place, Squadron Leader JH Iremonger who had lifted off from base at 1055 hrs with his No. 2 Flying Officer WL Miller, spotted a V1 and attacked it with several short bursts from his cannon. His shells riddled the flying bomb and it went straight into the ground, exploding into flames in a wood in the Crowborough area. Miller attacked the same V1 but saw no strikes and he returned to base at 1205 hrs followed by Squadron Leader Iremonger ten minutes later.

Throughout the afternoon the anti-flying bomb patrols mounted by the Squadron were all uneventful until 1835 hrs when Flying Officer JR Cullen and Flight Lieutenant EW Tanner soared into the air, climbing their Tempests rapidly to their patrol altitude. Directed by ground controllers, both pilots picked up and attacked V1s near Wrotham, but in each respect had to abort their attacks as the flying bombs went into the balloon barrage.

The last V1 destruction that day took place in the early evening. At 1905 hrs Squadron Leader JH Iremonger and Flight Sergeant JH Stafford were scrambled to intercept a flying bomb approaching the coast. They were vectored towards their interception point by ground control. Spotting the exhaust plume of a V1, Stafford dived on the target and realised this particular V1 was 'somewhat larger'.[30] Firing his cannon, he managed to bring it down north-east of Battle.

The Squadron resumed scoring against flying bombs in the early hours of 23 June when Pilot Officer Dansey destroyed the first V1 of the day. Flying with Flight Lieutenant HN Sweetman, he took off from Newchurch, climbing fast to gain height then turning towards the Hastings area. Within minutes Dansey spotted a V1 and rolled into his attack, swooping down on it from behind and firing several bursts. Climbing hard, he turned tightly and attacked again, seeing strikes all over it. The V1 exploded and Dansey returned to the patrol line and moments later was directed by ground control onto the coordinates of another V1 and attacked this one. Destroying it, he shared it with another Tempest pilot from No. 3 Squadron. Flight Lieutenant HN Sweetman returned to base at 0505 hrs and Dansey landed ten minutes later.[31]

Pilot Officer FB Lawless and Flying Officer NJ Powell took off from base at 0500 hrs on their anti-Diver patrol. Opening their throttles, the two pilots climbed their powerful fighters rapidly into the morning sky. Heading out over the Channel, the two Tempests turned towards the Hastings area vectored by control onto V1s approaching the coast in that sector.

Spotting the exhaust glow of a flying bomb, Lawless pounced on it, rolling his Tempest into a dive and attacking it with several bursts from his 20-mm cannon. 'The pilot saw his tracers strike the Diver and it exploded in mid air 10 miles north of Hastings,' the Squadron diarist recorded. Powell was back at base at 0550 hrs while Lawless landed twenty minutes later.

At 0600 hrs Pilot Officer RD Bremner and Flight Sergeant BM Hall soared off the ground. Scrambled to intercept flying bombs, they climbed rapidly away. Directed towards a sector where V1s were approaching the coast, Bremner attacked and destroyed one flying bomb while Hall attacked another. Diving on it, he fired burst after burst at the V1, peppering it with cannon shells. Eventually, the flying bomb slowed then went straight into the ground, exploding north-west of Battle.

More flying bombs were destroyed that day and Pilot Officer K McCarthy shot down two in a single sortie. Taking off with Flying Officer WA Hart at 1455 hrs, McCarthy opened the throttle and the Tempest shot into the air, the huge engine purring steadily. Rapidly gaining height, McCarthy picked up a visual contact of a V1 below him crossing in near Willington. He dived on it, giving it several short bursts. Levelling off behind the V1, he continued firing until the V1 went straight into the ground and burst into flames. Climbing back to patrol height, both pilots were directed towards another sector where V1s were approaching. This time, west of their base at Newchurch, McCarthy attacked another V1 and sent it crashing into the ground.

Later that afternoon at 1600 hrs Flight Sergeant OD Eagleson, flying with Flight Sergeant SJ Short, chased a flying bomb. Rapidly closing the range between his Tempest and the flying bomb, Eagleson fired short bursts at the V1. 'Seeing strikes on the V1 he saw it slow down then crash into the ground where it exploded between East Hoathly and Uxfield,' the Squadron diarist recorded.

At 1725 hrs Flying Officer WL Miller and Flying Officer R.J. Cammock were scrambled to intercept flying bombs approaching the coast. The Tempests were directed towards the sector by ground control. Spotting a V1, Miller dived on the target to close the gap between his Tempest and the flying bomb. Levelling off, he fired several bursts and sent the V1 crashing into the ground near Hastings where it exploded. Climbing back up to patrol altitude he picked up another V1, directed to it by ground control, and shot that down near Pevensey Bay while Cammock was engaging another flying bomb, which he shot down also near Pevensey Bay.

At 2140 hrs Flying Officer RJ Cammock was scrambled from Newchurch and roared off into the night sky towards the coordinates of another V1 coming in over the coast. Seeing the tell-tale glow from the V1's jet exhaust Cammock chased it, increasing the Tempest's speed. The range began to close until Cammock felt he could fire. 'He fired several short bursts at the Diver,' the Squadron diarist recorded. 'He saw pieces fly off the Diver and it went straight into the ground exploding near Edenbridge.'

While Cammock was attacking his flying bomb Flying Officer JR Cullen with Flight Sergeant J Steedman took off from Newchurch at 2155 hrs. Controllers on the ground directed the Tempests towards new coordinates and Cullen got a sighting of the V1 and immediately attacked it. However, another Tempest pilot from No. 3 Squadron took part in the same attack, eventually destroying the V1 after many bursts of cannon fire.

The following morning, Flying Officer RJ Cammock opened the scoring by destroying two V1s and his No. 2, Pilot Officer K McCarthy, destroyed another one. Throughout the rest of the day the Squadron mounted several anti-Diver patrols but were unable to intercept or destroy any flying bombs.

In the early morning of 25 June Flying Officer SS Williams shot down a V1 north of Newchurch. The rest of the day was uneventful until the evening when things changed.

That night at 2015 hrs Flight Sergeant SJ Short with Flying Officer RJ Cammock took off from Newchurch. Reaching their patrol altitude they turned, heading out over the Channel towards the area where V1s were approaching the British coast. Seeing the jet exhaust of a flying bomb below him Short gave chase, diving on it rapidly. He closed the range between himself and the flying bomb until he was able to give it several bursts of cannon fire, shooting it down north-east of Battle. Cammock chased a V1 and shot it down south of Maidstone. They were both back at base by 2140 hrs.

While Short and Cammock were flying their patrol Flying Officer JR Cullen with Flight Sergeant OD Eagleson took off from Newchurch at 2035 hrs. At their patrol height they were then directed towards their interception point. Spotting the glow from a V1 in the distance below him in the darkness, Cullen peeled off, rolling his Tempest into a dive. As the gap closed, he thumbed the firing button, sending a storm of shells into the doodlebug and saw them strike the wings and fuselage. Levelling out of his dive, he fired again, matching the V1's speed. The Squadron diarist recorded the incident:

> After a few short bursts of cannon fire the Diver went straight into the ground and exploded near Redhill.

He landed back at Newchurch at 2155 hrs, five minutes after Flight Sergeant Eagleson did.

At 2210 hrs Warrant Officer CJ Sheddan and Warrant Officer G Hooper were scrambled to intercept a V1 crossing the coast. In the darkness of night, they spotted the jet flame of the V1 against the backdrop of the clouds. Attacking it, Sheddan destroyed it 2 miles north of Newchurch airfield. He landed back at the base at 2320 hrs, just five minutes before Hooper did.

Cammock and Short were back up on patrol again at 2250 hrs. Vectored towards the Hastings area, both Tempests were at patrol height when Cammock spotted the flame of a V1. He pushed his throttle open and dived towards the target, building up speed before levelling off behind it. Riddling it with cannon fire, he saw strikes all over the V1, which went down 5 miles north of Hastings.

On 26 June only one V1 was destroyed by Flight Lieutenant McCaw. Flight Lieutenant HN Sweetman's Tempest was damaged by AA fire as he chased a V1 towards the gun belt. Unhurt, he managed to bring his damaged aircraft back to Newchurch.

The following day around dawn Flying Officer NJ Powell, flying as No. 2 to Pilot Officer EB Lawless, attacked two flying bombs. The second one was in conjunction with a Tempest from No. 3 Squadron, which was claimed by the pilot of that Squadron.

Early that morning at 0840 hrs Pilot Officer RJ Dansey and Warrant Officer JH Stafford rose into the air, soaring rapidly away from Newchurch. The two Tempests were directed to intercept an approaching flying bomb by ground control. Seeing the doodle-bug ahead and below them both Tempests peeled off, diving towards the V1 and firing several short bursts as they closed on the target. Pulling out of their dives, they could see their shells striking the flying bomb as they climbed away. Then suddenly another Tempest from No. 3 Squadron attacked and destroyed the V1 around 1000 hrs.

At 1005 hrs the Squadron mounted another anti-Diver patrol with Flight Lieutenant HN Sweetman and Flight Sergeant BM Hall taking off from Newchurch. As they levelled off at 6,000 feet Hall's engine began running rough, forcing him to return to base. Sweetman continued the patrol and spotted a V1 crossing the coast in the Rye area. Rolling into a dive, the Tempest's speed increased. He waited until he had closed the range at the moment when he became straight and level at the bottom of his dive, bringing the Tempest in behind the V1 then he began firing and saw strikes on the target. He turned sharply and climbed away, seeing the V1 crash north-east of Rye where it exploded.

There was a strange occurrence that evening. Warrant Officer CJ Sheddan and Flying Officer WA Hart took off at 1805 hrs, climbing rapidly away from their airfield at Newchurch. The Squadron diarist recorded:

Directed towards a Diver approaching the coast both pilots gave chase. Well out of range they closed the gap when the Diver began

losing height and crashed into earth without either of them firing a
shot. They returned to base at 1920 hrs their guns still fully loaded.

At 2045 hrs Squadron Leader JH Iremonger and Flying Officer
WA Hart were directed to intercept a flying bomb by ground
control. Reaching their designated patrol altitude, Hart spotted the
target below and pushed the nose of the Tempest forward, diving
on the flying bomb. Coming in behind it, he levelled off and fired
several bursts at it, seeing strikes on the engine and fuselage.
Under this hail of shells the fuel tank on the V1 blew up and the
robot aircraft exploded in mid-air.

The first V1 to be destroyed on 28 June took place between
0525 hrs and 0640 hrs when Flying Officer JG Wilson shot down a
V1 that exploded on the ground.

Later that morning at 0920 hrs another pair of Tempests took off
from Newchurch. Flying Officer JR Cullen and Warrant Officer
OD Eagleson were flying at their patrol altitude when ground
controllers directed them towards incoming contacts near Rye.
Catching sight of a V1 below him, Eagleson rolled the Tempest
into a dive, attacking the V1 with several bursts from his cannon.
The flying bomb crashed into the ground 6 miles north of Rye and
exploded.

Squadron Leader Iremonger was flying with Flying Officer
Cammock on an anti-Diver patrol between 1005 hrs and 1125 hrs
when Cammock picked up a sighting of a V1. He dived on it,
firing several bursts, and saw pieces fly off it before it exploded in
the air.

One hour and fifteen minutes later Squadron Leader Iremonger
was back in the air again, this time with Pilot Officer KA Smith.
They were vectored onto a high-speed V1 crossing the coast.
Iremonger dived on the target but was unable to close the gap. He
fired from 1,500 yards away, expending all his ammunition without any appreciable results. Smith also attacked another flying
bomb, firing two short bursts, but saw no results.

Sadly the day ended on a terrible note. At 2150 hrs Flying Officer
SS Williams and Flight Sergeant WT Wright took off from Newchurch, and climbed up to their allotted patrol altitude. Ground
control directed them towards a V1 contact. Getting a sighting,
Williams rolled into attack when he was hit by friendly anti-aircaft
fire. Breaking off the engagement, he managed to return his

damaged aircraft to base and land safely unhurt. Wright, however, was not so lucky. His Tempest crashed behind Beachy Head and he was killed. The Squadron diarist recorded the following in the Squadron history:

> He was posthumously commissioned on the 30th June, 1944. He was buried at Brookwood Cemetary on 4 July 1944. It is thought that the aircraft was damaged by pieces of the Diver breaking off and hitting the elevators, causing the machine to crash.

The following day, six V1s were shot down and destroyed by the Squadron, while on 30 June two events/observations took place. At 0725 hrs Flying Officer RJ Cammock and Flight Sergeant SJ Short took off from Newchurch. As they climbed they were directed towards V1s that were on their way to London. Short spotted one below him and rolled into the attack, opening fire as he manoeuvred the Tempest in behind the flying bomb, closing the gap. The Squadron diarist recorded:

> As he got closer he could see that the Diver appeared to have a long rod projecting from the nose. Although he fired several bursts he was unable to bring it down and returned to base at 0805 hrs.

An hour and twenty-five minutes after he landed he took off again on a second anti-Diver patrol and this time things were a little different. This time he was flying as No. 2 to Flying Officer WL Miller. At their patrol height and vectored towards their interception point by ground control, Short saw a flying bomb below him. He peeled off, giving his No. 1 the 'tally ho'. Diving on the flying bomb, he opened fire at short range with several short bursts from his cannon from behind and slightly above the V1. His shells hit home and the flying bomb suddenly blew up in the air. Trying to avoid flying into the debris, Short turned the Tempest tightly, climbing. But some of the debris from the V1 smashed into his Tempest, causing damage.

Nursing the battered fighter back to base, he crash-landed at the end of the runway. He was slightly injured but the aircraft was badly damaged.

June 1944 was over and from the arrival of the first V1s over England, 486 Squadron had been in action against them. They had destroyed 92½ flying bombs and flown 960 hours, of which 869 were operational hours and the rest were day training.

July 1944 opened with a bang for the pilots and ground crew of 486 Squadron. On 1 July Pilot Officer FB Lawless opened the scoring. At 0455 hrs Lawless, flying as No. 2 to Flight Lieutenant JH McCaw, climbed fast through the gloom of the early morning sky towards their patrol height. The pilots were in contact with ground control who were vectoring them towards interception coordinates. Lawless saw the V1 first and pushed the nose of the Tempest down into a dive, chasing the flying bomb. Gaining on it, he opened fire with his cannon and saw several strikes on the V1. But the flying bomb disappeared into cloud and he never saw it crash though this was later confirmed.

Nothing happened for the rest of the day until the early evening when Worthing Control vectored a pair of Tempests flown by Flight Sergeant BM Hall and Flying Officer BJ Cammock onto a V1 coming in near Horsham. Cammock dived on the target, firing at it until it exploded in mid-air at 1900 hrs. They landed back at Newchurch at 1915 hrs having flown a half-hour sortie.

At 1900 hrs Pilot Officer RJ Dansey and Warrant Officer CJ Sheddan were vectored towards approaching contacts by ground controllers. Sheddan spotted a V1 and gave chase, diving on it. He fired at it as he got closer and saw numerous strikes all over the flying bomb. The Squadron diarist recorded:

> The 'Diver' pulled up vertically. It climbed to 6,000 feet then went into a spiral dive to 1,000 feet, did a half circuit when Spitfires attacked. The Diver continued on a south south west course for a minute then dived to earth and exploded 7 miles west north west of Rye at 1915 hrs. Both pilots returned to base at 1925 hrs and the destruction of the flying bomb was officially listed as shared.

Just over an hour later, Flight Lieutenant LJ Appleton and Flying Officer TM Fenton lifted off from the runway at Newchurch and roared into the night sky at 2030 hrs. Ground controllers directed them towards the sector where radar stations and observers were reporting V1 activity. Both pilots spotted flying bombs and went in for their attacks. Diving on one, Appleton thumbed the firing button as he levelled off behind it, firing several short bursts from his cannon. Shells hammered into the V1 and it suddenly exploded in the air at 2106 hrs, 10 miles north-east of Pevensey. Appleton climbed and turned tightly to get away from the debris.

Both pilots returned to base at 2120 hrs and just after their wheels touched down another pair of Tempests tore into the night sky. Pilot Officers K McCarthy and KA Smith climbed to their patrol height to begin their patrol at 2120 hrs. Their patrol itself was uneventful until McCarthy's engine cut and he made a forced landing in a wood 4 miles north-east of Hastings at 2200 hrs. The Squadron diarist recorded:

> Although seriously injured, [with a] dislocated shoulder, fractured jaw and forearm, bruises and lacerations he cut his straps and extricated himself from the cockpit and was found supporting himself on the wing of the aircraft.
>
> He was admitted to the Royal East Sussex Hospital in Hastings and was later transferred to the Queen Victoria Cottage Hospital at East Grinstead. Pilot Officer Smith saw his No. 1 go down and reported the crash over the R/T and returned to base at 2205 hrs.

On 3 July Pilot Officer Bremner destroyed a V1 at 0910 hrs and managed to get back to base before the weather turned sour and visibility became very poor.

Throughout the day only two other patrols were mounted and nothing was seen. But at 1700 hrs Flying Officer JR Cullen and Warrant Officer OD Eagleson took off from Newchurch and within minutes were at their patrol altitude. Cullen picked up a V1 crossing in near Hastings and immediately attacked, diving the Tempest towards the target and firing his cannon as he closed the range. Peppered by cannon fire, the flying bomb went straight into the ground and exploded 4 miles north of Hastings at 1735 hrs. At the same time, Eagleson had attacked a V1 and shot it down. Both pilots finished their patrols and returned to base at 1755 hrs.

Five minutes later Flying Officer JG Wilson and Pilot Officer KA Smith began their anti-Diver patrol and Smith attacked and destroyed two V1s within ten minutes of each other.

As darkness closed in the cloud cover increased at low level, hampering visibility. Nothing was seen until 2230 hrs when Flying Officer WL Miller and Flight Sergeant J Steedman on anti-Diver patrol were directed towards interception coordinates by ground control. In the darkness of the night Miller picked up the glow from a V1's jet exhaust, checked his instruments to judge the range, then pushed his control column forward, diving the Tempest towards the target. Closing the gap, he fired several bursts but saw no results. Suddenly the Napier Sabre engine in the Tempest cut and he was left in silence with the aircraft dropping fast. 'Because of poor visibility he decided to abandon the aircraft,' the Squadron diarist wrote. 'The hood would not jettison and had to be wound back.' Baling out, Miller came down near Horsmonden, near Tonbridge in Kent.

The Squadron diarist recorded the following in the Squadron history:

His right shoulder muscles were bruised by the parachute shroud lines becoming tangled and his left ankle sprained through striking a fence on landing. The doctor who attended him afterwards sent him a bill for £1.1.0d.

More engine trouble plagued the Squadron the following morning when Flight Lieutenant HN Sweetman had to return to base with his engine running rough. Both he and Flying Officer HM Mason had taken off from Newchurch at 1035 hrs. Five minutes after take-off Sweetman turned back but Mason continued on the patrol, turning his Tempest towards the corridor between the gun belt and the coast. 'The pilot saw a Diver below him heading towards London and attacked it from dead astern seeing strikes on the wings and fuselage,' the Squadron diarist recorded. The V1 crashed into the ground near Brooklands and exploded at 1100 hrs. Mason returned to his patrol height and landed back at base forty minutes after destroying the V1.

At 1120 hrs another pair of Tempests shot off the runway, climbing into the morning sky. Flying Officer JR Cullen and Warrant Officer OD Eagleson reached their patrol altitude and were directed towards several contacts approaching from the Channel. Picking up a visual sighting of a flying bomb, Cullen peeled off chasing it. He closed the gap quickly and attacked it with several bursts, sending it crashing into the ground where it exploded 6 miles north of Hastings at 1142 hrs. While he was attacking his V1 Eagleson also dived his Tempest onto a V1, firing several short bursts at it. The V1 disappeared into some cloud and exploded on the ground near Sevenoaks and this kill was later confirmed and attributed to Eagleson. However, with his Tempest running low on fuel he could not get back to Newchurch so he landed at an airfield at Staplehurst.

The next engagement took place at 1523 hrs when Warrant Office WA Kalka destroyed one of two V1s on the same patrol. Taking off with Warrant Officer JH Stafford, Kalka had climbed to patrol height, picked up a visual contact and rolled into an attack within the space of twenty-eight minutes. Levelling out of his dive, he hammered the first V1 with cannon shells and it went into the ground west of Polegate and exploded. Climbing away, Kalka picked up another V1 and attacked it, sending it crashing in flames near Leatherhead at 1537 hrs.

At 1615 hrs Flying Officer FB Lawless, while on patrol with Flight Lieutenant Appleton, attacked a V1 and sent it crashing into the ground, exploding 6 miles north-east of Eastbourne.

As the evening wore on engagements with V1s increased. At 1850 hrs Flight Lieutenant HN Sweetman and Pilot Officer RD Bremner roared down the runway at Newchurch and shot into the air, their Tempests on full power. Climbing to 6,000 feet, they were directed by ground control towards several contacts. Sweetman dived on one flying bomb, seeing it getting bigger and bigger in his sights as the gap closed. He lined it up in his sights then fired his guns, seeing strikes on the wings and fuselage. It was sent crashing into the ground north-east of Eastbourne at 1905 hrs.

Bremner attacked another flying bomb, firing short bursts at it. This V1 hit the ground north of Hailsham at 1935 hrs.

While Bremner and Sweetman were attacking their respective flying bombs, Flying Officer NJ Powell and Pilot Officer FB Lawless had taken off for their patrol at 1950 hrs. Powell picked up a visual contact below him in the early evening gloom and peeled off, attacking the V1 with several bursts. He saw his shells hammer home and watched the V1 crash into the ground, exploding near Tunbridge Wells at 2010 hrs.

Ground control reported several contacts coming in from the Channel and several were attacked by Powell and Lawless as well as other fighters. Lawless claimed one damaged but it was not allowed. Both pilots returned at 2045 hrs.

Ten minutes before Lawless and Powell landed Warrant Officer JH Stafford and Warrant Officer WA Kalka took off to start their

German Fieseler Fi 103 flying-bomb (V1) in flight, as seen by the gun camera of an intercepting
F fighter aircraft, moments before the fighter destroyed the V1 by cannon fire.

(C5736 Imperial War Museum)

ut-away and annotated drawing of the Fieseler Fi 103 flying bomb (also known as FZG 76 or V1
apon).

(C4431 Imperial War Museum)

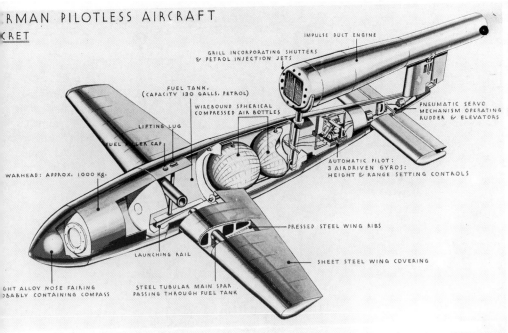

RMAN PILOTLESS AIRCRAFT

CRET

IMPULSE DUCT ENGINE

GRILL INCORPORATING SHUTTERS
& PETROL INJECTION JETS

FUEL TANK,
(CAPACITY 130 GALLS, PETROL)

WIREBOUND SPHERICAL
COMPRESSED AIR BOTTLES

PNEUMATIC SERVO
MECHANISM OPERATING
RUDDER & ELEVATORS

LIFTING LUG

FUEL FILLER CAP

AUTOMATIC PILOT:
3 AIRDRIVEN GYROS:
HEIGHT & RANGE SETTING CONTROLS

WARHEAD: APPROX. 1000 Kg.

PRESSED STEEL WING RIBS

LAUNCHING RAIL

SHEET STEEL WING COVERING

GHT ALLOY NOSE FAIRING
OBABLY CONTAINING COMPASS

STEEL TUBULAR MAIN SPAR
PASSING THROUGH FUEL TANK

AWING BASED ON INFORMATION TO DATE.   ISSUED WITH A.I.2.(g) REPORT No. 2243/16·6·44   P·C·CASTLE

Fieseler Fi 103 flying bombs being manhandled at a launching site. The bomb on the left has been placed on a conveyor trolley following servicing and is awaiting its move to the non-magnetic building Richthaus for course setting. The bomb on the right has been secured for transport on a site handling bogie. The background of the photograph has been obliterated by the German censor.

(CL3430 Imperial War Museum)

The lightly damaged launching ramp of the modified V1 launching site at Belloy-sur-Somme near Amiens, France.

(BU406 Imperial War Museum)

DANGER-GEVAAR
DO NOT TOUCH

V.II   S.H.A.E.F.

n display in Antwerp September 21st 1945.   *(Courtesy of Graham Berry)*

Squadron Tempest: An example of the mighty Hawker Tempest that shot down the majority of the
lying bombs during the summer and autumn of 1944.   *(Courtesy of Adrian Cooper)*

Civil Defence rescue workers stand on piles of rubble as the try to dig survivors out of collapsed buildings following V1 attack in the Highland Roa and Lunham Road area of Norwood, London, SE19. In th background, half-destroyed houses can also be seen.
(D21208 Imperial War Museu

PC Frederick Godwin of Gipsy Hill Police Station supplies tea and sympathy to a now homeless man after a V1 attack that sadly killed his wife and destroyed his home. He returned from taking his dog (also pictured) for a walk to find a scene of devastation. In the background, rescue workers can be seen searching the rubble and debris for any survivors of this attack, which destroyed almost an entire street.
(D2125 Imperial War Museum)

mpest Mark V, EJ743, on a test flight following completion at Langley, Buckinghamshire. This
craft served with No. 3 Squadron, RAF. *(HU2173 Imperial War Museum)*

ur Supermarine Spitfire F Mark XIVs, of No. 610 Squadron, RAF, based at Friston, Sussex, flying in
ose starboard echelon formation over south-east England. RB159 'DW-D' in the foreground is being
wn by the unit's commanding officer, Squadron Leader RA Newbury. With him are: RB167 'DW-
RB150 'DW-A' and RB156 'DW-G'. *(CH13817 Imperial War Museum)*

A de Havilland Mosquito IIF DD739/RX-X of No. 456 Squadron, flying from Middle Wallop, in fligl
The censor has scratched out the wing-tip antennae of the Airborne Interceptor radar.

(TR1090 Imperial War Museu

A Hawker Tempest V (foreground) and Hawker Typhoon of No. 486 Squadron, Royal New Zealand
Air Force, based at Castle Camps airfield, Cambridgeshire. *(CH13977 Imperial War Museu*

Tempest Mark V, JN682 'JF-Z', of No. 3 Squadron, RAF, parked at Newchurch, Kent, as a pair of aircraft takes off to patrol the Normandy beachhead.
(CH14095 Imperial War Museum)

Tempest Mark V prototype, HM595. The view shown is of the cockpit interior, port front.
(ATP10983F Imperial War Museum)

Airborne Interception Radar: AI Mark VIIIB installed in the nose of a de Havilland Mosquito NF Mark XIII night fighter. The transmitter box is at the top, mounted above the scanner hydraulic motor assembly. The rotating scanner is contained in the Perspex nose. The photograph was taken at No. 10 Maintenance Unit, Hullavington, Wiltshire.
(CH16610 Imperial War Museum)

Hawker Tempest Mark Vs of No. 3 Squadron RAF parked at Newchurch, Kent. The nearest aircraft, JN765 'JF-K', was lost on 1 July 1944 when it dived into the ground near Winchelsea, Sussex, after the pilot lost control in a cloud while chasing a Fieseler Fi 103 flying bomb (V1).

(HU92119 Imperial War Museum

Hawker Tempest Mark Vs of No. 486 Squadron, RNZAF, parked in their dispersal area by Will's Farm at Newchurch, Kent. In the foreground, JN754 'SA-A' undergoes an engine test.

(HU92145 Imperial War Museum

An RAF Supermarine Spitfire edging into position in order to tip the wing of a V1 flying bomb to alter its course.
(CH16280 Imperial War Museum)

casters were used extensively to bomb the V1 launching sites in Northern France.
(Author's collection)

Mark 9 Spitfire.

de Havilland Mosquito FB Mark VI, HX811 'TH-K', of No. 418 Squadron, RCAF, in a blister hanga
Holmesley South, Hampshire, after suffering fire damage following the explosion of a flying bomb
which HX811's crew shot down during a Diver patrol. *(CH20880 Imperial War Muse*

Two pilots of No. 486 Squadron, RNZAF, Warrant Officer OD Eagleson of Auckland, and Flying Officer RJ Cammock of Christchurch, stand by the tail of a Hawker Tempest four days after the Squadron's arrival at B60/Grimbergen, Belgium. Both pilots achieved high scores against flying bombs launched against the United Kingdom before the Squadron moved to Europe; Eagleson destroyed 21 and Cammock 20.5. *(CL1386 Imperial War Museum)*

Squadron Leader Joseph Berry DFC* 7 September 1944. *(Courtesy of Graham Berry)*

adron Leader Joseph Kendall, 486 Squadron. *from the John Kendall collection, courtesy of John Kendall)*

Pilots from 486 Squadron stand in front of and on the Hawker Tempest which was the main fighter used to stem the V1 menace during 1944.

(Courtesy of John Kenda

The American P47 Thunderbolt was used in limited numbers to engage the V1s. Everything that could be stripped from the fighters was including armour plating and bomb racks.

(Author's Collectio

A 486 Squadron Tempest peels off as it goes into a dive to attack a V1.
(Courtesy of John Kendall)

An example of the Hawker Tempest Mark II powered by the Centaurus radial engine which evolved into the magnificent Hawker Sea Fury.
(From the collection of Joseph Kendall)

Another view of the Hawker Tempest in action from 486 Squadron as it rolls into a dive.
(From the Joseph Kendall collection courtesy of John Kendall

The clipped wing Mark 9 Spitfire was one of the types that was successfully used in shooting down V1 flying bombs.
(Author's Collection

Spitfire Mark 9 was one of the fighters that successfully engaged and destroyed the flying bombs
re they reached London.   *(Author's Collection)*

American B17 Flying Fortress was used by the US Eight Air Force to pound V1 ski jump sites
ing daylight bombing raids.However, it was less effective against the smaller modified launching
ps.   *(Author's Collection)*

 No1 Squadron badge.

 No 501 Squadron badge.

No 3 Squadron badge.

No 605 Squadron badge.

Although it never had the effect that the Tempests had on the V1, the Gloster Meteors did manage to shoot down several flying bombs. The type shown is a later version of this jet fighter.

(Author's Collection)

patrol. Levelling off at their patrol altitude, they turned towards the corridor in constant contact with ground controllers who vectored them towards several contacts. Stafford attacked one, diving on it from behind and blasting it with shells that sent it into the ground in flames near Hailsham at 2055 hrs. Climbing rapidly away, he was directed towards another contact and saw it below him. Attacking this one he levelled out, seeing his shells striking the V1, which went into the ground exploding at 2135 hrs near Tonbridge.

Flying Officer Mason took off with Pilot Officer RJ Dansey at 2225 hrs. Levelling off from their climb to patrol height, they were directed towards incoming contacts and Mason had a sighting of the glow of a flying bomb's exhaust. Rolling into a dive, he fired several bursts at the V1 travelling fast below and in front of him. As he was diving and firing on this flying bomb another Tempest came roaring down, firing several bursts at the same target. Hammered by so many shells, it went straight into the ground and exploded. Mason was given a half share of this V1.

While Mason was busy chasing and destroying his flying bomb Dansey had been directed towards several contacts in the East-bourne area. He attacked one, diving onto the target and firing from around 800 yards away. Seeing his shells strike the wings and fuselage, he saw the V1 hit the ground 5 miles north of Eastbourne at 2305 hrs.

More engine trouble with the Tempests occurred the following day, 5 July. The first occurrence was at 1025 hrs when Flying Officer Mason turned back to base, cutting short his patrol because of a rough engine.

At 1335 hrs Warrant Officers G Hooper and CJ Sheddan took off from Newchurch. Directed towards contacts coming in over the coast towards London the two Tempests broke as Sheddan peeled away, attacking the first of three V1s. After destroying two he dived on a third. However, his engine cut due to an empty 20-mm shell case smashing into his radiator, causing a complete loss of engine oil. Struggling with the controls, he managed to crash-land at Battle in Sussex. The Squadron diarist wrote:

He was thrown out of the machine on impact. His injuries were nevertheless not serious, haematoma of the back, bruises and scratches. He was taken to the Royal East Sussex where he remained until rejoining the Squadron on 08 July.

The last V1 to be destroyed on 5 July fell to the guns of Flight Sergeant BJ O'Connor after he expended his ammunition attacking it. The V1 blew up in mid-air 6 miles south of Beachy Head at 1820 hrs.

In the early hours of 6 July O'Connor started another patrol at 0440 hrs with Warrant Officer Hooper. They were given coordinates for contacts approaching the coast and O'Connor peeled away, heading for the interception point. Diving on a V1, he sent it crashing into the ground with several short bursts and then a few minutes later attacked another V1 with another Tempest. He claimed one destroyed and one shared.

At 0640 hrs Warrant Officer OD Eagleson with Flight Sergeant J Steedman roared into the dawn sky. Picking up ground control, they pushed their throttles forward and climbed rapidly up to their patrol height. Moments later they were vectored towards interception coordinates and Eagleson peeled away from Steedman, diving on a flying bomb, attacking from close range as he levelled out. The V1 exploded on impact with the ground at 0720 hrs 4 to 5 miles north of Hastings.

Warrant Officer Hooper was back on patrol again at 1240 hrs, having taken off with Squadron Leader JH Iremonger this time. On reaching their patrol altitude both pilots were directed towards contacts approaching the coast. 'The pilot [Hooper] attacked a Diver with short bursts and saw strikes on the wings and fuselage,' the Squadron diarist recorded. 'The Diver went down near Friston at 1305 hrs.'

Hooper then destroyed another V1, which he shared with another Tempest pilot at 1310 hrs. Hooper chased another V1, this time out over the sea, firing the last of his 20-mm ammunition at it. Hammered by shells, the V1 staggered and went straight into the sea, exploding on impact some 16 miles south of Beachy Head at 1335 hrs. No other engagements took place that day, although patrols were mounted throughout the day and night.

On 7 July Flight Lieutenant HN Sweetman and Pilot Officer RJ Dansey took off from Newchurch at 0535 hrs, heading out over the Channel directed by ground control to interception coordinates. In the morning gloom, they picked up a sighting and both Tempests peeled off and dived on the target, each taking turns to attack it with cannon fire. The Squadron diarist recorded:

Strikes were seen by the pilots on the Diver as they chased it inland. After several bursts the Diver went into the ground and exploded 10 miles north of Beachy Head at 0610 hrs.

Over the next few hours standing patrols were carried out without any success until 1230 hrs when Flight Lieutenant HN Sweetman and Warrant Officer WA Kalka rocketed off the runway and roared into the sky, climbing to their patrol height. Heading inland between the gun belt and the coast, they were vectored onto a contact and Sweetman rolled his Tempest into a dive as he spotted the V1. Building up speed, the range closed and he lined up the flying bomb in his sights. At the bottom of his dive he fired several bursts at the V1, which went into the ground and exploded 6 miles north of Ashford at 1255 hrs.

The next V1 to be destroyed was by Flying Officer RJ Cammock who took off from Newchurch at 1630 hrs with Flight Sergeant J Steedman. Picking up a contact, Cammock attacked a V1 and shot it down 7 miles north of Pevansey at 1650 hrs.

Five minutes after Cammock and Steedman took off, Warrant Officer OD Eagleson took off on an air test and was directed onto a V1 coming in close to the base. Attacking with short bursts of cannon fire, the V1 blew up in mid-air directly over the airfield at 1650 hrs.

Nearly two hours later Squadron Leader JH Iremonger and Flying Officer J Cullen began their patrols when they took off from Newchurch. After being directed towards the sector where radar stations were tracking contacts, Cullen got a sighting of a V1. He dived towards it, chasing it as it approached the British coast heading inland. A few minutes later he was in range and fired his cannon hammering the V1 with shells, which sent it crashing into the sea 1 mile north of Beachy Head lighthouse at 1950 hrs.

On 8 July Flight Lieutenant McCaw shot down four V1s in the darkness of the night on a single patrol lasting from 2305 hrs to 2340 hrs. Two others were destroyed around the same time by Pilot Officer Lawless.

The following day, 9 July, the Squadron had no engagements with flying bombs until the late evening. At 2130 hrs Flying Officers RJ Cammock and J Cullen began their patrol when they were airborne out of Newchurch. In constant touch with ground control, they headed for the sector where the flying bombs were being tracked. Cullen spotted one and peeled off, diving on it and shooting it out of the sky. It crashed to the ground half a mile from Lydd at 2145 hrs. Climbing back up to patrol height, both pilots attacked another V1, shooting it into the sea south of Bexhill at 2200 hrs.

An hour later, Warrant Officer Hooper shot down a V1 at 2300 hrs into the sea south of Beachy Head. Ten minutes later he shot down another one into the sea south of Hastings.

Over the next three days no V1s were destroyed though the Squadron mounted regular patrols. On 12 July the lull ended and the Squadron started scoring again. The first V1 to be destroyed took place at 1300 hrs when Pilot Officer Hall dived on it, bringing his Tempest in behind and above the flying bomb before opening fire. Plastering it with cannon fire, he saw strikes on the fuselage and wings when suddenly the V1 exploded in mid-air north of Tonbridge. He turned and climbed hard to avoid debris from the V1 that came shooting back towards him.

At 1400 hrs Flying Officer SS Williams took off with Warrant Officer AA Bailey. Vectored onto an incoming flying bomb Williams peeled away, diving on the target. He fired at it several times as he closed the gap and levelled out. Stricken by so many shells the flying bomb climbed to 3,000 feet then dived straight into the ground and exploded at 1538 hrs.

Two hours later Pilot Officer Hall was in the air on another patrol when he dived on a flying bomb and fired at it from short range, sending it into the ground. It exploded east of Bexhill at 1620 hrs.

While Hall was attacking the V1 the pilot he had taken off with, Warrant Officer WA Kalka, destroyed four flying bombs on a single patrol. He attacked the first one from short range, his guns shooting it into the ground 10 miles north of Hastings at 1620 hrs, twenty minutes after both he and Hall had taken off from New-church. Nine minutes later, he shot down another flying bomb in the same way, diving from behind, levelling off and firing from close range from 800 to 250 yards away. He then climbed and turned away. The third one he spotted coming in over Bexhill heading for London and dived on it, firing as he levelled out. This flying bomb went straight into the ground after being hit by several strikes. It blew up 10 miles north-west of Bexhill at 1632 hrs. Five minutes later, he had shot down the last one of his patrol

10 miles north of Hastings. He had taken off at 1600 hrs and landed back at Newchurch at 1655 hrs, in which time he destroyed four flying bombs.

The following morning Flying Officer Mason, along with Flight Lieutenant HN Steedman, took off from Newchurch at 0930 hrs, roaring into the early morning air. Directed towards incoming flying bombs, Mason picked up a visual contact and dived towards the target, firing at it from short range. He saw his shells strike home and the flying bomb slowed then went into a fatal dive, crashing into the ground at Rye at 1004 hrs where it exploded. Climbing, he chased another V1 and several minutes later caught up with it, blasting it with cannon fire. He saw it crash north of Bexhill at 1032 hrs.

It was on 13 July 1944 that Sir Roderick Hill held the momentous conference that changed the conduct of the battle against the doodlebug. This was the day that Sir Roderick decided to move the anti-aircraft guns from protecting London to the coast, effectively hampering the area in which the fighters could operate.

Of course, at the Squadron level this change was not immediately apparent and it was business as usual for the pilots. At 1505 hrs that afternoon Pilot Officer WAL Trott destroyed a V1 at Tunbridge Wells. Firing several short bursts, he saw the V1 tumble to the ground with pieces flying off it. It exploded on impact.

The last V1 of the day to fall to 486 Squadron took place at 1715 hrs when Flight Sergeant BJ O'Connor rolled his Tempest into a dive and roared down on a target, opening fire as he came in behind it and seeing strikes on the wings and fuselage. The V1 crashed into the ground and exploded south-west of Malling.

On 14 July two Tempests flown by Flight Lieutenant JH McCaw and Warrant Officer OD Eagleson lifted off the runway at Newchurch at 0908 hrs. Directed by ground control towards incoming V1s, McCaw peeled away, rolling the Tempest into a dive as he caught sight of a flying bomb approaching Bexhill. Firing several bursts at it, he saw strikes on the enemy robot aircraft and watched it crash into the ground 10 miles north of the town where it exploded at 0945 hrs.

Eagleson also destroyed a flying bomb on this patrol. Chasing a V1, he opened fire and shot it into the ground 6 miles north of Eastbourne at 0955 hrs with several short bursts of cannon fire. Later in the afternoon Flying Officer Williams shot down a V1 between Westerham and Sevenoaks, sending it crashing into the ground at 1525 hrs.

At 1700 hrs Flight Lieutenant HN Sweetman and Flying Officer HM Mason took off from Newchurch to carry out another anti-Diver patrol. Reaching their patrol altitude, they were vectored towards approaching flying bombs and Mason rolled his Tempest into a dive. Picking up speed, he lined up a V1 in his sights and waited until the range closed. Thumbing the firing button, he let loose a storm of cannon shells that struck the flying bomb, sending it crashing into the ground at Bexhill at 1750 hrs.

While Sweetman and Mason were carrying out their patrol, Flying Officer JR Cullen chased a V1 near Hastings, firing several bursts from his 20-mm cannon at it. He saw strikes hit the fuselage and jet apparatus. Suddenly the flame went out and the flying bomb climbed up to 6,000 feet then dived to 500 feet where it levelled out then rolled over and went straight into the ground, exploding east of Hastings at 1832 hrs.

On 15 July only two V1s were destroyed, while the rest of the patrols were uneventful. The following day was not much better when one and a half were destroyed.

The next flying bomb to be destroyed was on 18 July 1944. By now the guns had been moved to the coast and were in operation.

At 1730 hrs Squadron Leader JH Iremonger and Flying Officer JR Cullen took off from Newchurch, their Tempests roaring into the sky, climbing fast to their patrol height. Directed by ground control towards incoming contacts, Iremonger picked up a visual contact of a flying bomb and both pilots peeled off, taking turns to attack the V1 as they dived on it. Plastered with cannon shells, the flying bomb suddenly exploded in the air west of Tenterden at 1735 hrs. Both pilots had a share in its destruction.

That night, Flight Lieutenant Sweetman fired several short bursts at a flying bomb as he dived on it, lining up the exhaust glow in his sights and blasting it with his cannon. As he levelled off he saw the V1 dive into the ground and explode between Hastings and Bexhill at 2250 hrs.

Though several patrols were mounted on the following day only one V1 was destroyed and then the weather turned bad with low cloud and poor visibility, which made operational flying very difficult.

By the afternoon of 21 July the weather lifted a little. Even though the weather over England and the Channel was bad at that time, the Squadron continued to mount standing patrols. One of them began at 1515 hrs when Flight Lieutenant JH McCaw and Flight Sergeant J Steedman lifted their Tempests off the runway and roared into the sky. Climbing up to their patrol height, McCaw attacked an approaching V1 below him and shot it down, sending it crashing into the ground at 1556 hrs.

The following day was much more successful. At 1300 hrs two Tempests roared away from Newchurch flown by Flight Lieutenant J Appleton and Flying Officer RJ Cammock. It was Cammock who picked up a visual sighting of a V1 approaching the coast. He chased it for a few minutes until he was within range when he opened fire, expending all of his ammunition with short concentrated bursts. He saw his shells striking the fuselage and engine, then suddenly the V1 exploded in the air 3 miles north of Ashford at 1315 hrs. Five minutes later he returned to base to rearm.

At 1545 hrs Flying Officer JR Cullen manoeuvred his Tempest in behind and above a V1 as he levelled out of a dive. Firing short bursts at it, the V1 staggered and dived into the ground, exploding near Sevenoaks.

Just as Cullen was touching down at Newchurch, Pilot Officer Dansey was taxiing out to the runway. Once Cullen was down, Dansey and Flying Officer HM Mason roared down the runway into the air. A few minutes later Dansey was chasing a V1 heading for London and after firing several bursts sent it diving into the ground 10 miles south of West Malling where it exploded on impact at 1637 hrs.

The last V1 of the day was shot down when Flying Officer JR Cullen attacked a V1 crossing the coast near Rye. Diving on it, he fired several times and saw his shells hitting home. The V1 crashed 10 miles north of the town at 2115 hrs.

On 23 July two V1s were shot down during Pilot Officer WAL Trott's afternoon patrol at 1520 hrs. After being directed towards the area where V1s were approaching, he attacked one and destroyed it at 1525 hrs. Five minutes later he destroyed a second one, both near the Etchingham area.

In the early hours of 24 July, Flight Lieutenant LJ Appleton attacked a flying bomb at 0526 hrs, which he shot into the ground 5 miles north-south-west of Canterbury where it exploded.

At dawn on 26 July Pilot Officer RD Bremner and Flying Officer WA Hart lifted their Tempests off the runway at Newchurch and climbed into the sky, heading towards their killing ground behind the gun belt that was now situated on the coast instead of defending London. Directed to intercept approaching flying bombs, Bremner saw one below him and attacked it. Firing his cannon, he saw shells strike the fuselage and the flying bomb slowed then dived into the ground bursting into flames 10 miles north-west of Rye at 0620 hrs, twenty minutes after he had taken off.

Hart got his sighting over Tonbridge and rolled his Tempest into a dive, blasting the V1 with cannon fire when he was within range. The flying bomb crashed 5 miles from the town at 0635 hrs.

Both pilots on the next patrol were also successful. Taking off at 0705 hrs, Flight Lieutenant JH McCaw and Flying Officer Cammock soared up to their patrol altitude. In constant contact with ground controllers, McCaw turned his Tempest towards the Channel as directed and picked up a visual contact of a V1 approaching the coast near Bexhill. Diving, he lined up the target in his sights, waiting as the range closed. Then he opened fire as he levelled out his shells, pounding the flying bomb that suddenly blew up in the air north of the town at 0745 hrs. Five minutes later Cammock, who had been chasing another V1, closed the gap between his Tempest and the doodlebug and he fired several short bursts at very close range. The flying bomb rocked from the impact of the shells and blew up in the air 10 miles north-east of Bexhill.

Flight Lieutenant V Cooke and Pilot Officer KA Smith began their patrols when they climbed into the sky at 0755 hrs. Heading for the coast, they were directed towards incoming flying bombs and Smith spotted one coming in fast below him. Peeling off, he chased it towards Pevensey, increasing the Tempest's speed. Within a few minutes he had closed the range between them and thumbed his firing button, sending a storm of cannon shells into the flying bomb. The V1 crashed into the ground 10 miles north of Pevensey at 0810 hrs.

Forming up with Cooke, they both went after another flying bomb and both pilots chased it inland. They took turns attacking it until the V1 fell into the ground where it blew up on impact at 0820 hrs 2 miles west of Battle.

Two more flying bombs were destroyed that night. Flying Officer JR Cullen took off from Newchurch with Squadron Leader JH

Iremonger at 2105 hrs. Directed by ground control to the corridor behind the coastal gun belt, Cullen intercepted a V1 as it crossed the coast missing the flak. He then chased it until he shot it down 8 miles north of Pevensey at 2210 hrs.

27 July was the last day of major engagements for pilots of 486 Squadron against flying bombs that month. The first flying bomb to be destroyed fell to the guns of Pilot Officer RD Bremner who shared in this kill with Flying Officer WA Hart. Both pilots took off from Newchurch at 1355 hrs and headed towards approaching flying bombs as directed by ground control. Getting a sighting on a V1, both pilots peeled off and dived their Tempests towards the target, opening fire as they reached minimum range and pulling out of their dives. One after the other they climbed and turned tightly and attacked again, diving on the V1, seeing strikes on the flying bomb. It went into a dive and crashed into the ground just north-west of Tenterden exploding at 1642 hrs.

The next patrol mounted by the Squadron that afternoon took off at 1720 hrs. Pilot Officer WL Trott and Warrant Officer OD Eagleson climbed their Tempests away from Newchurch and began their patrol. After thirty minutes they were directed towards approaching contacts and Trott saw a V1 below him. Pushing the control column forward he dropped the fighter's nose, diving towards the target, and attacked it with several short bursts, which sent it crashing into the ground half a mile south of West Malling at 1755 hrs.

Flight Lieutenant JH McCaw and Flying Officer R Cammock roared down the runway at Newchurch, soaring into the evening sky at 1840 hrs. Reaching their patrol height, each Tempest began patrolling and Cammock was directed towards an incoming V1. Spotting it in the distance below him, he rolled his Tempest into a dive to build up speed to catch the doodlebug. Closing the gap, he pulled out of his dive behind the V1 and opened fire with his cannon shells at the flying bomb. He shot it down at 1924 hrs, south of Tunbridge Wells. He then destroyed another V1 six minutes later in the same area.

While Cammock was racking up his score, McCaw attacked and destroyed another V1 at 1927 hrs.

At 2105 hrs Warrant Officer OD Eagleson lifted off the runway at Newchurch with Pilot Officer Trott, their Tempests roaring into the night sky. Within minutes of reaching their patrol height they were directed towards the area behind the guns and in front of the balloons. Seeing a V1 rapidly approaching, Eagleson rolled the Tempest into a dive, rocketing down on the V1. Quickly, the range between the two aircraft lessened until the Tempest was within firing range. Levelling out, Eagleson fired several short bursts from his cannon and saw his shells striking the fuselage and engine. Peppered with shells, the V1 suddenly blew up in the air 20 miles north of Ashford at 2122 hrs.

Flight Lieutenant JH McCaw was back up on patrol at 2230 hrs. Patrolling over the Ashford area, he picked up the glow from a V1 approaching rapidly. Diving towards it, he positioned the Tempest in behind and a little off to the side of the V1 and thumbed the firing button, unleashing several short bursts of cannon fire. He saw the V1 slow down and then dive into the ground in the Ashford area where it exploded at 2245 hrs.

As July 1944 ended August became a very slow month for the pilots of 486 Squadron and they began to take on other duties in place of some of their V1 patrols. By the end of the month they had been shifted to other duties entirely.

Flight Sergeant BJ O'Connor shot down the first V1 for the Squadron on 16 June and the last on 29 August. During this period they flew 2,443 sorties, covering 2,784 flying hours, and shot down 241 flying bombs. The Squadron experienced a great deal of engine trouble with the Tempest from 28 April 1944 to 31 August with twelve aircraft unserviceable or written off and eighteen pilots injured and seven slightly injured due to technical problems. They lost three pilots to other causes during this period as well.

CHAPTER NINE

Spitfires Engage: No. 1 Squadron

In the battle of the flying bombs the Tempests were the main players as they were the fastest aircraft capable of catching and destroying the V1s. Pilots flying these magnificent machines had higher scores than pilots flying other aircraft.

But several Spitfire squadrons were kept back for the battle to shoot down as many V1s as they could. This is the story of No. 1 Squadron and their battle against the V1.

June and July 1944 were busy months for Spitfire pilots of the Detling Wing. Flying the Mark IX LF with 25 per cent boost using nitrous oxide, they played their part in destroying as many V1s as possible. What follows are the most interesting combat engagements of that hectic and dangerous time and is indicative of the life of a Spitfire pilot fighting the unmanned menace that was the doodlebug.

In the early morning of 27 June 1944 a section of three Spitfires climbed into the sky from Detling at 0610 hrs. Flight Sergeant I Hastings, Flying Officer RW Bridgman and Flight Sergeant KC Weller each shared in the destruction of a V1. As they climbed to height, they were vectored onto the target coming in south-west of Lydd from the direction of Boulogne at 370 mph at 2,000 feet. Peeling off, the Spitfires dived on the target, picking it up at 0720 hrs over Dungeness and chasing it north-west, each one hammering away at it with their cannon and machine-guns. Finally, the V1 made an unstable turn to port and dived steeply into the ground where it exploded between a farmhouse and outhouses in the Filmwell/Wadhurst area at 0730 hrs.

The following evening, Flight Lieutenant TD Williams DFC was on an anti-Diver patrol with his section when Sandwich Control vectored him onto four V1s coming in over the Dungeness area at 2145 hrs. Rolling into a dive, Williams caught sight of the glow from a V1's jet engine and gave chase, rapidly closing the range as he dived on the target. Levelling off, he tucked his Spitfire in behind the target, which was flying at 345 mph at 1,500 feet. At 2210 hrs he was able to close the gap down to 300 yards and fired several short bursts at the flying bomb. 'I saw strikes and as I pulled away to starboard the Diver dived steeply and crashed near Williards Hill,' Williams reported. He also reported the fact that the AA coastal guns in the area were so trigger happy they nearly shot him down!

Early in the evening of 30 June Flying Officer K Foskitt of Blue Section took off from Detling at 1915 hrs, climbing rapidly. Picking up Sandwich Control, the Section was directed onto a V1 coming in 10 miles north-west of Folkestone at 190 mph at 2,000 feet. Diving on the target, Foskitt overshot the slow-moving V1, turned and came in again, overshooting a second time before he could attack. Turning back again, he came in from quarter starboard astern of the V1 and began weaving from side to side to keep his Spitfire behind the target. He fired a four-second burst and then a two-second burst from 300 yards away. He saw strikes on the jet engine and the rear of the fuselage. He reported:

> The size of the flame from the jet increased. The Diver then rolled on its back and went in exploding on some farm buildings. A P47 was making attacks from the port side without any apparent effect.

At 2115 hrs he was up again and this time under Beachy Head Control who put him onto a V1 coming in 5 miles south of Hastings. This one was flying at 300 mph at 1,500 feet and as Foskitt saw the glow from the jet engine he dived towards the target. Manoeuvring his Spitfire in behind the V1, he opened fire from 300 yards away. Thumbing the firing button three times, he let loose three one-second bursts of cannon and machine-gun shells that peppered the flying bomb. It dived straight into the ground, exploding about 1 mile north-west of Hasting in a wood at 2220 hrs.

At virtually the same time Flying Officer H Stuart, as part of Red Section, was vectored by Wartling Control onto a V1 coming in at 330 mph between 1,000 and 2,000 feet between Bexhill and Pevensey Bay. Peeling off, Stuart pushed the throttle forward and dived towards the target, bringing his Spitfire in behind the V1. He opened fire with a six-second burst from 200 yards away. He reported:

The Diver started gradually to lose height and went straight down. I saw the fuselage go bright red and the Diver turned over emitting much flame and exploded on the ground near some houses in the Bexhill area.

This took place at 2220 hrs.

In the afternoon of 4 July Flight Lieutenant TD Williams and Flying Officer DR Wallace roared into the sky from Detling, climbing rapidly away from base under the direction of Wartling Control. Vectored onto a V1 coming in 10 miles south-east of Rye, the two Spitfires turned and headed for the target. It was flying at 2,000 feet at 300 mph when the Spitfires made their first attack with Blue 1 (Williams) leading. Attacking from the rear starboard side, Williams fired a two-second burst of machine-gun and cannon fire at the V1, then climbed away as Wallace came in behind the V1 firing a three-second burst.

Again, Williams attacked the V1, firing another two-second burst while Wallace came in behind him, attacking the V1 with a four-second burst. They saw strikes hit the port wing and jet engine. Williams reported:

The glow from the jet engine increased considerably and fuel leaked from the starboard side. The Diver nosed down and dived steeply through the cloud crashing into the sea just off the coast between Rye and Dungeness.

Later that evening at 1915 hrs Flying Officer D McIntosh and Flight Sergeant KC Weller were directed by Hythe Control onto a V1 coming in 30 miles south of Rye at 300 mph at 2,400 feet. McIntosh went in first. 'I intercepted but owing to the low speed of the Diver, I overshot,' McIntosh reported. As he did, Weller attacked with a two-second burst and saw his shells strike the nose and wings. The two pilots each attacked again. McIntosh continued:

After the attack the Diver flew straight and level for a bit then turned on its back, banked to port and rolled out of control into the sea. The Diver appeared larger than usual, especially the jet propulsion unit.

The time was 1955 hrs when the V1 hit the sea.

At 1105 hrs on 5 July Flight Sergeant Hastings on an anti-Diver patrol was vectored onto a V1 by Wartling Control, coming in 15 miles south of Beachy Head at 320 mph at 2,500 feet. Rolling his Spitfire into a dive, he attacked from astern, firing a one-second burst at the target from 270 yards away. Climbing, he turned and attacked again, firing his cannon and machine–guns, this time blowing the outer section of the port wing off. 'The Diver dipped to port, made a steep climbing turn then dived to the ground crashing on the edge of the balloon barrage near Gatwick,' Hastings reported. Breaking away sharply, Hastings climbed his Spitfire hard to avoid the barrage cable but his wingtip clipped it and the Spitfire spun around. 'I managed to restore the aircraft to an even keel but saw the outer section of the starboard wingtip was cut off.'

Damaged as it was, Hastings headed for Gatwick, the closest airfield, and managed to land his Spitfire safely when he discovered that two opposite blades of the propeller were damaged. This was at 1300 hrs.

Fifty minutes after Hastings engaged his V1, Flight Lieutenant Stewart of Blue Section was vectored by Beachy Head Control onto another flying bomb coming in 6 miles south-east of Beachy Head at 320 mph at 2,000 feet. Pushing the throttle forward, Stewart peeled off, diving the Spitfire towards the target. He fired a five-second burst from 400 to 100 yards away, seeing strikes and smoke from both wings. The flying bomb went straight down into the ground, exploding east of Loughton at 1248 hrs.

On 7 July, Flight Sergeant HJ Vassie (Green 2) roared away from Detling with Green Section, climbing into the afternoon sky. Vectored onto V1s coming in south of Pevensey, Vassie caught sight of one flying at 1,500 feet at 350 mph. Peeling off from the others he dived towards it, he waited for the range to close. Then levelling out, he attacked from behind, firing several bursts at it from 300 to 200 yards away. The V1 slowed and nosed down, dropping 500 feet. He reported:

I followed it through cloud still attacking it. My ammunition exhausted I pulled up and away and lost sight of the V1 in cloud and shortly afterwards there was an explosion that lifted the aircraft.

In the afternoon Flying Officer HL Stuart (Red 1) took off from Detling at 1600 hrs, leading Red Section as they climbed away from base. Vectored by Kingsley Control, he saw the V1 5 miles inland from Eastbourne, travelling at 380 mph at 3,000 feet. Climbing to 6,000 feet, Stuart, with his No. 2, peeled off and dived onto the target, firing a four-second burst from 500 to 200 yards away from 10 degrees to port. He saw his shells hit home on the starboard wing and fuselage. 'Immediately following the attack the Diver made a diving turn to starboard and crashed on a house near a mental hospital north of Hailsham,' Stuart reported and this was later confirmed. The attack took place at 1630 hrs.

At 2113 hrs Pilot Officer EN Marsh attacked a V1 while under Beachy Head Control, which was flying at 350 mph at 3,000 feet 2 miles east of Eastbourne. Unlike the Tempests that could catch most of the V1s in level flight (but still most pilots dived on their targets) the Spitfires, even with the 25 per cent boost, had to dive steeply on their targets when they were flying at 400 mph or more and attack as they pulled out of the dive, passing over the target, turning, climbing and diving again on the flying bombs.

Marsh dived his Spitfire on the target, coming in from dead astern and firing two two-second bursts, shooting pieces off the port wing. The V1 dropped its wing but then regained stability and continued flying. Marsh attacked again with another two-second burst. 'The rear portion of the Diver disintegrated and, smoking badly, it dived steeply to earth exploding on impact,' he reported. The V1 hit the ground at 2135 hrs and Marsh touched down at Detling at 2214 hrs.

On 10 July Flight Sergeant Tate (Yellow 2) took off from Detling at 1400 hrs and tucked his Spitfire in behind Yellow 1 as they climbed away. Vectored by Kingsley Control, they picked up a V1 coming in 5 miles east of Tunbridge Wells at 350 mph at 2,000 feet. Peeling off, Tate roared down on the flying bomb, levelling off behind the V1, and from 400 yards away opened fire with four three-second bursts until he was 250 yards out. He saw pieces fly off the Diver as he climbed away. Suddenly, it exploded in mid-air 4 miles north-east of Sevenoaks at 1450 hrs.

The following day at 1959 hrs two Spitfires climbed rapidly away from Detling. Flight Sergeant I Hastings (Yellow 1) and Flight Sergeant Tate (Yellow 2) were vectored by ground control onto flying bombs coming south of Hastings. Peeling off, Hastings dived on one flying bomb flying at 310 mph at 2,000 feet. Coming in dead astern of the target, he levelled off and fired a two-second burst from 100 yards but saw no results. Chasing the V1, he fired a long four-second burst at it and as he did a Spitfire XIV from another squadron came roaring down in front of Hastings. 'I had to push the nose down to save hitting the Spit XIV,' Hastings reported. 'I saw strikes on the port wing and while the Spit XIV was still firing the Diver exploded in mid-air and we both flew through it.'

Yellow 2, Flight Sergeant Tate, attacked another V1 from 50 to 150 yards away with a long five-second burst 4 miles north of Hastings. This V1 was travelling at 350 mph at 2,000 feet when smoke started pouring from the jet engine. It crashed straight down into the woods 10 miles north of Hastings.

Later that evening at 2005 hrs Flying Officer FW Town rolled his Spitfire into a dive, roaring down onto a flying bomb coming in 6 miles north-east of Rye at 320 mph at 2,000 feet. From 200 yards away he fired a two-second burst at it from dead astern and saw his shells striking the jet engine. The V1 climbed 300 feet, rolled onto its back and then spiralled into the ground 7 miles north of Rye at 2105 hrs.

Over the next few days, the Squadron moved to Lympne.

They were operational again on 14 July when Sandwich Control vectored Flight Lieutenant Stewart onto a V1 1 mile off Camber, flying at 320 mph at 2,000 feet. Rolling the Spitfire into a dive, he headed for the target and attacked it with a half-second burst from three degrees starboard but saw no strikes. Climbing away, he turned hard and dived on it again from the same angle and fired another half-second burst. 'This caused a belch of flame from the rear of the Diver,' he reported. 'It banked slowly to port and dived steeply into the ground exploding near farm buildings.' This combat was seen by Blue 2 and confirmed at 1835 hrs.

The same time that early evening Flying Officer Marsh (Green 1) climbed away from Lympne into the early evening sky leading Green Section on an anti-Diver patrol. He was climbing fast and heading for the Channel as Swingate Control vectored Green Section onto V1s 5 miles off Cap Gris Nez, heading for Britain. Diving on a flying bomb travelling at 320 mph at 2,000 feet, Marsh attacked the target four times with two-second bursts. Flying in line abreast and slightly behind, Green 2[32] watched his leader attack the V1, seeing strikes on the port wing and jet engine. 'The final burst exploded the jet shooting out a ball of flame and the Diver winged over and spiralled into the sea at 1830 hrs,' Marsh reported.

The following day at 1645 hrs Flight Sergeant Vassie of Green Section climbed rapidly away from Lympne. Directed towards a V1 coming in north-west of Dover by Sandwich Control, Vassie climbed above the target flying at 345 mph at 2,000 feet. Rolling into a dive, he brought his Spitfire in behind the V1 as he levelled off and began firing several short bursts from 200 yards to 150 yards away. In all, he fired eight bursts at the V1, which finally went spiralling down into the ground where it exploded roughly 200 yards away from a house (which was damaged in the blast) approximately 5 miles east-north-east of Detling.

On 16 July Flight Lieutenant TD Williams was vectored by Swingate Control onto a V1 coming in at 360 mph at 3,000 feet south of Ashford. Diving on the target, he attacked the doodlebug from dead astern, firing a two-second blast of cannon and machine-gun fire, seeing strikes on the fuselage and wing roots. On his second attack he levelled off from his dive, coming in at the flying bomb at seven degrees and below the target firing another two-second burst. Williams reported:

The Diver dipped its starboard wing and made a slight diving turn to starboard. Then it pulled up on a 20 degrees climb to port went through some cloud and then I saw the Diver make a turn to starboard and go down.

It exploded in an orchard 2 miles south of Maidstone at 2000 hrs.

Another V1 fell to the guns of Flying Officer DH Davy on 22 July after he roared into the night sky at 2115 hrs vectored by Kingsley Control onto a target approaching from the Brookland area. He saw two Mustangs attacking it, achieving strikes on the target from 300 yards away, but it kept on going. As the Mustangs broke away, Davy dived on the target, attacking it from 20 degrees to port. Firing a single three-second burst, the flying bomb blew up in mid-air and the debris fell to earth 5 miles south-south-east of Ashford at 2300 hrs.

The following morning Flight Sergeant Vassie was up at 0510 hrs, climbing rapidly away from Lympne as Blue 2. He was tucked in behind his leader as they headed towards Dover where Swingate Control reported several V1s approaching. Seeing one flying at 355 mph at 2,000 feet, Vassie peeled off, diving towards the target now 15 miles south of the Dover Felixstowe Midway line. At 250 yards he levelled off astern of the flying bomb and fired a two-second burst before breaking off and attacking again, this time coming in below the V1 and behind it firing another two-second burst. Pieces flew off the jet engine and the V1 cartwheeled into the sea at 0555 hrs.

On 24 July Flying Officer K Foskitt (Black 1) and Flying Officer FW Town (Black 2) took off from Lympne at 2110 hrs picking up Sandwich Control. The Section was vectored onto V1s approaching Folkestone. Peeling off, Foskitt dived towards one doodlebug that was flying at 320 mph at 1,500 feet. Foskitt reported:

I saw the Diver coming in through the AA and held off while a Mustang went in to attack. The Mustang broke away and the Diver was still flying straight and level with the jet functioning.

Bringing his Spitfire in again, he fired a one-second burst from ten degrees starboard and line astern. He saw his shells hammer the V1 as he climbed away, now only 6 miles west of Ashford. 'The Diver heeled over to port and went into a slow dive to the ground.' Foskitt broke away quickly as the Mustang came back firing a burst while the V1 went into the ground and exploded on impact 20 yards from a brick works at 2140 hrs.

Town picked up a V1 flying at 360 mph at 2,000 feet. 'Guided by flak I saw the Diver and made a deflection attack,' Town reported. Diving on it, he fired a couple of two-second bursts from ten degrees starboard but saw no results. Climbing away, he brought the Spitfire around again and attacked from line astern, firing two more bursts at the target. 'The jet went out and the Diver went into a gentle dive and the jet started again during the dive. It crashed shortly after, exploding in a wood surrounded by open country.' That was 5 miles north-east of Ashford at 2140 hrs.

Flying Officer DH Davy (Yellow 1) and Flight Sergeant G Tate (Yellow 2) shared in the destruction of another V1 on 26 July. Taking off at 1350 hrs under Swingate Control, they climbed away from Lympne heading for the coordinates 10 miles west-north-west of Boulogne. Seeing the target flying at 330 mph at 2,000 feet towards Britain, they took turns attacking it, diving on it firing two two-second bursts. 'Yellow 2 attacked first,' Davy reported. 'Strikes were observed on the starboard and port wings. Then I attacked, seeing strikes on the port wing.'

As Davy went in, Tate had climbed above and turned to dive back down on the V1, firing another two-second burst that achieved strikes all over the flying bomb. Davy continued:

The Diver slowed to 250 IAS [indicated airspeed] and I then gave it another burst seeing strikes on the jet unit. The Diver dropped its port wing and begin to lose height and the Diver went into the sea exploding.

The V1 hit the ocean at 1420 hrs.

On the evening of 28 July Flying Officer Town destroyed two flying bombs. He took off from Lympne at 2115 hrs, climbing into the night sky. Vectored onto a V1 coming in from the Tenterden area, Town saw the flying bomb at 1,200 feet travelling at 380 mph and made two attacks from line astern, coming in sideways and firing a burst from 200 yards away. Town reported:

After the first attack, I saw strikes on the jet unit. The Diver dived down and I followed it firing two more bursts trying to explode it in the air but the Diver crashed in the ground in a field.

The V1 blew up on impact 2 miles from Staplehurst.

A few minutes later he saw the glow from a V1 shooting across the landscape north-west of Ashford flying at 320 mph at 2,100 feet, with two Mustangs and two Spitfires chasing it. Town continued:

Putting on full boost I passed all these aircraft after seeing one Spit fire a short burst at the Diver without effect. Closing in I gave the Diver one burst, seeing strikes on the tail unit.

The V1 glided steeply down and exploded 300 to 400 yards from a railway line near Lonham at 2225 hrs. Town was officially credited with 1⅓ V1s destroyed during that patrol.

CHAPTER TEN

The Germans Air-launch
the Flying Bomb

As the Allies began overrunning the V1 launching sites in
northern France and into the low countries in late 1944, the
Germans were ready to continue the V1 attacks by launching them from bombers taking off from bases in Germany.

Most of the following information came from a German informant
who provided the Allies with technical data on the modification
and use of the flying bomb being air-launched from modified
He 111 twin-engined bombers. Most of this information was backed
up later on when the Allies found an He 111 on Kohlenbissen Airfield, which had been blown up and partly burnt-out. The internal
equipment of the aircraft was surprisingly undamaged and it was
sent to England for examination.[33]

The Germans were already experimenting with air-launching
the flying bomb long before the campaign from their ramps in
northern France began. The first airborne launching of the V1 took
place at Peenemünde in 1943. The aircraft used was a Heinkel
He 111 and though this was used predominantly throughout the
war to launch V1s the Germans also used other aircraft such as
Do 217s, Do 215s, and Fw 200s.

In most cases the V1 was slung under the fuselage with its wings
forward of the landing gear. However, in the case of the Do 217 the
normal bomb bay was removed, giving the aircraft the appearance
of having some of the lower part of the fuselage cut away. On
the He 111, however, a single wire connection ran from the main
aircraft to the flying bomb.

The Germans did not overly modify the He 111 as these aircraft were capable of taking off and flying without difficulty, although they had to use the full length of the runway to do so. However, they did strengthen the starboard mid-wing section with additional metal sheeting around the mid-wing fuel tank.

Trials of air-launching the V1 took place during the day and night with the same launching procedures used each time. The He 111 would climb to a height of approximately 1,500 to 1,800 metres and fly on a course that the bomb would fly on, that is, pointing the aircraft in the direction they wanted to send the bomb. Once the V1 was released it would drop about 30 to 40 metres from the mother aircraft. Then the flame would appear from the exhaust of the jet engine, the small red lights on the trailing edge of each wing would light up and the bomb would be on its way.

The range of an He 111 with a flying bomb slung under the starboard wing was 640 miles, which gave it an action radius of 320 miles. Add to that the range of the flying bomb, which was around 160 miles, and you had a radius of action of 480 miles. In most cases the target was London so with the range of the He 111 and the flying bomb the bases for operating could be as far away as Magdeburg and Nurmberg in Germany, including the southern half of Denmark. However, as the Allies were gaining ground it would have been necessary for the He 111 crews to try to avoid them, so their bases were in the north-western part of Germany and Denmark.

Visual beacons were used on the Dutch coast, from which the pilots of the He 111 could plot a course out to sea.

The V1 was attached to the aircraft by a special carrier between the fuselage and the starboard engine. The carrier itself consisted of two lugs that held a T plate in place on the V1, which was the only point of contact between the flying bomb and the mother aircraft. To maintain the flying bomb's lateral stability the Germans had mounted two vertical metal struts, each with horizontal wooden battens on the ends that rested on the upper surfaces of the flying bomb's wings. The struts were tubes approximately 5 cm in diameter that partially protruded from under the wing by about 50 cm. Inside the tube was a coiled spring that was connected to the buffers that would rest on the wings of the V1. These struts were fixed to the fuselage and under the starboard wing aft of the engine nacelle.

The pilot could not see the flying bomb from his position and most pilots would not have seen much of the bombs as they were covered with a net that was only removed after the crew had boarded their aircraft.

The instrument used to start the V1's engine and release the bomb was called the Zahlwerk. It was a box that had a tachometer in it and was placed above and in front of the pilot and observer. The box was 20 cm in height and 10–12 cm in width and at its centre was a small illuminated window with five or six digits, each moving separately. The bombardier had a duplicated box in his position with the addition of a red and black button to the right and the release lever below it.

Approximately 2 to 3 metres outboard of the engine there was a metal tube on the leading edge of the starboard wing that protruded from the wing. The metal tube had a small propeller on the end of it and this tube was connected electronically to the Zahlwerk.

Also from a box inside the bombardier's position near the Zahlwerk was a tube. This tube went through the side of the fuselage where it formed a single right-hand loop where the end of the tube carried a small funnel-shaped mouthpiece, which was believed to have been the electrical connection for starting the V1's jet engine. This tube protruded through the fuselage out and under the starboard wing.

While the pilot went through normal flight checks the observer would set a number on the box before take-off. Once they were airborne and a certain point was reached in their course, the observer would then press a switch to the left of the box that would start the digits counting down by single units and the box in the bombardier's position would do the same.

The total time taken for the digits to run down from their original setting to zero was about fifteen to twenty minutes.

There was a red button that the bombardier used to push for stopping the propulsion unit if necessary. As the countdown reached 100 the observer would then tell the bombardier via the intercom when to push the various buttons and when to release the bomb, even though the bombardier had the same information in his position. At 25 the observer would give a warning via the intercom for the bombardier to get ready and he would then push the black button known as the *Anstellknopf*.

When the counter reached 0 approximately five to ten seconds later, the bombardier would pull the release lever and the V1 would be dropped. Should everything go badly wrong and the V1 needed to be jettisoned, there was a red lever in the roof to get rid of the bomb in an emergency.

The minimum safety height for releasing the bomb was set down at 500 metres or 1,650 feet. German pilots would usually fly very low over the sea at 100 metres or 350 feet. Shortly before releasing the V1 they would make a short climb to 500 metres, level out and increase speed, release the bomb and then dive back down to 100 metres. Most pilots added an additional 100 metres onto the 500-metre release safety height just in case.

Once the bomb was released the He 111 would suddenly rise steeply in the air. The pilot would have to level it out while the V1 dropped approximately 100 metres before starting on its course.

To avoid being detected by prowling enemy night fighters German pilots would dive their He 111 down to 100 metres but stay on the same course as the flying bomb. It was estimated that any night fighters would expect the aircraft to turn off its course to port or starboard rather than continue in the track of the bomb.[34]

Operational procedure for air-launching the flying bombs began on the afternoon preceding an operation, when the V1s were brought on a field railway from their dispersal areas to the servicing hangars. Here, special V1 armourers would sling them under the He 111s, after they had been fuelled etc., on an apron outside the hangar.

The bombers themselves were brought from their dispersal areas in pairs by the ground crew to their refuelling points and then taxied to the V1 hangar where the bombs were attached. Once this was done they were returned to their dispersal areas.

Only two of the crewmembers were briefed on the exact release points of the bombs during each operation and they were the observer and the wireless operator. No navigational aids were used at this time. However, originally when the Germans first started air-launching operations a sky marker was placed by a pathfinder aircraft. But after a few operations the Germans decided they didn't need pathfinders and left the aircrews to fend for themselves in the darkness of the winter nights over the North Sea.

The scale of the effort dwindled towards the end of 1944. At the beginning of November operations were being made by two

Gruppen with II *Gruppe* having started some three weeks before. About sixty aircraft would be out five times a week. But as December 1944 came the operations began to tail off due to lack of fuel. By the end of the month the fuel shortage was so acute that there was only ever enough fuel available for the next operation. No fuel stocks were held on the airfield.

Air Marshal Sir Roderick Hill's perspective forms a unique insight into the various phases of the battle against the flying bomb. In a secret report on the 'Air Operations of the Air Defence of Great Britain' he outlined his views on the German air-launched flying bomb campaign.

As early as 8 July, the Germans had experimented with launching the V1 from He 111s, operating from bases in Holland. These flying bombs came only at night.

As we have seen in earlier chapters Sir Roderick considered the threat of air-launched V1s to be as real as the main threat from launching sites and ensured he had the defences to meet this threat. He set up a gun box[35] between Rochester, Whitstable, Clacton and Chelmsford to supplement the coastal gun belt. Adding to this, he extended the balloon barrage to Gravesend and set up fighters to fly standing patrols over the mouth of the Thames. By the middle of August the gun box had 208 heavy guns, 178 40-mm guns, 404 20-mm guns and 108 rockets.

During July and August the defences picked up 120 flying bombs coming in from the east, which would have been from the direction of Holland. These flying bombs would have been launched from the air as the German bomber bases were in Holland until they were moved to Germany.

No more were sighted coming from this direction until the early hours of 5 September when another nine bombs approached London from this direction. By that time the launching sites in northern France had been overrun by the Allies so these new air-launched attacks meant that they had now entered a new phase in the battle against the pilotless aircraft – flying bombs launched from the air.

After that day, there was another lull in the attacks coming from Holland that lasted more than ten days. By this time, the Allied armies had captured every part of the continent where launching ramps that could fire off flying bombs within range of London either already existed or could be built. At the same time, British

Intelligence discovered that the German air-launching unit of the *Luftwaffe* was moving from its bases in Holland into Germany.

Many believed that the long ordeal of the flying bomb for London was now finally over. But it was not to be.

The Germans managed to do two things: increase the range of the flying bombs and therefore build ramps further away; and launch them from their modified He 111 bombers. 'That the Germans might still launch flying bombs from aircraft was not disputed by the Air Ministry or the Chiefs of Staff,' Sir Roderick recorded in his report.

The attacks resumed again at dawn on 16 September when at 0549 hrs a bomb fell in Essex. A few minutes later another bomb came down in Barking. For the next half-hour five more bombs approached Britain with one coming down in Woolwich and another near Felsted, while the remaining three were shot down by fighters.

The following evening three more bombs came over with two being shot down by fighters and by the guns. On succeeding nights more bombs continued to come over.

Up until this time the vast majority of bombs had been launched from ramps, which meant that the bombs would usually be coming in within a defined area. Hence the defences had been set up to cover the areas where the bombs would be crossing the coast. However, now that the ramps had been captured the Germans were able to exploit the mobility of air-launched V1s, making it harder for the defences to be able to predict where they would be coming from.

In fact, the German bombers launching the V1 were doing so well out over the North Sea by virtue of necessity to avoid Allied fighters and guns. So to meet the new challenge the existing gun belt and the gun box were fortified by Sir Roderick and General Pile who agreed to extend both the box and the belt by adding a gun strip from Clacton up to Great Yarmouth. Between 16 and 19 September sixteen heavy and nine light gun batteries began to move from their positions in the gun belt to the coast between Clacton and Harwich. Another 498 heavy and 609 light guns had been deployed in the box and in the gun strip by the middle of October.

This new deployment of the guns caused some problems, chief of which was that they could no longer have the same freedom of fire they had had in the south-east during the summer. The main reasons for this was the positions of Bomber Command's airfields and the intermittent character of the attacks. At the same time, Sir Roderick issued orders that aircraft flying below 6,000 feet during the hours of darkness were prohibited from flying over the gun box, but he could not prohibit them from flying over the strip in order to land at their airfields. The one caveat he did stipulate was that his headquarters needed to know beforehand of any low-flying aircraft coming in over the gun strip, so as to avoid them being shot down by their own guns!

The guns also had another restriction and that was now that the V1s were being launched by the He 111, the flying bombs were coming in around 1,000 feet rather than between 2,000 and 3,000 feet as they had been in the summer. Sometimes they were even lower than 1,000 feet and although equipment was coming online for controlling low-angle fire, it was at that time few and far between. This meant that General Pile had to position his guns in order to get the best results against low-flying targets, which meant sacrificing some of his early warning capability.

The fighters had their own restrictions, the main one being that the attacks were now taking place at night. Sir Roderick wrote:

There was a natural tendency to suppose that interception at night would be easier than in daylight. This was because the tongue of flame emitted by the bomb was so conspicuous in the dark.

It was not that simple. Not only did a pilot have to see the V1 but also to estimate its range, which in the blackness of night was extremely difficult. Anyone who has tried to judge his or her distance from a light on a dark night will understand how difficult this was, especially since the flying bomb and the fighter were both travelling at high speeds. A simple rangefinder was developed to solve this problem and proved to be very valuable to the pilots, but it was the skill and experience of the pilots that overcame the challenges of night-fighting. Some pilots took to it, showing remarkable ability in flying and fighting at night, while others simply could not get to grips with it.

Two fighter types were used in these night operations against the flying bombs. The twin-engine Mosquito night fighters flew in the areas in front of the guns, while the Tempest day fighters piloted by specially trained night fighter pilots operated between London and the gun belt, gun box and the gun strip.

The Mosquito could only catch a flying bomb in a dive, even with its additional boost. But throughout this phase of the battle against the flying bombs Mosquito night-fighter crews shot down a total of twenty-one bombs.

Sir Roderick wrote in his report:

The Tempest which had been outstandingly successful during the main attack in the summer now operated with the aid of a searchlight belt extending from Saffron Walden and Sudbury in the north to Southend and Brightlingsea in the south.

The Tempests brought down more than fifty flying bombs operating inside the searchlight belt. Most of the V1s they destroyed fell into open country. Out of some 600 flying bombs that had been detected heading towards London during the months from September 1944 to January 1945, only 205 got past the defences, with only sixty-six falling in Greater London.

In addition, Mosquitoes were also dispatched to patrol the areas where the German He 111 bombers were launching their flying bombs over the North Sea in order to shoot down the launching aircraft. In itself this was a difficult task because the Germans would fly very low indeed, only climbing to around 2,000 feet to launch their flying bombs. They would then immediately dive down again and head for home. The Mosquito night fighters also had to fly a few hundred feet above the sea, which hampered the ability of their onboard radar to pick up their targets. The land-based radar stations that controlled the fighters usually were unable to detect the German bombers until they climbed to the height for releasing their bombs. They would be at this height for only a few moments before they dived away.

A number of experiments were tried to overcome some of these limitations. One included using a naval frigate to act as a controller for the fighters but this bore little fruit. Another was to use one of the Mosquitoes equipped with ASV Mark V radar as a controller for the other fighters and this began to bear fruit right at the end of this phase of the battle.

Once again, it came down to the skill and perseverance of the night fighter crews who shot down sixteen of the *Luftwaffe*'s He 111 launching aircraft, with another four as probably destroyed and another four damaged between 16 September 1944 and 14 January 1945. We will go into this in more detail in the next chapter.

These losses, combined with the hazardous operations of launching flying bombs at almost sea level, put severe strain on the *Luftwaffe* unit operating these machines. At the same time, the Germans seemed to be either unaware of the small numbers of flying bombs that were now reaching London or they had resigned themselves to having an extremely low return for the work they were putting in to keep some sort of offensive going against Britain. During the winter of 1944/5 they increased the scope of their activities.

Despite the success of the defences against the flying bombs, the most worrying thing for the British was that the air-launched flying bomb had mobility as its primary advantage. The guns could not be everywhere at the same time and the Germans could use the bombs against other targets besides London. They did just that.

There was also a new, deadlier, more frightening menace now raining down on Britain – the V2 rocket. 'At that time,' Sir Roderick wrote, 'the country was being bombarded with rockets as well as flying bombs.'

During the winter of 1944 Sir Roderick was responsible for co-ordinating offensive and defensive countermeasures against the V2s and the V1s. Although the tactical and strategic air forces were very busy with many different tasks, he was able to send fighters and fighter-bombers to pound the launching areas of the rockets. The bases in north-west Germany from which the He 111 bombers operated for air-launching the flying bombs were beyond the range of all the aircraft he had at his disposal.

Intelligence reports kept a close eye on the *Luftwaffe* air-launching unit. As the Germans began to increase their activity Sir Roderick asked Bomber Command to attack the bases from which these aircraft operated. This was done by squadrons from Bomber Command and from the American Eighth Bomber Command.

Also, Sir Roderick rapidly deployed fifty-nine gun batteries to areas between Skegness and Whitby based on intelligence reports showing an increase in the air-launching unit's capability.

Without warning, on Christmas Eve 1944 around fifty He 111s took off from their bases and headed towards the British coast. They launched their bombs in the direction of Manchester. Thirty bombs crossed the coast and only one reached Manchester, while six came down 10 miles from the city centre and another eleven came down within 15 miles of the centre. That night thirty-seven people were killed and another sixty-seven seriously injured.

Fortunately, the Germans were not able to mount an attack like this again, but Sir Roderick immediately ordered guns to be deployed north of the Wash. He then set up plans for the defence of Tees-Tyne and Forth-Clyde but did not have the resources to properly defend these areas. If the Germans had followed up the attack on Manchester with other attacks north and south of the Wash, they would have caused considerable chaos.

Sir Roderick reported:

Either this did not occur to the Germans, or such an enterprise was beyond the capabilities of an organisation whose spirit was shaken and which was running short of fuel. No more bombs came from north of the Wash; and three weeks later the air-launching unit ceased operations.

As far as the Germans were concerned 9/KG53 had between eighteen to twenty modified He 111s available for fifteen crews. By the end of December this *Staffel* had suffered no loss of aircraft or crew.

However, II/KG53 lost twelve aircraft in two operations in mid-December due to several V1s detonating just after the bombers lumbered into the sky, making the *Gruppe* non-operational for almost a fortnight.

One of the first units to start air-launched flying bomb operations was III/KG55, which moved to Grottkau from Russia in September 1944. Here, they received their new He 111 H-16s and H-20s, which had been modified to carry the V1. They were not new airframes.

For the Allies, intelligence on the activities of the *Luftwaffe* air-launching unit came from a wide variety of sources. As we have seen earlier in this chapter, there was first-hand evidence from the informants working near or on the air bases who could provide details about the equipment used, as well as times of take-offs and landings. However, there was also the visual identification of flying bombs actually released by the He 111s over the North Sea near the English coast.

Indeed, in a report from the Port Fisheries Captain in Grimbsy dated 5 January 1945, three skippers of fishing trawlers provided eye-witness accounts of flying bombs launched from German bombers.

The first was from Skipper Gorringe of the S/T *Gurth* who was 7 miles south-east of the Dowsing Spar buoy on Sunday 24 December 1944. He reported seeing a flying bomb released from an aircraft at 0445 hrs. He believed the flying bomb flew off at approximately 100 to 150 feet on a west-north-west course. That same morning he saw four or five flying bombs crash and explode into the sea instead of flying on.

Later that same day trawler Skipper Petherbridge of the S/T *Remagio* reported that he heard a loud explosion and saw a big flash at approximately 1915 hrs. At the time the *Remagio* was sailing 5 miles east-south-east of the Dowsing Spar buoy when the skipper saw the explosion though it was some distance away in a north-westerly direction.

The skipper of the S/T *Scouter* was 14 miles east of the buoy when he saw two aircraft circle overhead between 0500 and 0600 hrs. At first, according to his report, he thought they were friendly aircraft but when they launched their flying bombs he realised they were not. The German bombers released their V1s about a mile or two west of the trawler's position and both began flying at a height of approximately 150 feet. In all, the skipper of the *Scouter* reported seeing eighteen or so bombs. However, none of them were as close as the two mentioned above and one of the V1s he witnessed being launched crashed and exploded into the sea.

Interestingly, little evidence of air-launched flying bombs from He 111s was seen in photographs taken from high-flying photo-reconnaissance aircraft. For example, in an interpretation report dated 2 November 1944 of He 111s at Boblingen Airfield, it could not definitely identify that any of the He 111s on the airfield were modified to carry flying bombs. There was no evidence of any activity to suggest this.

In another interpretation report (dated 10 October 1944) of He 111s at Barth and Garz airfields, there was a possibility that the He 111s at Garz were modified.

In most cases no statement can be made on possible modifications owing to lack of definition. One He 111, however, seen directly outside the hangar previously associated with Hs 295 glider bombs appears to have three light-coloured patches on it.

The report also stated that a large amount of development was taking place on that airfield at Garz, which included the construction of shelters for very large and small aircraft. However, no flying bombs could be identified in the photographs of the airfield.

A report dated 8 October 1944 regarding the interpretation of photo-reconnaissance photos of Greifswald airfield showed some interesting results. Firstly there was a large number of He 111s on the airfield where since before April 1944 the airfield had been devoted mainly to Ju 88s and other twin-engined aircraft. 'Thirty-three He 111s were visible at Greifswald on 5.10.44 dispersed near the southern hangars and also in the newly developed dispersal area to the north of the airfield,' the report states.

But no definite statement that these He 111s had been modified for carrying V1s could be made. 'Several appear to have the three light-coloured patches on the forward fuselage which may possibly indicate such a modification.'

This report also stated that there was no evidence of flying bombs in the photographs.

A further interpretation report, No. L.244, dated 9 September 1944 seemed to point towards the He 111s being modified to carry flying bombs. However, none of the interpretation reports could certainly state that He 111s were, in fact, used for launching flying bombs.

'Some He 111s may have an additional fitting between the dorsal turret and the nose a fact which may be significant if flying bombs are carried above He 111s,' the report states.

'The appearance on the fuselage of an He 111 seen on air photographs depends upon the position of the movable wind-shield on the dorsal turret and of the sliding hatch on the upper part of the nose.' Definition of the aerial photographs taken by reconnaissance aircraft varied substantially. Where the definition was poor these components were indistinguishable, but where definition was good they appeared as two light-coloured patches on the fuselage.

However, in some photographs three light-coloured patches were visible on the fuselage between the trailing and leading edges of the wing. The report stated:

This, indicates the presence of either a glazed or light-coloured surface, a marking, or some modification involving the alteration of the skin, at a point between the dorsal turret and the nose.

One interesting entry of the report stated that a long, light-coloured object was seen on top of an He 111 based at Venlo. However, the quality of the photographs was poor and the light-spread could have been a protective covering rather than a flying bomb mounted on top of the bomber.

Indeed, the British felt that there was evidence to suggest that the Germans had experimented with air-launching flying bombs from on top of the bomber. But, as we have seen with evidence from the German informant, they were launched from under the starboard wing.

In interpretation report No. L.228, dated 2 August 1944, the reconnaissance photographs showed two flying bombs near the south-eastern hangars. The closest aircraft to the V1s were He 111s and Dornier 217s.

A top-secret report dated 31 July 1944 entitled 'Flying Bombs from Dutch-Belgium Area' suggested that the Germans were indeed launching flying bombs from He 111 bomber aircraft. The report states that on the evening of 30 July 1944 nine He 111s took off at 2125 hrs heading outwards off Blankenberge, Belgium, at 2105 hrs. Another eight He 111s were spotted outward off Blankenberge at 0115 hrs flying at 200 metres. Another three were seen off Walcheren.

That same evening ten flying bombs were seen from the Ostend area and twelve more were seen coming from the Dutch Islands area. The report concludes that the number of flying bombs reported that evening closely coincided with the number of He 111 flights out.

The inference is therefore that the scale of effort is directly connected with the number of He 111s operating; taking this further that the flying bombs are actually launched from the aircraft.

That no launching sites had been detected in the area at the time the report was written and radar tracks showed that the launchings had taken place from beyond the coast, also added to the conclusion that the Germans were using He 111s to launch flying bombs.

In a report from Intelligence Headquarters Air Defence of Great Britain dated 11 September 1944, the accuracy of air-launched flying bombs was discussed. The report states:

In order to achieve any degree of accuracy of aim it is essential that the position of the aircraft is accurately determined at the time of launch. So far the aircraft have made use of visual beacons to pinpoint themselves on crossing the coast and their overseas flight has been only about 25 miles, probably dead reckoning to sufficient accuracy.

However, the report states that the likely operational range of the He 111s could be as high as 400 miles, which without any navigational aids would mean the pilots would have to use dead reckoning. This would certainly impact on the accuracy of the flying bomb.

In 1944 the He 111 was an extremely vulnerable aircraft to heavily armed Allied fighters and bombers. The He 111 was slow and lacked real defensive armament, therefore even though the maximum range of the aircraft meant it could release its flying bomb at the English coast and hit virtually anywhere within the UK that scenario was very unlikely. Its vulnerability meant that it was unlikely these aircraft would go anywhere near the British coast. The report states:

The problem, therefore, becomes that of how close to the English Coast could the He 111s approach without being attacked which in turn depends on the range at which they would be detected.

Launchings had taken place below 2,000 feet, which meant that a radar station on the British coast situated 400 feet above sea level would be able to detect an aircraft approaching from 75 miles away. But as Sir Roderick Hill stated in his report, most of the radar stations on the British coast had difficulty detecting the He 111s flying below 2,000 feet.

It was not until the Allies overran the main launching points and received information from German informants that they realised the enemy was indeed using He 111 bombers to launch flying bombs from the air. Only the fuel shortage curtailed the use of these aircraft, though one must wonder how long these airfields would have remained intact under the air superiority enjoyed by the Allies. The likelihood was not for long.

CHAPTER ELEVEN

Mosquitoes into the Fray

In order to tell the full story of the Mosquito crews' efforts against the flying bomb I have used a variety of sources, including Martin Bowman's excellent book *The Men Who Flew the Mosquito*. The Mosquitoes began their air war against the V1 on the evening of 14 June 1944 when Flying Officer Schultz of 605 Squadron was passed by a flying bomb while he was on a mission over the sea. The V1 was going in the opposite direction. Immediately, Schultz turned his Mosquito on its tail, rammed his throttles through the gate to catch up and the aircraft surged ahead. When he was within range he fired a burst at the target and destroyed it, but he was going so fast he flew straight into the debris and returned to Manston with most of the skin of his Mosquito burned off.

Mosquito crews were not briefed on the coming V1 menace so they had no idea what to expect. For example, on the night of 18/19 June 1944 Flight Lieutenant RW 'Dickie' Leggett with Flying Officer J Midlane took off from Hurn near Bournemouth on a routine patrol. Coming in to land at the end of that patrol, they were refuelling when they were told to get off again as quickly as they could to intercept a pilotless aircraft. Scoffing in disbelief, they took off and climbed away, put onto patrol by a GCI station at 1,500 to 2,000 feet. A lot of choice words flowed over the RT from Leggett who was already fed up from the previous two-hour patrol that had resulted in nothing at all. Then suddenly everything happened at once. Sighting an aircraft going at high speed with a huge flame coming out the back, it shot past going at 90 degrees to them. The Mosquito was travelling at 220 mph while the buzz bomb roared past them at 400 mph. Leggett turned as quickly as he could and rammed the throttles forward but by then the V1 had left them in its wake. Furious at not being briefed or prepared for the new menace, they landed back at Hurn and reported what they had seen.

Switched to anti-Diver patrols on 25 June 1944, 85 Squadron Mosquitoes had their engines upgraded with the injection of nitrous oxide mixed with the petrol that gave the aircraft greater speed. Both squadrons operated against the V1s until 20 August when they were switched over to bomber support duties from Swannington.

The Mosquitoes without nitrous oxide injection had to dive down on the doodlebugs at full speed, flat out and do the best they could. But, in order to avoid collisions with other night fighters trying to do the same thing, pilots had been briefed to switch on their navigation lights. This also made them a sitting target for enemy Fw 190s that sometimes flew along or behind the V1s at night.

The end of June 1944 saw 605 Squadron with a tally of thirty-six V1s and in the following month another twenty-nine fell to their guns.

On the night of 6/7 July 605 Squadron pilot Flight Lieutenant Brian 'Scruffy' Williams and Warrant Officer SF Hardy took off on an anti-Diver patrol at 0145 hrs. They saw a group of eight V1s heading for Britain. Williams attacked the first one from 6,000 feet, 8 miles south of Dungeness. He dived towards it, firing a burst at it. The doodlebug exploded and as Williams climbed away he was directed towards another flying bomb, this time 5 miles north-north-west from Le Touquet. Peeling off, he dived towards it, gradually closing the gap until he was in range. He then fired a short burst from his cannon and the shells ripped the flying bomb apart, sending debris all over the sky. Fifteen miles east of Dungeness he attacked another V1 and shot it down.

On 18 August Williams was again in the thick of it, directed towards the Continent where the V1s were being launched. He sighted the glow from several V1s crossing the French coast at 2,000 feet between Le Touquet and Boulogne, heading for Britain. Coming in dead astern behind one he chased it across the Channel until he closed the range 4 miles out from Dungeness and fired a short burst with his cannon, completely destroying the bomb. Turning back towards the Continent, he was 10 miles out from

Le Touquet when he destroyed another V1 from above and astern, firing two short bursts at it.

By September 1944 the Allies were racing across France and the launching sites in the Pas de Calais area had been overrun. The Germans switched to air-launching V1s from Heinkel bombers of III/KG3 based at Venlo and Gilze Rijen in Holland.

But the Germans suffered a setback in the doodlebug blitz in September 1944 when III/KG3's airfields were overrun by the Allies, forcing them to move to airfields in Germany. That then meant only the radar-equipped Mosquito night fighters were able to counter the threat.

The first He 111 H-22 fell to Mosquitoes of 409 and 25 Squadrons when they shot down the enemy aircraft over the North Sea on 25 September. Three nights later, Wing Commander LJC Mitchell and his navigator Flight Lieutenant DL Cox of 25 Squadron had further success.

Taking off from their base at Coltishall at 0055 hrs, they climbed rapidly into the night sky. Their Mosquito was fitted with the AI Mark 10 radar unit and they were on patrol over the North Sea looking for the Heinkels. Forty miles east of Great Yarmouth, they spotted a V1 being launched from a Heinkel at 3,500 feet and immediately gave chase. They informed Greyfriars Control of their position and Control came back and told them the Heinkel had turned to port. Dropping 600 feet in a rapid turn, Cox found the contact on his radar 2½ miles ahead. Closing fast, Mitchell brought the Mosquito down to 200 feet above the sea and at 1,300 feet got a visual sighting of the German bomber confirming it as a He 111. Coming in behind the enemy aircraft, Mitchell thumbed the firing button and his cannon burst into flame, the shells ripping into the Heinkel, which exploded and sent debris into the night sky and right into the path of the Mosquito. Mitchell turned the Mosquito quickly, catching sight of the wreckage of the Heinkel crashing into the sea. He orbited the area, watching the enemy machine burn for two or three minutes before it sank.

Climbing rapidly back up to their patrol altitude, Mitchell and Cox saw another V1 being launched from a Heinkel. Rolling into a dive, Mitchell tore after the flying bomb, informing Greyfriars Control. But instead of chasing and destroying the V1, they vectored him onto the launcher. Eventually, after flying around in the dark, Cox obtained a fix and directed Mitchell onto a converging course with the enemy aircraft. For what seemed an eternity they waited for the range to close to a mile then Mitchell executed a hard turn to port, closing in behind the enemy bomber.

The German seemed to be completely oblivious of the Mosquito stalking him. Dropping down to 150 feet, the Mosquito roared over the waves at 220 mph, heading towards the enemy machine. At 1,500 feet Mitchell and Cox got their visual confirmation that it was, indeed, an enemy machine. Mitchell closed to 600 feet then hit the firing button, sending a short burst of cannon fire at the Heinkel. As the shells pounded into the enemy aircraft pieces flew off the right wing. Closing rapidly, Mitchell fired another burst and this time the He 111's port engine erupted in flames and the enemy machine smashed into the sea, burning fiercely. Searching for survivors, Mitchell circled the Mosquito over the wreckage until 0615 hrs but there was no sign of life.

The Mosquitoes used for this work had their normal armament modified. The nose of the day fighter version of the great twin-engined 'Wooden Wonder' normally housed four machine-guns and four 20-mm cannon under the fuselage. However, to house the onboard radar, the machine-guns had been removed and the nose modified into a bubble-type of installation. This was the NFXVII version. This left the four cannon as the main armament for the aircraft. However, unlike aircraft like the Tempest and Mustang that had their guns in the wings, the cannon under the nose in the fuselage were much more concentrated and the resulting fire from them was extremely powerful.

On the night of 30 October Squadron Leader LWG Gill and his navigator Flight Lieutenant DA Haigh roared into the early morning sky from Coltishall at 0725 hrs in a Mosquito NFXVII and were immediately vectored by Hampton Control towards enemy aircraft to the east. Pushing the throttles forward, the Merlin engines roared into full power and the Mosquito headed towards the coordinates. Picking up a contact 2 miles away, Gill turned hard right, 7,000 feet away from the enemy machine. Through the broken cloud base the Mosquito crew caught fleeting glimpses of the He 111. Then suddenly it released its V1 and turned left, descending rapidly. But the Mosquito was faster and Gill closed to within 1,000 feet, when he fired a long burst at the enemy bomber, cannon shells ripping into the right engine and fuselage. Bits and debris broke off, scattering in all directions. Gill fired again and saw more shells hammer into the enemy aircraft's tail.

But the Heinkel would not die. Instead, it dropped down to sea level and straightened out. Frantically seeking cover in the low cloud the Heinkel began to climb but there was no hiding place from the radar-equipped Mosquito. Contact was momentarily lost until Haigh picked up the enemy aircraft again and Gill brought the Mosquito within 4,000 feet. The German pilot, *Feldwebel* Warwas of 4/KG53, turned violently, climbing again for cloud cover with one of his engines smoking. But it was a useless gesture. From 1,000 feet away, Gill pumped another long burst into the Heinkel, which floundered, caught fire and dropped like a rock into the sea.

The pair attacked another He 111 H-22 eleven minutes later but this time the result was inconclusive. Firing a long burst before his ammunition ran out, Gill could see several shell strikes all over the enemy machine, but as it dived to get away from the Mosquito it disappeared into the cloud base at 600 feet. Gill and Haigh were unable to confirm that the Heinkel had crashed into the sea.

Despite the losses in October the Germans decided to continue the air-launching raids and added II/KG53 and III/KG53 to I/KG53 for these operations.

A 68 Squadron Mosquito took off from Coltishall on the night of 5/6 November 1944 piloted by Flight Sergeant Neal with Flight Sergeant Eastwood as his navigator. The radar-equipped Mosquito climbed rapidly into the night sky, heading out over the North Sea to intercept some incoming enemy aircraft. Eastwood picked up a contact flying at 1,000 feet 1 mile away from them. They had no difficulty finding the Heinkel carrying the V1. The machine was travelling at 150 mph so Neal initially overshot the enemy and turned back to their patrol line. Picking up contact again, they closed from 2 miles to 1,000 feet, then to 500 feet. At 1,500 feet the Heinkel released its flying bomb and then gradually lost height, turning to starboard.

Keeping the contact on radar, Neal followed the German machine while Eastwood expertly worked the radar controls, bringing Neal ever closer to the target. At 200 yards' range flying at 900 feet over the sea, they caught sight of the enemy bomber and Neal let loose with a two-second burst. The Heinkel rolled over, diving steeply to starboard crashing into the sea.

A Mosquito was despatched at 1825 hrs from Coltishall on 10/11 November to intercept an enemy aircraft coming in over the North Sea. Climbing into the night sky, Flight Lieutenant GF Simcock and navigator Flying Officer NE Hoijne headed over the dark, rough waters towards their unknown contact. Vectored by Neatishead Control and then Hopten Control they caught sight of a flying bomb being released. Turning in the direction of the sighting, they carried on and soon obtained a contact heading east bearing across their course from starboard to port. Flying at 1,000 feet, Simcock turned the Mosquito towards the Heinkel that was 3 miles away. The Heinkel turned widely to port and began losing height, dropping down to 200 feet. By now the weather had turned against them and they followed the bomber in a heavy shower, buffeted by the wind and rain getting a visual on their target at 800 feet.

The Heinkel then dropped to 150 feet above the rough waves and Simcock decided to open fire immediately rather than waiting any more. Firing at 600 feet to 400 feet he could see his cannon shells striking the port engine, wing root and port side of the fuselage. A large flash from the port engine sent a piece flying back towards the Mosquito. Hoijne reported seeing another flash from the port side fuselage as the aircraft immediately slowed down and went into a steep portside bank. Avoiding collision, Simcock broke away sharply as the Heinkel dropped now below 100 feet. Breaking hard to starboard, Simcock turned to port in an effort to regain the contact on radar but they picked up nothing. Searching thoroughly about 75 feet above the wave tops, they scanned the area as best they could in the darkness and under the heavy weather but saw no sign of wreckage. He reported it as a probably destroyed.

German losses continued to mount with another He 111 being shot down by Mosquitoes on 10/11 November when Flight Sergeant A Brooking and Pilot Officer Finn of 68 Squadron caught one over the sea and shot it down. Nine days later another Mosquito, this time from 456 (RAAF) Squadron, chased a Heinkel, catching up with it 75 miles east of Lowestoft. Pilot Flying Officer DW Arnold and his navigator Flying Officer JB Stickley closed within 400 yards of the enemy bomber. Arnold thumbed the firing button as his cannon burst into life. The ventral gunner on the Heinkel returned fire, striking the Mosquito's right propeller.

Arnold fired another burst as the Heinkel turned away, hitting the bomber's starboard engine, which suddenly caught fire. Climbing to 1,200 feet, the burning Heinkel began to break up, rolled onto its back and did a stall turn into the sea, the flames almost immediately extinguished by the waves.

Early dawn on 25 November 1944, a Mosquito crew from 456 Squadron, pilot Flying Officer FS Stevens and observer WAH Kellett, took off from Ford at 0655 hrs, heading out over the North Sea towards Holland. On the horizon they saw two bright flashes 1,000 feet below them from flying bombs being air-launched. Climbing, Stevens dived the Mosquito down to 1,500 feet as Kellett reported two contacts. Latching onto the closest one, they took off in hot pursuit, diving down to 500 feet.

One Heinkel weaved continuously as it headed for home. In the gloom, the Mosquito crew had difficulty seeing the enemy bomber but the return fire from the Heinkel's gunners helped them to identify its presence. At 800 feet shells from the enemy aircraft's gunners shot past the Mosquito, but Stevens continued following the enemy aircraft bringing the Mosquito closer to the enemy machine and they were able to identify the aircraft as an He 111. At that point Stevens fired a two-second burst from his cannon, peppering the enemy machine with shells. The starboard engine immediately burst into flames. But not content, Stevens moved in closer firing another burst that ripped right through the fuselage, which exploded in flames. Turning hard to starboard to avoid collision, the flaming aircraft fell as the crew baled out and crashed into the sea 10 miles out from Texel. German search and rescue crews picked up all the survivors.

At 0550 hrs on the night of 23/24 December 1944 Dick Leggett and his navigator Midlane took off from Coltishall (they had been at Hurn and then returned to Norfolk), and climbed into the early morning sky heading for the North Sea.

On that night, they saw the flash of light from the launch of a V1 from a Heinkel. There could be several Heinkels attacking in one go and on this night that was the case. The Germans would fire off the V1 then turn to port and rapidly lose height heading for home. Heavy rain and low visibility made it hard to see the enemy but the Germans always came when the weather was bad.

Following the Heinkel, Leggett maintained his position above and behind the fleeing enemy aircraft. Closing steadily through the dark, the German started to turn away as if knowing the Mosquito was on his tail. Leggett closed in again with his guns and gunsight geared to 200 yards, but because of the bad weather was not able to get a visual contact.

Leggett dropped the Mosquito away while the navigator picked up the contact again, and Leggett turned continuing to stalk the German bomber. He started getting concerned as they were off Den Helder in Holland after following for a full fifty-five minutes. Eventually, as the dawn was coming up, Leggett closed within about 300 yards of the enemy aircraft and fired a long burst of his cannon while in the slipstream from the enemy aircraft. He observed several strikes on the Heinkel. The stricken aircraft crashed in Holland, killing four of the crew with only one of the two gunners surviving.

Another Mosquito from 68 Squadron claimed the last He 111 H-22 V1 air launcher to be shot down.

Some 1,200 V1s were air-launched against Britain but only 638 approached the coast and KG53 had lost seventy-seven Heinkels, sixteen claimed by Mosquitoes.

CHAPTER TWELVE

Night Fighters:
No. 96 Squadron

osquitoes of 96 Squadron began their war against the
flying bomb from West Malling on 14 June 1944. The
Squadron history has an interesting entry on that day.

*Well, well, whatever will happen next! At 0342 hrs the air raid
message was sounded, the All Clear going at 0400 hrs. At 0415 hrs
Red was sounded again and this time the news came from Biggin
that the Hun was sending over pilotless aircraft.*

Once the Mosquito crews were flying their anti-Diver patrols
they were in constant contact with various ground control centres
within their sectors. In most cases they would be given general
coordinates from the ground controllers and the Mosquito crews
would pick up the contact on their onboard AI radar sets, then
track the target until obtaining a sighting.

At 0520 hrs more than fifteen flying bombs came roaring over
in two waves headed for London. 'Flight Lieutenant Mellersh was
just coming in to land when he saw one crossing the airfield
at 1,500 feet going quite slowly and flashing a yellow light from
the tail at 0500 hrs,' the Squadron diarist recorded in the official
Squadron history. Another V1 flew across the airfield a few
minutes' later and crashed 5 miles south.

The Squadron did not see any action against the flying bombs
until 16 June when Flight Lieutenant Ward and his navigator
Flying Officer Eyles took off from West Malling at 2302 hrs pushing

their Mosquito hard, to 3,000 feet. They were directed onto a flying bomb coming in at 300 mph over the Channel from Boulogne towards Dungeness. Turning, Ward dived the Mosquito onto the target, firing several bursts of cannon fire at it. Finally, the V1 dived into the sea and exploded.

However, while Ward and Eyles were attacking their V1, Squadron Leader Parker-Rees and his navigator Flight Lieutenant Bennett took off at 0135 hrs, directed by ground control towards Dover. Bennett picked up a contact flying at 280 mph at 2,000 feet on a north-westerly course. Climbing the Mosquito, Parker-Rees turned and roared down on the flying bomb, attacking from behind, firing several bursts at it until it exploded in mid-air.

The entry by the Squadron's diarist for that night said:

... the robot bombers started to come in strength tonight. The ack ack was terrific and the fighters couldn't get anywhere near them though the CO went up specially to find one and was hit by our flak himself!

The Squadron diarist then suggests that the best name to describe the V1 was 'Chuff-bombs'. In addition to Parker-Rees and Ward each destroying V1s, that night several other Mosquitoes were also on anti-Diver patrols. They engaged several doodlebugs, firing their cannon, but with limited success. The Squadron was yet to get into its stride.

The night of 18 June was busy for all the fighters defending Britain. As we have seen, the Tempests, Spitfires and Mustangs were up in force that night as were the Mosquitoes. As with all the other squadrons it was a busy night for 96 Squadron. 'Only two crews failed to fire at Divers but most of the attacks were abortive because of speed or flak,' the Squadron diarist recorded.

Flight Lieutenant Gough with his navigator Flight Lieutenant Matson took off at 2241 hrs on an anti-Diver patrol heading across the Channel where they picked up a V1 off Calais flying at 2,500 feet at 300 mph. Gough had climbed the Mosquito to patrol altitude and was now flying higher than the V1. He rolled the twin-engined fighter into a dive. They rapidly closed the gap and attacked the target, seeing their shells strike the flying bomb, which suddenly blew up in mid-air. They landed back at West Malling at 0145 hrs on 19 June.

At 0156 hrs another Mosquito crew, Flying Officer Ball and Flying Officer Saunders, picked up a V1 10 miles off Hastings over the sea, which was flying at 2,000 feet after ground control had directed them towards the area. Ball reported:

We attacked from 4,000 feet. We saw strikes and the Diver began to lose height rapidly and the firing of its engine became erratic. We broke off the engagement as the Diver disappeared into cloud and the anti-aircraft guns opened up.

Other patrols during the early hours of 19 June were more successful. Squadron Leader Green and his navigator Warrant Officer Grimstone destroyed two. The first they picked up 10 miles north-west of Hastings, travelling at 3,000 feet at 340 mph. Well above it, Green rolled the Mosquito into a dive, increasing his speed. When he was in range he levelled out behind the V1 and fired several bursts, which resulted in the doodlebug going straight into the ground where it exploded on impact.

Returning to their patrol altitude and position, they were vectored onto another V1 coming in 10 miles south of West Malling, travelling at 320 mph. Green climbed the Mosquito as Grimstone called out the coordinates from his radar set, directing Green towards the target. Seeing it, he dived the Mosquito towards the V1, closing the gap to 300 yards when he opened fire. This time the Diver blew up in mid-air, the debris damaging the nose of the Mosquito.

Already airborne on an anti-Diver patrol, Squadron Leader Bradleigh and Flying Officer Ayliffe attacked and destroyed a V1 off Dungeness from 700 yards away. Seeing their shells strike the target, it dived into the sea and exploded as it hit the waves.

In the evening Mosquito crew Flying Officer Goode and Flying Officer Robinson roared away from West Malling at 2247 hrs, climbing into the night sky. Vectored onto coordinates where flying bombs were coming in, they picked up a contact on their radar set and tracked it until Goode caught sight of the glow of a jet engine and dived towards it. 'We saw strikes on the port side,' Goode reported. 'We had to break away as ack ack opened up: on turning in again the Diver had disappeared.' It was never confirmed as destroyed for them and they landed back at West Malling at 2340 hrs.

Another Mosquito crew, Flight Sergeant McLardy and Flight Sergeant Levine, attacked a flying bomb at 2249 hrs from 1,500 feet away north-east of Beachy Head. 'The Diver dived steeply to starboard with clouds of black smoke,' McLardy reported.

'A grand time was had by all,' the Squadron diarist recorded, 'including Flight Lieutenant Gough and Squadron Leader Chandleigh who were credited with damaging flying bombs.'

During the day on 19 June the Squadron moved from West Malling to Ford. Late that night Mosquito crew Flight Lieutenant Primavesi and Flying Officer Wilson, roared away from Ford at 2300 hrs. Directed by ground controllers, they tracked a contact on radar. The only light they had was the glow from their instruments as Wilson directed Primavesi towards the V1. Finally, seeing the glow from the flame of the flying bomb heading north-north-west at 1,500 feet at 290 mph, Primavesi turned the Mosquito towards the target. He dived on it, firing several bursts from 1,500 feet away, seeing strikes all over the flying bomb, which rolled and dived into the ground exploding on impact.

Also on patrol that night were Flight Lieutenant Kennedy and his navigator Flying Officer Morgan who were directed to a V1 coming in towards the coast, at 2,500 feet and 290 mph. Kennedy rolled the Mosquito into a shallow dive as Morgan tracked the target on the Mosquito's AI set. Seeing the glow from the V1's exhaust, he lined it up in his sights and closed the gap, opening fire from 1,100 feet away. Firing short bursts, they saw their cannon shells striking the V1 until it slowed then dived into the sea, crashing and exploding on the water at 0012hrs. Forty-eight minutes later they were back at their base at Ford.

Later in the early hours of 20 June Flight Lieutenant Ward and Flying Officer Eyles took off at 0250 hrs, climbing rapidly into the gloom. Picking up a contact coming in off Beachy Head, Eyles directed Ward towards the target. Ward pushed the throttles forward, increasing the aircraft's speed and climbing the Mosquito to get above the V1, which was travelling at 3,000 feet at 320 mph. They saw the glow from the exhaust and Ward rolled his aircraft into a dive, tearing down on the target. Firing several bursts at the flying bomb, Ward and Eyles saw their shells strike the fuselage and wings. Suddenly the fuel tank on the flying bomb burst and it fell into the sea where it exploded on impact.[36] 'We celebrated the move to Ford by adding three more chuff bombs to our store,' the Squadron diarist recorded that day.

On the evening of 20/21 June two more V1s were destroyed. Flight Lieutenant Mellersh and his navigator Flying Officer Stanley picked up a contact while on their patrol that was coming in at 2,500 feet at 320 mph east of Dover. Following the contact, with nearly full speed on, Mellersh climbed the Mosquito to get into position where he could dive on the target. Through the clouds they saw the glow from the V1 and attacked it. Lining up the exhaust glow in his sights as he dived the Mosquito, Mellersh opened fire with his cannon at 1,000 feet away and saw strikes on the flying bomb. It went down and exploded on the sea at 0035 hrs.

While other Mosquito crews were on patrol, only Wing Commander Crew and his navigator Warrant Officer Croysdill managed to chase a V1 coming in at 3,000 feet flying at 320 mph near Dungeness. Crew pushed the throttles forward, increasing the Mosquito's speed, the nitrous oxide giving him the precious few more miles per hour. Closing the gap, he dived towards the target, firing short bursts of cannon fire from 1,000 feet away. Continuing to fire as the Mosquito got closer, he saw his shells plaster the V1, which rolled and dived into the sea, exploding on impact at 0200 hrs. They returned to their patrol position and landed back at Ford at 0355 hrs. The Squadron diarist recorded:

Both Mosquitoes have holes torn in their underside near the cannon ports either by blast or vibration for they were travelling well over 300 ASI. Squadron Leader Parker-Rees fired several long bursts but made no impression and several others engaged similarily.

Only Squadron Leader Caldwell managed to destroy a V1 on 22 June. The entry in the Squadron history for that day is an amusing one. 'Squadron Leader Caldwell was the only one to engage,' the diarist wrote. 'He had four tries, two went down, one was frightened, and the other got away.'

The following day, however, was much different. In all, eight V1s were destroyed and the destruction began in the early hours. Squadron Leader Green led the way with three destroyed. His first came while he and his navigator Warrant Officer Grimstone were directed towards the coordinates of approaching flying bombs. They picked up a contact on their radar travelling north-west near

Friston at 1,500 feet at 300 mph. Tracking the V1, they gave chase, with Grimstone directing his pilot towards the contact until they obtained visual contact with the bright glow from the jet engine against the early morning gloom. Attacking it with several bursts, Green's shells burst the fuel tank and sent the flying bomb into the sea where it exploded.

The second V1 they picked up coming in at 320 mph over land near Worthing, flying on a north-westerly course at 1,500 feet. Again, they chased the V1, tracking on their radar then picking the visual contact in the darkness. Concentrating on the flame of the V1's jet engine, Green dived towards it and fired his cannon, sending it smashing into the ground where it burst into flames at 0359 hrs.

Their third V1 of the day was picked up over the sea on their radar near Hastings, travelling north-west at 2,000 feet at 280 mph. Green climbed the Mosquito up to patrol height while Grimstone tracked the contact on the radar, softly calling out the coordinates to Green. Once they had spotted the flying bomb, Green dived on it[37] and shot it down, peppering it with cannon shells that sent it falling into the sea where it exploded at 0415 hrs.

While Green and Grimstone were attacking their various targets, Squadron Leader Chudleigh and his navigator Flying Officer Ayliffe were already on patrol when they were directed towards Beachy Head where they picked up a contact over the sea between Beachy Head and Dungeness, flying north-west at 2,000 feet at 320 mph. The Mosquito was already well above the V1 and as they gave chase, Chudleigh dived towards the target firing several bursts at it. The V1 glided down slowly and crashed into the sea. Climbing away, they picked up another contact in roughly the same location as the first one, but travelling at 3,000 feet at 350 mph. Again, they tracked it, waiting until they had a sighting and were above the flying bomb. Seeing the glow of the jet engine in the darkness, Chudleigh dived the Mosquito onto the target, closing the gap between them until he was able to fire several short bursts. They saw strikes on the V1, which dived straight into the sea where it exploded at 0300 hrs.

Also on patrol in the early hours of that morning were Flight Lieutenant Gough and Flight Lieutenant Watson when they picked up a contact on their aircraft's radar near Dungeness. The V1 was travelling at 4,000 feet at 380 mph. Rolling the Mosquito into a steep dive, Gough gave chase and gradually overtook it, firing several bursts and seeing sparks all over the target. It began to glide down to 2,000 feet then it dived straight into the ground, exploding on impact at 0430 hrs.

Sub Lieutenant Wakelin and navigator Sub Lieutenant Williams picked up a V1 while on patrol, coming in 15 miles off Beachy Head. The V1 was flying at 360 mph at 3,000 feet and the Mosquito was well above at patrol height. Giving chase, Wakelin dived the Mosquito down behind the V1 and levelled off, lining up the jet exhaust in his sights. Closing the gap, he fired several long bursts and they saw pieces fly off the V1, which slowed down and began losing height. It exploded into the sea at 0200 hrs.

Flight Sergeant McLardy and his navigator Sergeant Devine took off from Ford at 0045 hrs and while all the others were attacking and destroying their V1s, McLardy and Devine were on patrol. But at 0300 hrs they picked up a contact on their onboard radar coming in near Lympne at 340 mph at 2,500 feet. Attacking it, McLardy fired several bursts, seeing sparks all over the V1. 'Then the enemy aircraft slowed down to 220,' McLardy reported. 'It began losing height down to 1,000 feet. Then after another burst it went in and exploded on the ground.'

Flying was hampered by low cloud on the evening of 24 June and it was not until the early hours of 25 June that the Squadron was able to resume hunting for V1s. Flight Lieutenant Mellersh and navigator Flying Officer Stanley were on patrol from 0200 hrs when they picked up a V1 on their radar, coming in over the sea off Dungeness at 2,000 feet flying at 300 mph. Heading in a north-westerly direction, the V1 shot towards the coast with the Mosquito above and behind giving chase. Pushing the throttles forward, Mellersh increased speed, diving on the target. From 1,000 feet he fired his cannon at the V1, seeing several strikes that sent the flying bomb straight into the sea where it exploded on impact at 0230 hrs.

Climbing away, they picked up another contact on their radar, which was travelling north-west over the sea at 2,000 feet at 300 mph not far from Dungeness. Chasing it, Mellersh waited until the gap slowly closed between them. Then from 800 feet and behind the V1, he fired a long burst at the target. 'I saw strikes but the Diver flew on with a train of sparks about a mile long,' Mellersh reported. 'It finally became a mass of flame before crashing onto the sea.' This was at 0305 hrs and the Mosquito was back on land at Ford at 0320 hrs.

While Mellersh was attacking his V1 another Mosquito crew, pilot Flight Sergeant Bryan and navigator Pilot Officer Friis, picked up their first contact of the night at 0328 hrs, which was travelling at 320 mph at 3,000 feet coming in near Eastbourne. Tracking it on their radar, they chased it until Bryan got a visual fix on the target and rolled the Mosquito into a steep dive, building up speed. He levelled off above and behind the V1, firing several bursts from his cannon from 2,000 feet away. Shells ripped into the flying bomb, which exploded in mid-air just as Bryan pulled the control column back, climbing the Mosquito hard to avoid flying through the debris. A few minutes later, with the Mosquito still climbing, they picked up another V1 on their radar. This one was coming in off Beachy Head, travelling at 320 mph at 1,000 feet in a north-westerly direction. Well above it, Bryan dived the Mosquito towards the target, rapidly closing the gap until he was 1,200 feet away when he opened fire with his cannon. The shells smashed into the V1 and it went straight into the ground, exploding on impact at 0340 hrs.

But Wing Commander Crew suffered damage to his aircraft while he was chasing a V1. The Squadron diarist recorded:

The C.O. was chasing one when the nose of his aircraft split open and he reported baling out. Warrant Officer Croysdill got out from 7,000 feet and Wing Commander Crew from 5,000 feet. Both landed safely near Wartling though Warrant Officer Croysdill hurt his ankle.

On the night of 25/26 June twelve patrols were flown by 96 Squadron and six V1s were destroyed. Flying Officer Goode and his navigator Flying Officer Robinson had a good night, destroying two V1s. Roaring into the night sky from Ford at 2240 hrs, they climbed rapidly away. Ground control directed them towards a sector where the V1s were approaching. They picked up a contact on their radar and began tracking it. Heading north-west, the V1 was flying at 3,000 feet at 320 mph when Goode gave chase. Rolling the Mosquito into a shallow dive, the gap closed rapidly and Goode fired several bursts at the flying bomb, sending it crashing into the ground. Climbing away, they returned to their patrol line and were vectored onto another contact.

Robinson tracked it on the Mosquito's radar, seeing that it was flying at 3,000 feet at 240 mph. Above the target, Goode brought one wing up, diving towards the V1. He then levelled off behind it and fired, seeing strikes on it. The flying bomb faltered and went straight into the ground, exploding on impact.

At the same time, Flying Officer Ball and Flying Officer Saunders picked up a V1 coming in north of Bexhill flying at 310 mph at 2,000 feet. Well above the target, Ball dived down on the target and as he levelled off above and behind it he opened fire. The V1 was sent straight down into the ground from the hail of shells where it exploded at 0050 hrs.

Squadron Leader Caldwell and Flying Officer Rawlins were directed onto coordinates while they were on patrol. Tracking it on their AI set, they gave chase to a V1 coming in 12 miles north of Hastings at 322 mph at 2,500 feet. Diving on it, they attacked the V1, which hit the sea and exploded at 0045 hrs.

Squadron Leader Green and Flying Officer Thorning attacked a V1 flying in a north-westerly direction at 310 mph at 1,500 feet. They took off from Ford at 0300 hrs and climbed into the darkness. They picked up the contact over the sea as it was coming in for the coast and headed in that direction. Spotting the flame from the V1's jet engine they attacked, diving on the target. They fired several bursts at it and saw shells strike the wings and fuselage. The V1 dived towards the sea and exploded just before hitting the water.

Bad weather made any operational flying prohibitive on 27 June. But the day after that the Squadron flew ten patrols and destroyed four flying bombs. Flight Lieutenant Mellersh and navigator Flying Officer Stanley took off from Ford at 0100 hrs and climbed up to patrol height. They picked up a contact 20 miles south-east of Dungeness – the V1 was travelling at 310 mph at 2,000 feet in a north-westerly direction. Increasing the Mosquito's speed, Mellersh gave chase and saw the glow of the V1's jet exhaust in the distance.

Rolling into a dive, he closed the gap and from 900 feet away opened fire. The V1 went straight into the sea and exploded at 0320 hrs.

Wing Commander Crew and navigator Sergeant Jaeger picked up their V1 coming in at 330 mph at 2,000 feet south of Hastings. In the gloom Crew saw the V1 and attacked, diving on it. Levelling out behind the target, his twin Merlins were at near full power. Finally, he fired from 250 yards seeing strikes on the V1, which dived straight into the sea and exploded at 0340 hrs.

South of Dungeness at virtually the same time, another Mosquito crew, Flight Sergeant Bryan and Flying Officer Friis, attacked a V1 coming in at 320 mph at 2,000 feet. Bryan fired on the V1 but saw no strikes. 'The Diver orbited losing height and then crashed into the sea,' he reported. However, there is nothing to indicate if his shells had caused some damage or if the V1 had been damaged before.

At 0315 hrs Flight Lieutenant Ward and Flying Officer Eyles roared into the morning sky from Ford, climbing rapidly. Vectored onto approaching contacts, they picked up a V1 on their radar, which was coming in 6 miles south of Dungeness flying at 370 mph at 3,000 feet. Climbing the Mosquito to get above the V1, they tracked it as it headed north-west. Ward then rolled the aircraft into a dive, then levelled out behind it closing the gap to 500 feet. He then fired several bursts and saw his shells rip both the wings off the flying bomb. 'It dove like a bomb and exploded on the sea,' Ward reported.

On the evening of 29/30 June many patrols were mounted to bring down flying bombs. Several Mosquito crews sighted V1s but they were flying in and out of cloud, making attacks very difficult.

July was a busy month for the Squadron but the month began very slowly. The first day the Squadron mounted eleven patrols. They saw many flying bombs but made no contact at all. The following day there was bad weather and low cloud made flying impossible.

But on 3 July the Squadron destroyed eight flying bombs. At 0055 hrs Flight Lieutenant Mellersh and navigator Flying Officer Stanley took off from Ford, their Mosquito roaring into the night sky. That night V1s were coming over in waves and Mellersh was directed to coordinates by Wartling Control over the sea 40 miles south of Beachy Head. Picking up a contact on their onboard radar, they gave chase to a flying bomb travelling at 260 mph at 1,000 feet. Diving on it, Mellersh levelled out the Mosquito, closing the range to 1,000 feet when he fired several very short bursts of his cannon. They saw strikes all over the fuselage and the V1 slowed and went straight down into the sea where it exploded at 0125 hrs.

Climbing away, they were directed back out to sea by Wartling Control and picked up another V1 on their radar, this one was coming in at 300 mph at 2,000 feet. As they tracked the V1 they caught sight of the bright glow from the jet exhaust and Mellersh rolled into a dive, attacking the target with several bursts. The V1 turned sharply, climbing rapidly, then suddenly dived into the sea and exploded on impact at 0200 hrs.

The third V1 they picked up 10 miles south of Beachy Head, which was also travelling at 300 mph at 2,000 feet on a north-westerly course. Levelling out from a dive above and behind the V1, Mellersh closed the gap. The Mosquito was flying at high speed because of the dive. At 1,000 feet he fired, seeing strikes, and the V1 dived into the sea at 0220 hrs.[38]

At 0105 hrs Flight Lieutenant Dobie and navigator Flying Officer Johnson were directed by Beachy Head Control onto coordinates 15 miles north of Dieppe. Picking up the contact on radar, they chased the V1, which was flying at 3,500 feet between 250 and 270 mph. Dobie was well above the V1 and on an intercept course with it. Peeling off, he dived the Mosquito towards the doodlebug. He came in behind and to the side of the flying bomb, firing from only 350 feet away. Shells hammered into the target. 'The fuel and air bottles appeared to blow up and the Diver exploded on the sea at 0245 hrs,' Dobie reported.

While Dobie was successful in his attack on a flying bomb, so was Wing Commander Crew. He and his navigator, Sergeant Jaeger, had taken off at the same time as Dobie had at 0105 hrs. But Wartling Control directed him onto coordinates north of Beachy Head. They tracked a V1 on their radar flying at 1,500 feet at 330 mph. Crew closed the gap, seeing the V1's glow below him. Pushing the nose down, he dived the Mosquito towards the target and opened fire. He saw strikes hit the V1, his shells bursting the fuel tank. Suddenly the flying bomb caught fire and began to glide down, burning as it did before hitting the sea and exploding at 0220 hrs.

Climbing and turning, Jaeger picked up another contact on his radar and again they gave chase. Wing Commander Crew pushed the throttles forward, heading for an intercept course with the V1, which was coming towards Beachy Head at 340 mph around 2,000 feet. Peeling off, Crew dived the Mosquito towards the target, firing short bursts of his cannon. His shells peppered the jet engine, causing it to burst into flames. It slowed down, losing height as it glided down into the sea and blew up at 0228 hrs.

His last V1 of the patrol Crew destroyed over Beachy Head, having fired several bursts that sent it crashing into the sea at 0247 hrs.

Along with Wing Commander Crew and Flight Lieutenant Dobie, Flight Sergeant Bryan and his navigator Pilot Officer Friis lifted their Mosquito off the runway at Ford at 0105 hrs. Wartling Control directed them onto coordinates near Hastings where they picked up a V1 coming in at 2,000 feet, flying at 330 mph. Diving to intercept the target they engaged the flying bomb 10 miles north of Hastings, firing several bursts. Shells tore into the fuselage, damaging the V1 and sending it straight into the ground where it burst into flames on impact at 0215 hrs.

On the evening of 3/4 July Squadron Leader Chudleigh and navigator Flying Officer Ayliffe took off from Ford at 2248 hrs, lifting into the darkness of the July night. Climbing, they picked up a target coming in over the coast at 360 mph at 1,500 feet on a north-westerly course. Chudleigh climbed the Mosquito, positioning his aircraft ahead and above the V1, allowing it to overtake him as it passed underneath. Pushing the control column forward, he then dived on the target, firing at it from 600 to 500 feet away as he levelled out. He saw strikes on the fuselage and jet engine. It went straight down and crashed into the sea where it blew up at 2350 hrs.

Climbing away, Chudleigh turned the Mosquito back towards his patrol line when they were vectored by control onto another set of coordinates. Ayliffe picked up the contact on radar that was coming in from the sea at 350 mph at 3,000 feet. Again, Squadron Leader Chudleigh positioned the Mosquito so that it was above and ahead of the V1. As the flying bomb shot underneath them, Chudleigh attacked and sent this one straight down into the ocean where it exploded at 0010 hrs.

Their last V1 destruction of the evening came forty minutes later after Ayliffe had picked up the flying bomb on radar, which was travelling at 350 mph at 2,000 feet. This time Squadron Leader Chudleigh attacked by 'cutting off the vector using a quarter attack,' he reported. Rolling into a dive, he attacked it from the side instead of behind from 500 feet away. This V1, struck by so many of his shells, blew up in mid-air so suddenly that Chudleigh had little option but to fly through the debris that was blown back at him. The debris hit the Mosquito, damaging it, but they were able to limp back to base and landed at 0110 hrs.

Patrolling at the same time were Flight Lieutenant Head and navigator Flying Officer Andrews who were initially vectored onto a sector where flying bombs were coming in over the sea towards London. They made radar contact on a V1 that was coming in at 280 mph at 2,000 feet. Spotting the glow of the flying bomb's jet exhaust, Squadron Leader Head climbed, ensuring the V1 was under them. As it passed below, he rolled the Mosquito into a dive towards the target, attacking it with short bursts. Suddenly, a long sheet of flame shot out from the V1 as it dived straight into the sea and exploded on impact at 2330 hrs.

A few minutes later they picked up another V1 contact on their onboard radar. This one was flying much faster than the first, at 350 mph at 1,500 feet. He waited until the V1 flew past below them. Then he peeled off, rolling the Mosquito into a shallow dive and fired several long bursts. The V1 did a vertical dive for 500 feet and then it crashed on the land.

Eleven patrols were flown on the night of 4 July right through into the morning and for the most part they were uneventful, except for Flight Lieutenant Dobie and navigator Flying Officer Rawnsley who had taken off at 2240 hrs from Ford. Directed towards coordinates by control, Dobie climbed the Mosquito to 7,000 feet. A V1 was coming in at 4,000 feet, travelling at 250 mph. Rawnsley picked up the contact on his radar tube and they tracked it. Once they had a visual contact of the flying bomb, Dobie rolled the Mosquito into a dive, tearing down towards the target. He opened fire from 1,000 feet away and saw strikes hit the flying bomb. As Dobie levelled the Mosquito out the V1 exploded in mid-air and some of the debris damaged the Mosquito's tail. This action took place at 2347 hrs and though the Mosquito was slightly damaged they landed safely back at Ford at 0015 hrs.

At 0158 hrs, Lieutenant Lawley-Wakelin and Royal Navy Lieutenant Williams climbed into the night sky from Ford at 0158 hrs on their Anti-Diver Patrol. Heading out to the Channel, they picked up a V1 coming in a north-westerly direction towards London flying at 2,500 feet at 350 mph. Tracking the flying bomb on their radar, Lawley-Wakelin climbed to 9,000 feet and got a visual contact of the V1s jet exhaust far below. Diving, he waiting until he was close enough before opening fire from 1,000 feet away. Hit by the Mosquito's cannon fire, the V1 dived into the sea and exploded at 0350 hrs. They landed back at Ford at 0441 hrs.

At 0300 hrs on 5 July Squadron Leader Parker-Rees and Flight Lieutenant Bennett were vectored onto a sector where V1s were coming in. They tracked a flying bomb heading towards the coast at 350 mph at 3,000 feet. Parker-Rees soon picked up a visual contact and dived on the target, opening fire from 1,000 feet as he levelled out and seeing strikes on the wings and fuselage. The V1 went straight into the sea and exploded on impact at 0354 hrs. Turning, he climbed the Mosquito and Bennett soon picked up another contact within the same sector. This V1 was coming in at 340 mph at 2,000 feet, also heading towards London. In the darkness, they tracked the enemy flying bomb and finally picked up a visual contact of the exhaust and dived on the target. At 800 feet away and astern of the V1, Parker-Rees fired a few short bursts of his cannon, seeing strikes on the Diver. It went straight down and exploded on impact with the water at 0415 hrs.

Another Mosquito crew on patrol at the same time destroyed a V1. Flight Lieutenant Ward and navigator Flying Officer Eyles chased a flying bomb that was travelling at 350 mph at 1,500 feet. Eyles tracked the V1 on his radar set until they both had visual contact. Then, Ward peeled off and dived the Mosquito towards the target, firing bursts from his cannon from 1,500 to 800 feet, peppering the V1 with shells. It slowed and dived into the sea where it exploded at 0425 hrs.

Wing Commander Crew and navigator Sergeant Jaeger took off at 0100 hrs on 6 July from Ford and shot down three flying bombs on this patrol. The first one they picked up several miles off the coast, travelling north-west at 335 mph at 1,500 feet. Crew brought the Mosquito down behind the flying bomb and fired from only 600 feet away, which sent the V1 crashing down onto the water. Climbing the Mosquito, Crew remained in the same sector, gaining as much height as he could, while Jaeger picked up another contact. This doodlebug was flying in roughly the same direction as their first one was at around 340 mph at 2,000 feet. Using the same method, he attacked this one from 900 feet away, seeing strikes on the fuselage and jet engine. The V1 slowed and then crashed into the sea at 0315 hrs. Ten minutes later another V1 hit the sea and exploded, a victim to Crew's cannon fire. They returned to Ford at 0350 hrs.

On 6 July Flight Lieutenant Ward with his navigator Flying Officer Eyles took off from Ford at 2255 hrs, climbing hard into the night sky. Directed out over the Channel towards France, they picked up a V1 coming in at 390 mph at 1,500 feet. They tracked the V1 until they could see its glow and then Ward pushed the throttles forward to get maximum speed from the Mosquito. He reported:

I attacked by diving hard from 3,000 feet. I was above and firing deflection bursts of 10 degrees off from astern from 1,500 to 500 feet. The Diver crashed into the sea at 2345 hrs and we landed back at Ford at 0105 hrs.

Also on patrol was Flight Lieutenant Dobie with navigator Flying Officer Johnson. They tracked a V1 on their radar set that was heading in on a north-westerly course at 350 mph at 1,500 feet. Seeing the flying bomb's glow in the night sky, Dobie rolled into a dive. He reported:

I fired the first burst from 1,000 feet away at 3,000 feet height. The Diver immediately started to dive steeply. I then fired a second burst from 1,900 feet away the height now 1,500 feet. The chase was abandoned because of a thunderstorm and the Diver was still going down the height below 1,000 feet.

The night of 8 July was a record one for the Squadron. For the first time a single Mosquito crew destroyed six flying bombs over two patrols in a single night. The crew comprised Squadron Leader Chudleigh with navigator Flying Officer Ayliffe. They roared into the night sky at 2300 hrs from Ford, climbing fast. Vectored out over the Channel off the south-east coast, they tracked their first V1 coming in at 380 mph at 3,000 feet. Chudleigh levelled out of his dive dead astern of the flying bomb and opened fire from 800 feet away, seeing strikes on the jet engine and fuel tank. Burning, the V1 went straight down into the sea and exploded at 2330 hrs.

Climbing to gain as much height as possible, they picked up another contact on their radar. Now halfway across the Channel, they tracked the oncoming V1, which was flying at 380 mph at

2,000 feet. Peeling off, Squadron Leader Chudleigh dived on the target, bringing the Mosquito directly behind the flying bomb and fired from only 800 feet away, seeing strikes from his cannon on the fuselage and wings. The V1 exploded in the sea at 2350 hrs.

The last V1 for this patrol was picked up in roughly the same area, this time heading for Britain at 340 mph at 2,500 feet. Chudleigh destroyed this V1 from 800 feet away. Under the hail of cannon shells the V1 blew up in mid-air at 0005 hrs.

Several Mosquito crews were on patrol that night but the next men to destroy a V1 were Flight Lieutenants Goigh and Matson. They were patrolling off the coast of Dungeness when Matson picked up a contact on his radar. Turning, Goigh climbed the Mosquito to intercept the V1, which was on a north-westerly course, flying at 340 mph at 2,000 feet. Seeing the V1's exhaust glow in the darkness, Goigh dived on the flying bomb from behind and slightly off to the side. From 800 feet away he opened fire and sent the V1 crashing into the sea just off Dungeness at 2350 hrs. They finished their patrol at 0126 hrs when they landed back at Ford.

Patrolling over the Channel, Flight Lieutenant Ward and Flying Officer Andrews tracked a V1 travelling north-west at 340 mph at 2,000 feet. Climbing, Ward searched the sky for a visual contact while Andrews directed him towards the interception point. Finally seeing the V1, Ward brought the Mosquito around above and behind the flying bomb, then rolled into a dive and opened fire from 1,500 to 1,000 feet away directly behind the V1. They saw strikes on the flying bomb and it crashed into the sea, exploding on impact some 20 miles south of Beachy Head at 0030 hrs.

Now into the very early hours of 9 July, another Mosquito crew patrolling at that time comprised Flying Officer Goode and navigator Flying Officer Robinson who attacked a V1 flying at 5,000 feet at 320 mph some 25 miles north of the Somme Estuary. Goode brought the Mosquito in from behind at 5 degrees and fired his cannon from 1,200 feet away. The V1 exploded in mid-air.

Squadron Leader Chudleigh's second patrol began when his Mosquito roared into the early morning sky at 0315 hrs on 9 July. Vectored towards the French coast near Le Tougquet, they picked up a contact heading towards Britain at 260 mph at 3,000 feet. While his navigator Flying Officer Ayliffe directed him towards the V1, Chudleigh searched the gloom for the tell-tale glow of the flying bomb's jet exhaust. Sighting it, Chudleigh brought the Mosquito around above and behind the V1 and dived on it, firing short bursts from 1,000 feet to 600 feet away, seeing strikes. The enemy aircraft dived into the sea blowing up on impact at 0430 hrs.

Almost immediately Ayliffe picked up another V1 in the same area, this time travelling at 380 mph at 3,000 feet towards Britain. Climbing hard, they gave chase as Ayliffe directed Chudleigh towards his interception point. Within moments, Chudleigh saw the V1 and attacked from above and behind, diving on it to pick up speed. From 1,000 feet to 600 feet away he fired bursts from his cannon, the shells ripping into the flying bomb's jet engine and fuselage, which sent it crashing into the sea close to the shore west of Dungeness at 0435 hrs.[39]

Climbing away, Squadron Leader Chudleigh turned the Mosquito back towards France, his throttles open in the hope of picking up another contact. Moments later, Ayliffe began to track another V1 travelling at around 380 mph at 3,000 feet. After several minutes of chasing the flying bomb as Ayliffe called out the coordinates, Chudleigh dived on the target, attacking from 1,000 feet to 600 feet away. His cannon shells sent the Diver crashing into the sea where it blew up at approximately 0500 hrs. They landed back at Ford after a very eventful patrol at 0524 hrs.

In the very early hours of 10 July another Mosquito crew, Warrant Officer McLardy and Flight Sergeant Devine, chased a V1 that was flying on a north-westerly course across the Channel at approximately 325 mph at 1,500 feet. Coming in behind and above the target, McLardy attacked from 1,500 to 800 feet away, seeing strikes on the flying bomb, which went straight into the sea some 15 miles south-east of Dungeness at 0213 hrs.

On the night of 10 July Squadron Leader Parker-Rees and navigator Flight Lieutenant Bennett took off from Ford at 2250 hrs. Climbing to around 9,000 feet, they were vectored onto a V1 coming in at 1,500 feet at 380 mph near Worthing. Tracking the V1 on their radar set, Bennett directed Parker-Rees towards the target. In the gloom they saw the flame from the V1's exhaust and Parker-Rees dived on it from 8,500 feet, he opened fire from 1,000 feet away as he levelled out at 400 mph-plus above and behind the V1. Plastering it with cannon shells, the flying bomb caught fire and crashed into the sea, exploding on impact at 2311 hrs.

Flight Lieutenant Ward with Flying Officer Eyles destroyed two V1s that night. Patrolling off the coast of Worthing at around 5,000 feet, they picked up a flying bomb heading towards the English coast at 320 mph at 3,000 feet. Well above the target, they tracked it, getting closer by the minute. Peeling off, Ward rolled the Mosquito into a dive and attacked the V1 from behind, waiting until he was only 700 feet away before levelling off and firing his cannon. The V1 went straight into the sea at 2325 hrs. Climbing back up to 5,000 feet, Eyles saw another contact on his radar screen, travelling at 300 mph at 1,500 feet. Again, they gave chase, Eyles directing Ward towards interception. Getting a visual sighting, Ward dived on the flying bomb, attacking it from dead astern again from 700 feet out. The German doodlebug was sent into the sea where it blew up on impact at 2346 hrs.

At 0056 hrs on 11 July Wing Commander Crew with navigator Flight Sergeant Jaeger lifted their Mosquito off the runway at Ford into the night sky. Climbing rapidly away, they levelled out at 4,000 feet and were soon vectored towards V1s coming towards Worthing. Tracking one on their radar, they flew over the sea off the coast near Worthing, chasing a V1 that was flying at 360 mph at 1,500 feet north-west. Seeing the target below them in the gloom, Crew dived on it and from only 450 feet away he opened fire, hammering the V1 with cannon shells. The flying bomb blew up in mid-air and Crew managed to avoid the debris as he turned hard, climbing away as the debris fell into the sea at 0225 hrs.

In the very early morning hours of 17 July Squadron Leader Parker-Rees with navigator Flight Lieutenant Bennett roared into the early morning sky at 0105 hrs, climbing rapidly from their airfield at Ford. Picking up Wartling Control, they were vectored towards France. Several minutes later Bennett saw a contact on his radar tube flying just under 300 mph between 1,000 and 2,000 feet. Parker-Rees reported:

We first saw the Diver flying north of Abbeville flying due north. We flew parallel up the coast and attacked it off Cap Gris Nez. The Diver caught fire in the air and exploded on the sea.

Parker-Rees had attacked it from directly astern at 300 feet away. This action took place at 0213 hrs.

Climbing the Mosquito away from those coordinates, they picked up another contact, which was north of Abbeville at 700 feet at 240 mph heading towards Britain. Attacking it from behind and above at only 300 feet away, they saw strikes on the target as Parker-Rees reported.

We first saw it north of Abbeville on a more westerly course than the first Diver. After a short burst the Diver lost height and then the light went out and we saw an explosion on the sea.

However, their adventure did not end there, as when they began to attack a third V1 things went wrong as the Squadron diarist recounts.

They were forced to bale out while attacking a third presumably because they were fired on as Squadron Leader Parker-Rees saw tracer coming from beneath his nose. Still all's well that ends well and they were picked up by HMS Obedient *after six hours in the water.*

Flight Lieutenant Ward and navigator Flying Officer Eyles destroyed another flying bomb. The Squadron diarist had this to say about that day. 'Well at last we've bridged the gap and got to the century.'[40]

Taking off from Ford at 0320 hrs they climbed rapidly away, directed by Fairlight Control towards France where several V1s had been launched. Eyles picked up a contact on his radar that was flying at 280 mph at 1,000 feet. Ward dived on the target, attacking it from dead astern from 800 feet away. Cannon shells ripped into it and the V1 exploded in mid-air 18 miles north of Boulogne at 0400 hrs. They touched down at Ford at 0545 hrs.

At 2230 hrs on 18 July Mosquito crew Lieutenants Richards and Baring took off from Ford airfield under Wartling Control. Climbing rapidly into the night sky, they headed out to sea and soon Lieutenant Baring picked up a radar contact that was heading towards the coast at 800 feet between 340 and 350 mph. Well above it, they tracked its trajectory as Richards brought the Mosquito in behind the flying bomb, diving to 1,000 feet. He fired his cannon and they saw several strikes on the V1. The flying bomb turned slightly to port then blew up in mid-air 4 miles south of Dungeness at 2330 hrs. They finished their patrol twenty minutes later when Richards landed the Mosquito back at Ford.

At 0130 hrs Flight Lieutenant Mellersh and Flying Officer Stanley lifted their Mosquito into the air, climbing rapidly away while Fairlight Control directed them towards V1s that were coming in near Beachy Head. Over the Channel they tracked a V1 flying very low at 900 feet at 350 mph heading for England. Mellersh manoeuvred the Mosquito in a position above and behind the V1 then dived on the target, attacking from 1,000 feet away directly behind it. The V1 exploded into the sea 8 miles south of Beachy Head at 0125 hrs. Climbing away, they continued patrolling until 0330 hrs when they landed back at Ford.

Fairlight Control directed another Mosquito crew, Flying Officer Goode and Flying Officer Robinson, onto a V1 that was flying at 320 mph at 2,300 feet. Tracking it on their radar, Robinson directed Goode towards an interception. Seeing the V1's glow in the early morning gloom Goode increased their speed, diving on the target, and fired from 1,200 feet away. Cannon shells ripped into the V1's port wing tearing it off and the flying bomb went straight into the sea where it exploded at 0115 hrs.

Also on patrol was Squadron Leader Caldwell with navigator Flying Officer Rawlins who under Wartling Control picked up a V1 that was heading towards the coast at 300 mph at 3,500 feet. As they tracked the flying bomb, Caldwell increased the Mosquito's speed, trying to get behind and above the V1. After several minutes he picked up the flame from the V1's jet engine and rolled into a dive, attacking the V1 from directly behind at 900 feet away. The flying bomb exploded in mid-air at 0115 hrs. Caldwell and Rawlins returned to Ford airfield at 0351 hrs.

Squadron Leader Chudleigh increased his score on the same day, climbing his Mosquito into the early morning sky at 0245 hrs. Directed by Wartling Control towards a V1 flying north-west over the Channel towards the coast at 280 mph at 1,500 feet, he gave chase while his navigator Flying Officer Ayliffe tracked it on their radar. Bringing the Mosquito above and behind the V1, Chudleigh rolled his Mosquito into a dive, attacking the flying bomb from a distance of 750 feet. Squadron Leader Chudleigh reported:

The petrol exploded in the air. The flying bomb exploded on the sea but the starboard engine began giving trouble so we returned to base with it feathered.

Squadron Leader Green with Squadron Leader Cook as his navigator destroyed three flying bombs that morning. Taking off from Ford at 0250 hrs, they climbed away picking up Fairlight Control who directed them towards their first V1, which was coming in at 340 mph at 2,000 feet. Green climbed the Mosquito and dived on the target, attacking from dead astern from 600 feet away. The V1 exploded in the air at 0415 hrs and as Green climbed and turned, Cook picked up a radar contact. It was another V1 flying on a north-westerly course at 350 mph at 1,500 feet. Again, Green brought the Mosquito in behind and above the target then dived down, attacking it from 900 feet away, his cannon fire ripping the port wing off the flying bomb. The V1 went straight into the sea and exploded on impact at 0430 hrs. Climbing to 3,000 feet, they patrolled for another thirty minutes. Cook picked up a radar contact that was a V1 coming in at 300 mph at 1,500 feet. Orbiting the target, Green brought the Mosquito in behind the V1 and dived on it from 2,000 feet, firing at it from 900 feet away and seeing strikes on the flying bomb, which blew up when it hit the sea at 0505 hrs. They landed back at Ford at 0530 hrs for tea.

On the night of 20 July the Squadron had more success against the flying bombs. Wing Commander Crew with Warrant Officer Croysdill as navigator took off at 2355 hrs. Directed by Wartling Control to intercept a fast-moving V1, which was heading for the coast at 360 mph between 1,500 and 2,000 feet, Crew climbed his Mosquito as hard as he could to gain precious height while Croysdill directed him towards interception. After several minutes Crew managed to bring the Mosquito above and behind the V1 then rolled into a dive, lining up the glow of the jet exhaust in his sights. Levelling off 200 yards away from the target he opened fire with his cannon, seeing strikes on the flying bomb, which crashed into the sea at 0140 hrs. Turning away from the crash scene, he climbed the Mosquito while Wartling Control directed them towards another target.

This V1 was heading towards the coast at 1,000 feet at only 300 mph and Croysdill tracked it on their radar set. Again, Wing Commander Crew positioned the Mosquito above and behind the V1 then dived on it, building up speed. He closed the gap and levelled out 200 yards away, firing his cannon. The V1 was hit several times and crashed into the sea where it blew up at 0207 hrs.

In the early hours of 21 July Squadron Leader Chudleigh destroyed the first of two V1s while under Wartling Control. The first V1 Chudleigh and his navigator Flying Officer Ayliffe attacked was flying at 360 mph at 1,500 feet. Using standard attacking procedure, Chudleigh manoeuvred the Mosquito into a diving position above and behind the target. Diving on it, he fired several short bursts of cannon fire from 300 yards away and the flying bomb exploded in the air over the sea at 0424 hrs.

Climbing, Chudleigh turned towards another V1 coming in on a north-westerly course at 360 mph at 1,500 feet, directed by Ayliffe who was tracking the contact on his radar. He brought the Mosquito in from above and behind then dived on the target, firing again from 300 yards away. The V1 was sent crashing into the sea where it exploded at 0506 hrs.

On the evening of 21 July another Mosquito crew, Flying Officers Goode and Robinson, scored again for the Squadron when they destroyed a V1 just off the coast near Hastings. Wartling Control had directed them towards a V1 coming in at 2,800 feet flying at 300 mph. Tracking the contact, Robinson directed Goode towards it. Goode then attacked the V1 by diving on it and opening fire directly behind the flying bomb from 2,000 feet away. After firing several bursts the flying bomb exploded on the sea at 2315 hrs.

Bad weather on 22 July made flying impossible but the following day the Squadron destroyed five more flying bombs. Low cloud again hampered operations over the next two days when only three V1s were destroyed out of twenty-one patrols.

On 26 July five V1s were shot down but the night was a disaster for the Squadron. The Squadron diarist made the following record:

Flight Sergeant Bryan and Sergeant Jaeger were reported missing after R/T contact had been lost by Wartling. They were on patrol over the Channel but the exact position they went in was not known. So searching was extremely difficult. Nothing was found but an empty Mae West.

Another Mosquito crew, Lieutenant Richards and Lieutenant Baring, had difficulty when they developed engine trouble while on a search and rescue mission. The Squadron diarist recorded:

While making for the coast they were shot up by the Diver Guns. Evasive action caused the port engine to go completely and they crashed landed at Friston each with both engines feathered.

Luckily Richards and Baring were safe but the aircraft was written off.

From 27 to 29 July the Squadron destroyed eight more flying bombs but the night of 30 July was another bad one. Flying Officer Black and his navigator Flight Sergeant Fox baled out off Boulogne at 0457 hrs. The Squadron diarist recorded:

Flight Lieutenant Ward and Flying Officer Eyles thought they saw a torch flashing in the approximate position. They also reported seeing two vessels six miles south of that position. Flak ships. Wing Commander Crew flew with Flying Officer O.D. Morgan to continue the search at dawn. They broke cloud 4 miles off Boulogne and while doing an orbit at 400 feet were fired on by approximately 6 guns. [They suffered one direct hit behind the cockpit rendering their R/T useless.] They returned on the AI beam and crash landed at Friston on one wheel.

Luckily the crew were safe but the Mosquito was wrecked. Three more flying bombs were destroyed that night, bringing the Squadron's total to 138 destroyed.

August began badly for the Squadron when one Mosquito crew was killed on the edge of the airfield as the weather clamped down around midnight on 1 August. Flying Officers Bell and Saunders crashed as they were attempting to land in visibility so poor they couldn't see more than 100 yards.

Over the next few days the Squadron continued to increase the number of flying bombs destroyed with Flight Lieutenant Mellersh destroying seven in one patrol alone on 4 August.

By 12 August the Squadron had destroyed 162 flying bombs. On 13 August Flight Lieutenant Gough attacked and destroyed a V1 and while chasing another one saw his shells hammer the flying bomb but was unable to bring it down and had to break off the engagement. Flight Sergeant Gallavin had the same thing happen as well when he dived on a V1, firing from around 1,000 feet away. He saw strikes on the fuselage but the V1 did not go down and kept on going. Only Flight Lieutenant Head managed to bring one down that night and he had to cut his patrol short due to engine trouble.

But 14 August was another bad night for the Squadron as the diarist relates.

Flight Sergeant Read, taking Warrant Officer Gerrett for his operational night trip took off about 45 degrees off the runway for unknown reasons or causes. The aircraft went through a blister hangar and crashed into a brick wall catching fire outside Squadron Headquarters. Both of the crew were killed.

On 21 August the entry in the Squadron history indicates the Squadron's luck was changing as one V1 was shot down. The Squadron diarist recorded:

There were several chases but the cloud conditions 9/10 interfered with them and Flight Lieutenant Gough and Flight Lieutenant Matson were the lucky crew. The Diver went down into cloud after being hit and the pilot broke away to avoid the gun belt but Flight Lieutenant Goode saw it crash.

Four days later after no activity the Squadron diarist wrote 'A sudden outburst of Diver activity, perhaps the last fling.' They mounted eleven patrols that night but the weather, cloud from 2,000 to 6,000 feet and heavy rain, made it very difficult to attack the flying bombs. Four were destroyed that night.

For the next three days no anti-Diver patrols were mounted by the Squadron but on 27 August they were up again as several flying bombs came over in a batch at early dawn. Flight Lieutenant Mellersh and his navigator Flying Officer Stanley dived on one while over the Channel, attacking it from short range with short bursts of cannon fire. The V1's engine cut out and it did a steep climbing turn to port before diving into the sea where it exploded on impact. Vectored onto another one, they gave chase but were unable to catch it. 'Flight Lieutenant Kennedy chased another Diver off Cap Griz Nez but could not close sufficiently before reaching the gun belt,' the Squadron diarist recorded.

By 30 August the Squadron diarist wrote 'By the way things are going in France we shall soon be finished with chuff-bomb chasing.'

But the words were written too soon as the following day around 0600 hrs a wave of V1s came over and Flight Lieutenant Dobie and Flying Officer Johnson were the only crew to bring one down. The rest chased several but broke off the engagement as they were too near the gun belt. Control warned Flight Lieutenant Kennedy that he had an aircraft on his tail. Pushing his rudder he turned the Mosquito hard 'obtaining a contact but he was called off because of his open exhausts.'[41]

In the first week of September patrols were mounted in bad weather but no contacts were made and no flying bombs were seen. To illustrate the diminishing menace of the flying bomb the Squadron diarist wrote:

> We are going to start cross-country flights in training for Intruders. I wonder if the war will last long enough for us to get organised on it again. It will be a change to get some Huns after so long chasing chuffers.

Though the menace had diminished the Squadron continued to mount patrols right up until the move to RAF Odiham on 24 September. From here they mounted anti-Diver patrols against the air-launched V1s. Their first night at the new airfield was a memorable one. During the patrols Flight Lieutenant Mellersh with navigator Flight Lieutenant Stanley dived onto a flying bomb from astern, firing several short bursts at it. The V1 climbed suddenly to 8,000 feet into cloud. It then reappeared and crashed, exploding on impact, observed by Flight Lieutenant Kennedy. Flight Sergeant Dunn and his navigator Warrant Officer Stephens caught sight of a V1 launched from an aircraft about 5 miles from their position. Giving chase, they were unable to get a contact on the enemy aircraft. 'Looks like we may be in for some fun,' the Squadron diarist wrote.

Over the next three days only one V1 was destroyed as poor visibility hampered patrols. On 29 September four flying bombs were attacked. Launched from enemy aircraft, they were coming in very low and although four were attacked only one was destroyed, shared by Flight Lieutenant Kennedy and two Tempests of 501 Squadron. 'All the Divers were flying at 500 feet or less,' the Squadron diarist recorded. 'Ken said he could see the details of the countryside by the light of the chuff.' The month ended with one more V1 destroyed.

Although patrols were mounted they were uneventful and nothing was seen until 13 October when Squadron Leader Caldwell was vectored onto a unknown contact. He saw two flying bombs launched but was unable to get a fix on the launching aircraft. Turning, he dived on a V1 and opened fire, seeing strikes on the target and pieces flying off it. It finally crashed west of Chelmsford and blew up.

Poor weather reduced the number of patrols the Squadron mounted for the rest of the month but no sightings of V1s were seen. However, they were beginning to see more and more contrails of V2 rockets.

They continued to mount patrols from Odiham and for the whole of the month of November they saw no more V1s, but did have increased sightings of the V2 rockets.

The Squadron destroyed its last flying bomb on 5 December, bringing the total destroyed to 180. On 12 December 96 Squadron was disbanded. 'It had a proud record throughout,' wrote the Squadron diarist. 'In the fight against the flying bombs in 1944 they played their finest part.'

At 0213 hrs on 14 January 1945 the last air-launched flying bomb crashed in Britain when it exploded on the ground at Hornsey.

CHAPTER THIRTEEN

Anti-Aircraft Command

The V1 attack on London had tapered away and then finally ceased by the first week of September. Although so much of the credit for blunting the attack has gone to the RAF, the contribution of General Pile's AA Command was greater. The combination of the RCA584 radar and the Mk 9 Predictor essentially an analogue computer, the first of a genus, together with the skilful deployment of the AA guns reinforced by the 'Z' (rocket) batteries, had proved lethal for the V1, especially when the proximity fuse became available which detected the target directly and ensured that detonation of the charge took place in close proximity to it. This device, developed initially by EMI and Pye, was produced in huge quantity in the USA, providing with the SCR584 a second reason for thanking US industrial strength for saving so many lives in London.

J Heslop-Harrison, *Autobiography: War Service Part 5 'Anti-Aircraft Command'*[42]

Astonishingly, at the height of the war staff officers from the Army and the RAF were at each other's throats, apparently trying to score points with their own arms or with their immediate superiors. Looking through all the documents and research, one finds it hard to understand how men of real substance would waste so much time competing with each other when the fate of the nation and the fate of so many thousands of civilians hung in the balance.

And what was it all about? In this case, who made the decision to move the anti-aircraft guns from the area south of London to the coast. This was a move of all the guns, not just a few. The Army, in the form of the Royal Artillery, took credit for the idea, while the RAF maintained the idea came from them. We shall see.

In earlier chapters we discussed the report written by Sir Roderick Hill about the defences and the move of the guns to the coast. In his report Sir Roderick made no mention of the rivalry between the RAF and Anti-Aircraft Command. Perhaps, that rivalry was at a level below General Pile and Sir Roderick or perhaps Sir Roderick was magnamious and did not wish to sully anyone's name. Nevertheless, rivalry did exist.

In a letter from Air Vice Marshal GH Ambler to TCG James of the Air Ministry dated 21 January 1947, Ambler sets out his feelings on the matter of 'competition' between the arms. 'It seems to me that certain persons have decided to compete in order to gain personal credit for the success of the operations against flying bombs,' he wrote.

He continued that responsibility for the plan for moving the guns to the coast away from London was on the shoulders of Air Marshal Sir Roderick Hill and that all the credit for the successes made for the operation should go to him. It was Sir Roderick through the medium of Sir Robert Watson-Watt who suggested the plan to General Pile.

Air Vice Marshal Geoffrey Ambler wrote a letter to the Air Ministry in September 1945 outlining the sequence of events leading up to the redeployment of anti-aircraft guns to the coast.

On 6 July 1944 the Commander-in-Chief of Fighter Command, Sir Roderick Hill, called a conference to discuss the difficulties that were affecting operations between Anti-Aircraft Command and the fighters in the war against the flying bomb. As we have seen, there was much disparity between the two arms. Cooperation was not successful and this conference was to try to find a way forward. The major decision that came out of the conference was that the guns should be confined to the area immediately south of London and that any guns on the coast that had been used against ordinary enemy aircraft were also to be moved into the area.

Air Vice Marshal Ambler was not happy about taking the guns away from their current positions around the coast and bringing them all into the area south of London. Presumably, this was the area over which the flying bombs flew in order to get to London.

Ambler believed that concentrating the guns in this area was the wrong way forward. 'I was not altogether happy in my own mind about the removal of the guns to London,' he wrote. 'I therefore decided to do a full appreciation and make a précis of it afterwards to the C-in-C.'

His appreciation, which he finished on the evening of 12/13 July 1944, showed that it would be better for all the anti-aircraft guns to be moved to the coast. This was in direct opposition to the action that had been started from the conference a week earlier. Already the trucks were moving, towing the guns from the coast up towards the zone in the area south of London. Ambler was advocating the immediate cessation of this activity, turning the trucks around and sending them back to the coast!

In a meeting the following day with scientist Sir Robert Watson-Watt, Ambler discussed his idea and concerns for the deployment of the anti-aircraft guns.

> *I told him that I had not consulted anybody in drawing up this appreciation and therefore felt some uneasiness as I did not want to draw a red herring across the trail which was already fairly confused.*

However, Sir Watson-Watt agreed with Ambler that the trucks should be turned around and sent back to the coast, with all the guns from London following. He believed, as Scientific Advisor, that this was the right action and subsequently both men met with Air Marshal Sir Roderick Hill. They convinced him that the right action was to move the guns to the coast.

Sir Robert Watson-Watt then agreed to advise Sir Fredrick Pile of the new decision to redeploy the guns. He met with General Pile who agreed to the redeployment. Ambler wrote:

> *This was the first approach to AA Command on this matter and at no time to my certain knowledge previously had any suggestion come from AA Command that the guns should be moved to the coast. There is no doubt whatsoever that the proposal to move the guns to the south coast came from Fighter Command and not from AA Command.*

That afternoon, 13 July, Sir Roderick Hill convened the conference that made the decision to move all the guns to the coast.

According to Ambler's letter, Sir Roderick gave instructions to General Pile to move the guns to the south coast and to have them ready by 17 July. Ambler wrote:

> *I have always felt that the decision to re-deploy the guns in the heat of battle and with all the politicians standing on their hind legs and yelling was a most courageous and gallant act on the part of Sir Roderick. It was, I remember, a very dramatic moment when he gave the instructions for the re-deployment at the conference which he did entirely on his own authority and with full knowledge of the risks he was taking. I also felt very strongly that he never received the proper credit for this act.*[43]

However, General Pile's version of events is somewhat different. Shortly after the war General Pile wrote a dispatch on the Anti-Aircraft Command during the war and suggested that the plan to re-deploy the guns came from a staff officer within the AA Command. General Pile wrote:

> *Neither the fighters nor guns were being given full scope, for the guns had to ensure that the break on their radar tubes was not a friendly plane before opening fire while the fighters in pursuit of a V.1 often had to give up the chase when the pilot approached the gun zone.*

General Pile continued that his Technical Staff Officer Lieutenant-Colonel Radcliffe suggested that the plan of moving the guns from the coast should be re-examined.

> *This plan had always seemed to us to have great advantage from the gun point of view, but it was turned down because it was considered that the fighters would be much limited if they had to break off an engagement on approaching the coast and starting it again if the target got through the gun zone.*

It was clear to him at the time that unless there was a radical re-arrangement of available resources two-thirds of the V1s would get through to London, which they did. However, this passage was written after the war in January 1946, so one has to look at it with some scepticism. 'The fighters were still having only limited success,' Pile continued. 'That success was much better than the guns were experiencing.'

Referring to the meeting that took place on 13 July, General Pile wrote that the plan was agreed 'and before nightfall advance parties were already on their way to the coast'.

Also on 13 July 1944 staff officer TCG James of the Air Ministry, Sir Robert Watson-Watt and scientist John Cherry met and James suggested that the means of intercepting flying bombs with fighters using radar was the wrong way. 'We were trying to modify existing radar stations to do the job without really analysing the problem from first principles such as time, speed, distance and height.'[44]

James felt that the deduction that all the anti-aircraft guns should be moved to the coast was the correct one compared with a decision that had been reached a few days before that the guns should all be moved to London. James wrote in his letter to Sir Robert Watson-Watt:

> What matters from the point of view of posterity is this – you, a scientist, thinking along purely scientific lines, reached the conclusion that the guns ought to be moved to the coast. I believe that this fusion of thought gave us both the confidence we required in order to convince us that without a shadow of a doubt, the guns should be moved to the coast.

He then states that the fusion of thought from a scientist and a staff officer, both approaching the problem from different angles but coming up with the same answer, made it easy to convince Sir Roderick that this redeployment of anti-aircraft guns was the right move. 'I never had any doubts of the plan being successful,' he wrote.

In a letter to TCG James dated 14 September 1945, Air Vice Marshal Ambler mentions the meeting between Sir Robert Watson-Watt and TCG James on 13 July in which they both came to the same conclusion that the guns should be redeployed to the coast. 'It would not be too much to say that in Sir Robert Watson Watt's view you and he had independently arrived at the same conclusion.'

Perhaps the best illustration of events is the letter from Air Marshal Sir Roderick Hill to TCG James dated 5 October 1944 regarding Air Vice Marshal Ambler's account. In his letter, Sir Roderick stated that it was his decision to redeploy the guns at the conference of 13 July. 'The exact words I used,' he wrote. 'So far as my memory serves were these: Look here, Tim, what would you say to moving the guns to the coast?' This question was directed towards General Pile, whose response was that it was exactly what he had always wanted to do.

After the unanimous approval at the meeting Sir Roderick made the decision to move the guns and Anti-Aircraft Command was ordered there and then by telephone to re-deploy the guns. With the battle of the flying bombs at its peak, this move was very risky. 'I knew it would mean that for a few days a large proportion of the guns would be out of action,' Sir Roderick continued in his letter. 'If bad weather prevented the fighters from doing well, the total taking would drop badly.'

At the same time, Sir Roderick felt that by splitting the fighter defences between the gun zone at the coast and London the number of flying bombs destroyed by fighters alone would also drop. 'An inevitable reduction in flying bombs destroyed by fighters would have to be accepted as the price of an increase in flying bombs destroyed by guns.'

Another problem was that there was no proof that the guns would achieve the significant destruction of V1s as was hoped, despite predictions from the scientists and service personnel involved. Sir Roderick also knew that if he submitted the question of redeployment to the Air Ministry and subsequently to the Chiefs of Staff, the decision would take weeks if a decision came at all. This was because it was so highly controversial, as it was in direct opposition to what the politicians wanted, and it was also impossible to substantiate the proposal with any practical experience.

As C-in-C of Fighter Command, Sir Roderick was in a far better position than anyone else to make a decision on the deployment of anti-aircraft guns and fighters to fight the doodlebug menace. 'I was the only person who could have seen the job through with the power to put it into execution.'

If the results of moving the guns to the coast had been unsuccessful it would not have been General Pile or the War Office who would have suffered. 'It would have been the Secretary of

State for Air, whom I committed and, above all, me who got it in the neck.'

Sir Roderick based his decision on the appreciation given to him by Ambler who already had misgivings about the decision to put all the guns near to London. Sir Roderick wrote:

He was of the utmost moral support to me during the interval between making the decision and the results becoming apparent when I was torn with anxiety and exposed to criticism and a certain amount of discredit.

Despite the differences the redeployment decision was smoothly and quickly put into operation by Anti-Aircraft Command and within hours personnel and equipment were on their way to the coast. Sir Roderick commented:

It was a formidable task indeed. The flying bomb attack developed while new gun laying equipment was being introduced with which personnel were not familiar. The method of bedding the static guns with a steel mattress had only just been devised. In the face of these and many other difficulties, AA Command, training their men and women while they fought, performed a feat so prodigious that it must surely rank among the great exploits of the Royal Regiment of Artillery.

The result of moving the guns to the coast enabled both guns and fighters to have a free hand in destroying the flying bombs. The fighters could set up a corridor picking off V1s that approached the coast and those that got through the curtain of guns, while the ack-ack guns could fire away at will. More V1s were shot down by the guns than before, while the fighters were vectored onto V1s coming in before reaching the guns, meaning that those the fighters couldn't attack would be picked up by the guns.

However, public opinion at the time, according to TCG James, was that the decision to move the guns had come from Anti-Aircraft Command. However, all the correspondence that flowed between James, Air Vice Marshal Ambler, Sir Roderick Hill, Sir Robert Watson-Watt and General Pile was to finally set the record straight.

Nevertheless, history shows that although both fighters and anti-aircraft guns shot down a fair number of flying bombs, the majority still got through. But for every flying bomb that went down, the lives of hundreds of people were saved so in the end it doesn't matter who did what, it only matters that lives were saved and that the flying bomb menace didn't bring Britain to its knees.

CHAPTER FOURTEEN

Last Gasp

T he end of the air-launched flying bomb was not the end of the German flying bomb offensive. Indeed, they had one more card to play.

After losing the launching ramps in Northern France as the Allied armies liberated more and more areas of the continent, the Germans were forced to use different methods of launching the V1. We have already talked about their subsequent offensive of launching the flying bomb from their He 111 bombers. The other main method of continuing the offensive against England was that the Germans were working on increasing the range of the V1 so it could be launched from ramps much further away.

The Allies discovered that the Germans were working on methods of construction of the flying bombs that would enable the V1s to fly further than they already did, from fragments of some of the bombs fired by the Germans into Belgium in February 1945. Reconnaissance photos showed two launching sites in south-west Holland, one at Ypenburg near The Hague and the other at Vlaardingen 6 miles west of Rotterdam. A third site was built near the Delftsche Canal but this was not discovered until later.

This attack was a postscript only and lighter than anyone expected. To meet the threat the gun defences were reinforced between the Isle of Sheppey and Orfordness.

On 27 February 1945 orders were given for ninety-six heavy guns to be moved from the northern part of the gun strip to this new area. By 4 March nine batteries out of twelve had been deployed in their new positions. The deployment of the remaining three became unnecessary as the expected attack was too light to warrant the move.

Sir Roderick also earmarked six Mustang squadrons to meet the new threat. Each of these fighters had their engines boosted. Three of these squadrons along with a Meteor squadron were borrowed from the Second Tactical Air Force and operated between the guns and London, while the rest operated in front of the guns. At night the Mosquitoes patrolled over the sea and the Tempests flew behind the guns aided by the searchlight belt.

The first bombs launched from the new ramps in south-west Holland reached English shores in the early hours of 3 March. At 0301 hrs the first bombs from this area got through the defences and crashed at Bermondsey. Six more bombs that came over were all destroyed by anti-aircraft fire. After this brief flurry of activity no more bombs arrived for another nine hours, when the attacks began again on an intermittent basis and lasted until noon on 4 March. Ten bombs came over during this period and only two reached London. The rest were destroyed.

In the early hours of 5 March the attacks began again and lasted until 29 March on a spasmodic basis. So light was the attack and so effective were the guns at this time that Sir Roderick released five of the six Mustang squadrons and the Meteor squadron from flying bomb duty to go back to their normal operations. In total, only 125 flying bombs came over during these few weeks and only thirteen reached London. The rest were destroyed, eighty-six of them by anti-aircraft fire.

On 23 March 1945 Typhoons bombed the launching site at Vlaardingen, while on 20 and 23 March Spitfire fighter-bombers bombed the site at Ypenburg. Essential components at each of these sites, buildings and storage areas were destroyed during these attacks.

The last gasp of the German flying bomb offensive took place between the evening of 28 March and noon of the following day when twenty-one bombs approached Britain and twenty of those were shot down. The one remaining bomb that got past the defences crashed in the village of Datchworth 25 miles from London Bridge. It was the last flying bomb to fall on British soil.

APPENDIX 1

The State of Fighter Command

The Crossbow threat has proved serious; it is causing public alarm and is reducing production. Subject to the needs of the battle, therefore, we must do all we can to defeat it.

Assistant Chief of the Air Staff (Operations) Air Marshal WA Coryton

I n a report to the Secretary of State for Air the state of the aircraft being used by Fighter Command was outlined. Trials were underway for Spitfires, Mustangs and Mosquitoes to use N_20 or nitrous oxide. The speed of Mosquito XIX and XXX models had been increased by 10 mph at 3,000 feet but the weight of the equipment amounted to 600 lb, discounting the advantage in speed.

'The RAF have also found that appreciable increases of speed can be achieved on Mustangs, Spitfires and Tempest types by "cleaning up" the aircraft,' an Air Ministry report dated 27 July 1944 stated.

The same report indicated that the British jet fighter, the Gloster Meteor, had not yet gone into action against the flying bomb. It had trouble with its cannon ejector chutes, which at the time of the report had just been fixed.

The use of smoke shells had been ruled out since the guns had been redeployed.

The fighters operating in the rear of guns obtain good preliminary indication of the tracks of flying bombs from gunfire bursts. Inland

the R.O.C. are using Snowflake rockets, but the main system of control of fighters overland is by R/T running commentary. This is operating successfully.

In an Air Ministry report dated 12 August 1944 it outlined the advances made with Meteors. No. 616 Squadron then operated seven Meteor 1 aircraft from Manston. By the date of the report the Squadron had flown thirty-eight sorties and had destroyed three V1s.

'The previous trouble with the cannon and ejector chutes, defects were found in the ammunition feed system,' the report stated. At that time, 616 Squadron was to have a complement of Meteor 1 aircraft and Meteor 3 aircraft with the more powerful jet engines. By August the Squadron had six Mark 1 aircraft on strength; by September they received one more Mark 1 and two Mark 3 aircraft and by October another four Mark 3 Meteors were to be delivered.

The same report indicated that technical problems existed with the use of nitrous oxide on the piston-engine fighters. Also, the backfiring problems on these aircraft that resulted from the use of 150 grade fuel had been cured by the date of the report. 'All engines capable of using this type of fuel, which are being used on anti-Diver operations are being modified.'

Four Tempest squadrons, four Mustang squadrons, two Spitfire Mk 9 squadrons, three Spitfire 14 squadrons, two Mosquito XIX squadrons and one Mosquito XII squadron were all modified to use the 150 grade fuel.

At the time there were fifteen day fighter squadrons (including seven Meteor 1 aircraft) flying against flying bombs. There were also five AI Night Fighter Squadrons, two Intruder Squadrons, five Tempest aircraft of FIU (Fighter Interception Unit) and six American Black Widow aircraft operating in the night fighter role against the flying bomb.

By 1 September operations with the Meteor had increased. Flying from Manston, 616 Squadron now operated eight Meteor 1 aircraft and since 11 August had flown 151 sorties, destroying seven flying bombs. All of the armament problems had by this time been overcome.

However, the use of nitrous oxide injection in Mosquitoes was limited to high altitude and had not yet been sanctioned for use at low altitude, which is where they would operate.

In an Air Ministry report dated 1 September 1944, information on how the backfiring problem experienced using 150 high-grade fuel had been corrected. 'The majority of aircraft which are being used on anti-Diver operations have been modified to take the higher boost allowed by the fuel,' the report stated. Tests were under way to modify the manifolds of the Merlin 25 engines in the two Mosquito Intruder Squadrons to take advantage of the increased boost. 'At present this high boost can only be used when stub exhausts are fitted; this precludes the employment of the aircraft on normal Intruder work.'

Another step taken to improve the performance of the Mosquitoes was to re-engine them with the Merlin 25 instead of the Merlin 23. This step was put in hand quickly.

At the same time the other fighters were in the process of being cleaned up. Steps taken to do this included:

(i) Removal of all the paint, smoothing down of extrusions and the filling in of holes with a special kind of filler

(ii) Improvements to streamlining, removal of unnecessary items in the air stream such as the backward leaning mirror and, in the case of the Mustangs, removal of the bomb racks and their fittings

(iii) Crews looking after these aircraft wore rubber soled shoes to avoid any danger of scratching the aircraft during servicing.

The report also mentioned that the number of day fighter squadrons operating against the flying bomb had dropped to nine. There were four night fighter squadrons, one Tempest squadron and two Mosquito intruder squadrons flying in the night fighter role.

Day fighter squadrons on anti-Diver operations had been reduced as a result of the reduced scale of the German attack and also the lack of launches from sites south of the Somme, subsequently reducing the area in which the fighters had to operate. Some of the day fighter squadrons had been taken out of the fight in order to support Bomber Command's attacks on the Ruhr. 'The fighter squadrons concerned will be operating from their original airfields and can revert to "Diver" work in an emergency,' the report continued.

Tempests and Mustangs were used to provide experimental and operational flying for the Experimental Control Unit at Fairlight.

Performance of Various Fighter Aircraft at 2,000 Feet

Type of aircraft	Engine	Boost	Max speed at combat rating	Remarks
With 130 grade fuel				
Tempest V	Napier Sabre 2	9 lb	383 mph	
Tempest V	Napier Sabre 2	11 lb	396 mph	Modification to automatic boost required and engine not yet cleared for 11 lb boost
Spitfire XII	Griffin 2, 3 or 4	12 lb	354 mph	
Spitfire XIV	Griffin 65	18 lb	370 mph	
Mustang III	Packard Merlin V1650/7	18 lb	370 mph	
Mustang III	V1650/3	18 lb	362 mph	
Mustang II	Allison F4/R	60″ hg	390 mph	
With 150 grade fuel				
Spitfire XII	Griffin 2, 3 or 4	15 lb	365 mph	Clearance for 15 lb is doubtful as the crankshaft is not up to the same strength as Griffin 65
Spitfire XIV	Griffin 65	25 lb	399 mph	Not cleared
Mustang III	Packard Merlin V1650/7	25 lb	400 mph	Not cleared

APPENDIX 3

Spitfire Power at 1,000 Feet

The power required to fly Spitfires at 350 mph and 400 mph at 1,000 feet

350 mph = 1,850 hp
400 mph = 2,800 hp

The maximum power developed by a Spitfire IX at 1,000 feet at 18 lb boost	1,700 hp
The maximum power developed by a Spitfire IX at 1,000 feet at 25 lb boost	1,910 hp
The maximum power developed by a Spitfire XIV at 18 lb boost	1,980 hp
The maximum power developed by a Spitfire XIV at 25 lb boost	2,200 hp

APPENDIX 4

Recollections

Throughout this book we have heard the voices of the pilots, politicians and senior military men who were involved with the Battle of the Flying Bomb. But the book cannot end without the remembrances of the ordinary people who had to endure the terrible menace of the V1.

What follows are just a smattering of people's memories of the V1 and the terror it caused in their hearts when they heard it coming over and, especially, when they heard the engine stop. They never knew until the V1 exploded if this time it would be them.

When the war started I was 3½ and in 1944 when the flying bombs were coming over I was 8 years old. It is difficult to know what you remember and what you were told you remembered by mums and dads. During the original blitz we spent a lot of the time down in the air raid shelter in the garden but by 1944 the air raids had slackened off quite a lot. There were hardly any really.

One night in mid-44 there was this horrible noise outside. It's difficult to explain what it was like, a bit like a motor bike with no exhaust pipe. We went out in the garden to see what was going on and caught in the searchlight of the sky was one of these things coming over. We didn't know what it was. It carried on going. More and more come over during the following days. And one of these come over during the daytime making this horrible noise and it suddenly stopped. Then it just crashed, just straight down and crashed not too far from where we lived in East Dulwhich near the Dulwich Library.

I can remember Uncle Will in the air force at home. Mum was there and granddad was there and they were very worried about what was going on. I didn't really know what was going on. I had been brought up in wartime and I didn't really know what peace was. All these bombs and guns and bangs and Christ knows what.

The V1 exploded. All of a sudden there was this bloody great bang and it shook everything. Maybe three quarters of a mile away. We saw more coming over and we didn't think they were coming down in our part of London we thought they were going up to the main part of London, Whitehall and all that.

When they came over there was hardly any air raid sirens going it was just the noise. They didn't all come in on the same line either they were quite well dispersed around.

The nearest one to us was about 400 yards away. Fortunately there were two rows of houses between us and they took the blast. They were about 400 yards as the crow flies. The worse one at the time and I don't know much about it was the flying bomb that landed on the Co-op in Lordship Lane and about 20 people died. There was some connection with the family, someone's fear that they were there.

I'm not too sure if it was a distant friend of the family or whether it was just a good friend. There were about 20 to 30 people killed and it was the equivalent of today's supermarkets where you queued up for things.

There were a couple of light hearted things. Mrs Brooks next door was deaf. And [if] we heard one coming over I used to shout 'there's a doodlebug coming over Mrs Brooks' and she used to give me threepence.

Quite a lot of V1s came down in our area. At the time it didn't make much sense to me but there was talk amongst the grown ups that I picked up was that they thought they were aiming for a particular area. It was the bottom part of East Dulwich, Dulwich Hospital and East Dulwich Railway Station and West Dulwich Railway station. There was some talk that there was something down there that the Germans were after.

But on reflection now the gyroscopic sights on the doodlebugs weren't really that efficient for them to pick things out.

Another one that landed fairly close was when my dad was on leave and went to have his hair cut. When it came over he fell to the ground and covered his head and came back with half a hair cut and all covered in dust.

But it was frightening for a kid. Early on in the war you had the air raid warning siren and went down in the shelter and that was it. But with these you didn't know. You heard the noise and went out and looked up and if the noise kept on going you knew you were ok but if the noise stopped that's when you got worried because you knew it was going to crash down.

The worse thing was not knowing when they were coming and where they were going to land. They just sort of dropped.

Dave Sanderson (Sandy), jet engine mechanic 96 Squadron

You would hear them. They made a horrid sort of noisy motorbike sort of noise and you just prayed that they wouldn't cut out and they wouldn't fall on you. It was a horrible feeling but you prayed please let them go further and fall on somebody else that sort of thing.

I lived in Surrey and we had them there. I heard the explosions. We didn't have any windows blown out. But there were neighbouring roads that had damage. I'm almost 80 now.

The worst was the V2 because you never knew when they were coming they just exploded without any warning.

The thing about the doodlebug was that you could see them, hear them and there was this awful feeling, please don't let the engine cut out. That was the worst part of it because you knew once the engine cut out it was going to land somewhere.

I was at school then.

I do remember that was the one thing that worried my father more than anything else was the V2s. It was the only thing that seemed to get to him because there was no way of knowing when they were coming.

Patricia Johns

My father was on air raid duty one night. He'd gone off in the middle of the night, my mother said come in my bed and keep warm. After a while my father came back and said there were some very strange aircraft about. We'd heard these things around and they weren't British planes and we were told the next morning that they had no pilots in them.

Towards the end of the war we just didn't bother going into the air raid shelter but we did at the beginning of the war.

You could hear these things coming of course because they sounded different from any other aircraft and if the engine stopped you knew it was going to come down possibly somewhere not very far away.

One day I was playing the piano in the day time and I heard one of these planes fairly overhead and then the engine stopped and I just dived out of the house down to the air raid shelter because it was so close I was afraid it was going to come down so close.

If it just went over that's all right it's nothing to worry about but if it stopped then there was something to worry about.

I was about 17 at that time. I was in school till I was about 18.

But with the V2s you had no warning at all. They were just explosions. I had been out walking on a Sunday afternoon and there was an enormous explosion not very far away. We had gotten pretty blasé about air raids by that time. I didn't go to look to see where it was.

But a friend was talking to somebody on the phone at the same time and the phone went dead. It turned out the V2 had dropped on the friend's house and the friend he had been talking to was killed. Those were more frightening because you had no warning at all.

Anne Bouteau

I was eight and a half years old, living on a small estate of semi-detached houses, near the De Havilland airfield, in Hatfield, Herts., with my sister (aged 13), mother and father. Father worked at De Havilland, as did pretty well everyone on that estate, which had been built as homes for their employees in 1936, when De Havilland set up in Hatfield. Our house was on the long side of a T-junction, Selwyn Drive, with the start of another road, Selwyn Crescent, just opposite. In the first house on the right of Selwyn Crescent, which was perhaps 150 yards from our house, lived my best friend, another girl of eight, Irene Knight.

Irene's father was away in the RAF, and she lived there alone with her mother. They had a Morrison Shelter in their back garden, and on that day, she and I had been playing house inside it, and planning to spend the night in it for what is nowadays called a 'sleepover'. When I went home and announced this to my mother, she would have none of it. 'Oh no, you're not! There's a war on, and I want you at home with us.' Was I cross! And the more so, because we were expecting a visitor next day, who would sleep in my bedroom, the small one at the front of the house, over the front door. My mother had prepared the room for the guest, and so I would have to sleep in the back bedroom, with my horrible sister. (Not really horrible, but at that time, aged 8 and 13, we had little in common, and neither of us liked having to share a bedroom).

After supper, came bath time, this being Friday, the one day in the week when enough coke could be found to heat the boiler, and all the family would bath, in sequence, using the same water, topped up. I, the youngest, was first. My bath over, my mother was tucking me up in bed when the air-raid warning went. 'Aren't you just going to have a bath?' I asked, but my mother said 'No, not while there's an air-raid on.' I remember saying 'Oh, nothing ever happens in Hatfield,' though I knew my father always stood on the front step, during air-raids, and had been able to see the brightly lit sky over London when there were serious raids. I lay in bed, feeling thoroughly disagreeable (not being allowed to sleep at my friend's house, and having to share with my sister), listening to the sounds of aircraft engines. Then suddenly, one of them cut out. My father, from the front doorstep called out 'Take cover' . . . but, in my rebellious mood, I didn't . . . until a chunk of ceiling fell on my head. I did get my head under the covers then!

I lay in bed, now heavy with plaster on it, and very quickly, my mother was there, uncovering me, to see my head streaming blood. She went to carry me downstairs, but the front door had blown in, and lay on the staircase, blocking her way. She never could make out, afterwards, how she had ever got UP the stairs. We got downstairs somehow, and she carried me to the back room, where everything was covered in soot; she blew the soot off a chair, to sit me down. We had friends further along the road, out of the line of the bomb-blast, and we spent the night there . . . Doctors came from local hospitals, and visited each house, treating the minor wounds, and giving me a magnificent huge white bandage round my head.

My friend's house, and the one to which it was attached, was completely razed by a direct hit to the side of it, both Irene and her mother killed, as I would have been, had I slept there. And, since the front wall of our house had collapsed with the blast, I would probably have been killed had I been in my own bed under the window in the front bedroom. My guardian angel (if any) had had a busy day!

Our house was not habitable for at least a year, as I remember from the disruption of our family life that ensued, staying with various friends and relations until a council house was found for us, near to de Havilland, so that my father could get more easily to his essential work, making Mosquitoes.

We assumed that they were being aimed at the de Havilland works, where those vital Mosquito aircraft were being built. I don't think any ever found that, though there may have been one which landed on the airfield, causing no damage. Talking to other residents of the estate much later I learnt what a lot of damage many houses had sustained. I was always surprised, as an adult, when I heard of IRA bombs, which seemed to do so little damage, by comparison. They didn't sound to me like proper bombs at all!

Wendy English, remembering the events of Friday
22 September 1944

APPENDIX 5

The Aircraft

T here were many aircraft used in the fight against the doodle-bug but I have concentrated on three main types: the Tempest, the Mosquito and the Spitfire. While mention is made throughout the book about the Mustang, it seemed only right that some facts about the aircraft and others should be included here.

De Havilland Mosquito: The Night Fighter Version
The Mosquito was the brainchild of Geoffrey de Havilland and he originally saw it as an unarmed bomber. In the prewar years this concept was unthinkable by the officials of the day. Also, that the bomber was made of wood was considered by the government as a retrograde step, as all operational aircraft of the time were constructed of metal. Design work began in late 1938 in Salisbury Hall a few miles away from the company's headquarters at Hatfield, in order to work unhindered by officialdom.

Designated DH98 by the design team, headed by RE Bishop, the project soon became known as the Mosquito. An order for fifty Mosquitoes was awarded to de Havilland on 1 March 1940, thanks mostly to the good offices of de Havilland's only ally in the government, Sir Wilfred Freeman, Air Member for Development and Production at the Air Ministry.

There were many advantages to wooden construction, one being the great weight saving, as well as freeing up a skilled workforce for work on the metal aircraft. Semi-skilled workers employed by the furniture manufacturers around the country could build the Mosquito. From the beginning of the design work to when the aircraft entered production was less than two years – a remarkable achievement.

208

Wood construction also cut down on the design stage, speeding up the development of the prototype. As a result, the aircraft was put into production very quickly.

The Mosquito's wing was one piece, consisting of front and rear spars with interspaced ribs covered by plywood skins of birch, separated by spruce stringers on the top of the wing's surface.

Built in two halves, the fuselage consisted of two skins of plywood separated by a thick layer of balsa wood. All the necessary equipment was first installed into the fuselage, then the halves were glued together. Once glued together the fuselage and the wing were coated in a madapolam covering using red dope. Then the fuselage and wing were covered in a standard paint finish.

This construction proved to be stronger than metal and was able to take more punishment. It could also be easily repaired. Because there was less internal reinforcement than with metal aircraft, more fuel and armaments could be carried.

On 25 November 1940 the prototype made its maiden voyage with Geoffrey de Havilland Jr at the controls. The success of the aircraft was easily seen and subsequent orders meant that production had to be moved from Hatfield to the de Havilland factory at Leavesden, followed by the Standard Motors factory at Coventry, Airspeed at Portsmouth and Percival Aircraft at Luton all switching over to Mosquito production. Production lines were also set up at the de Havilland factory in Toronto, Canada, at the end of 1942 and at the company's Sydney factory in Australia in 1944. Altogether 7,781 Mosquitoes were built: 6,535 in Britain, 1,034 in Canada and 212 in Australia.

The Mosquito was the first true multi-role aircraft, although the term was not used in 1940. Nearly fifty different versions of the Mosqutio were built ranging from bombers, fighter-bombers and fighters, to photo-reconnaissance, mail-carrying, night fighter and ground attack. One version of the Mosquito was fitted with a 57-mm cannon capable of firing twenty-five shells in twenty seconds that wreaked havoc over all theatres of war by day and by night. By November 1944 Mosquito crews had shot down 659 enemy aircraft.[45]

More than 2,700 of the FBVI fighter-bomber version were built. It was armed with four machine-guns and four cannon, as well as carrying two 250-lb bombs in the internal bomb bay and two 500-lb bombs on under-wing racks. This weaponry, plus a range of more than 1,000 miles and a level maximum speed of 358 mph, made it quite a formidable weapon indeed.

No. 157 Squadron was the first of the Mosquito fighter squadrons to be formed. The first operational patrol took place on 27 April 1942 when Mosquitoes were sent to intercept enemy aircraft attacking Norwich.

By June 1943 twelve squadrons were equipped with Mosquitoes in the night fighter role, defending British skies. On D-Day six Mosquito squadrons patrolled over the beaches of Normandy as part of 85 Group Tactical Air Force. By early 1944 Mosquito fighters were in use against the flying bomb.

The FII was the first version of the Mosquito used as both a day and night fighter, equipped with AI radar for the latter role. This version flew for the first time in May 1941 and was used for intruder work for Fighter Command and Coastal Command.

The dedicated night fighter version was a modification of the FII and was designated the NFXII. The four machine-guns in the nose were replaced with the AI Mark VIII radar in a thimble nose, leaving the four cannon.

The next night fighter version was the NFXIII, which was able to carry under-wing drop tanks or bombs and had a range of 1,260 miles at a maximum speed of 394 mph. The NFXV was a high-altitude version with two-stage Merlin engines. The next version was the NFXVII, which was equipped with the AI Mk 10 radar. The NF30 was a development of the NFXIX and was also fitted with two-stage Merlin engines that gave it a top speed of 424 mph and an operational ceiling of 35,000 feet.

North American Aviation Mustang III

The North American Aviation Mustang's early stages of development were disappointing. It was built to a British specification and order. Designed, built and flown in 100 days, the prototype's first flight took place in October 1940. Having passed all its tests, it was put into production for the end of the year. November 1941 saw the delivery of the first production Mustang I to the RAF and the first two batches of Mustangs amounted to over 600 aircraft. However, on America's entry into the war a proportion of Mustangs were diverted to the US Army Air Forces.

Fitted with the Allison V-1710 F3R liquid-cooled engine with 1,000 hp at 12,000 feet and 1,150 hp for take-off, the Mustang I was a disappointment. The initial armament was four .50 calibre machine-guns and four .30 calibre machine-guns, with two of the .50 calibre machine-guns mounted in the fuselage on either side of the engine crankcase, synchronised to fire through the propeller. The rest of the guns were in the wings. But as a high-altitude fighter, the performance with the Allison engine was poor and the aircraft was relegated to low-altitude reconnaissance fighter missions. The aircraft was posted to the RAF Army Cooperation Command where it made its first operational sortie on 27 July 1942.

The Mustang II was essentially a designation to mark the change of armament to four .50 calibre machine-guns in the wings. Later versions of the Mustang II did have an uprated Allison V-1710-81 engine rated at 1,125 hp at 15,500 feet with around 1,200 hp for take-off.

But like the Mustang I, the Mustang II was also a disappointment. It was not until the Mustang II was fitted with the Merlin 61 engine and four-blade airscrew by Rolls-Royce in Britain that the performance dramatically increased, making the Mustang the legend it is today. So successful was the conversion to the Merlin engines that North American Aviation immediately began re-designing the aircraft so it could take the Packard-built Merlin 68 with a two-stage two-speed supercharger and aftercooler. To take the new engine, the airframe was strengthened, the radiator installation redesigned, new ailerons installed and streamlined bomb racks for long-range drop tanks were fitted under each wing. These racks could also carry 500-lb bombs. The bomb load was later increased to carry two 1,000-lb bombs.

The Mustang III (designated P51B and P51C for the Americans) was put into production in 1943. By January 1944 the Mustang III was in action in the skies over Europe with both the Americans and the British. By placing the Merlin engine in the Mustang, the performance had increased to more than 420 mph maximum speed, close to that of the Tempest, and it was the second most capable aircraft to be able to deal with the V1.[46]

Supermarine Spitfire
Perhaps the most iconic and famous fighter to come from the Second World War, the Spitfire was developed and designed by

RJ Mitchell who incorporated the experience gained from designing high-speed seaplanes that won three successive Schneider Cup Trophy Contests in the 1930s. These seaplanes established world speed records.

Along with the Hawker Hurricane, the Spitfire was instrumental in stemming the German air assault on Britain during the Battle of Britain. The soundness of the design meant that it could be upgraded and redeveloped. Throughout the Second World War the Spitfire served as a first-line fighter. However, against the V1 two Marks of Spitfire were predominantly used – the Mark IX and the Mark XIV.

Mark IX
The Mark IX was a development of the Mark VC and would have been fitted with the Merlin 61, 63, 63A, 66 or 70 engine, depending on the variant. It came into service in late 1942 with the standard armament of two 20-mm cannon and four machine-guns in the wings. There were three versions: the standard fighter designated the F.IX with the Merlin 61, 63 or 63A engine; the LF IX was a low-altitude version with the Merlin 66 engine and was distinctive as it had clipped wings; while the high-altitude version was designated the HF IX and had the Merlin 70 engine. Later Mark IX versions were adapted to take the 'E' wing, which consisted of two 20-mm cannon and two .50 calibre machine-guns as well as racks for two 250-lb bombs. Often, the LF IX would have the 'E' wing adaptation. Later Marks were also fitted with a larger, pointed rudder.

As we have seen, these aircraft were boosted in order to engage the V1s.

Mark XIV
This version of the famous fighter was considerably different to the Mark IX in that it had a completely different engine, the Rolls-Royce Griffin 65 with a two-speed, two-stage supercharger and five-blade constant speed Rotol airscrew. A new cowling was designed to take the new engine. It also had a new fin and rudder of larger area and came in three versions: the standard fighter F.XIV; the standard fighter with the 'E' wing (F.XIV E); and the fighter reconnaissance version with the 'E' wing armament, clipped wings and bubble sliding hood (F.R.XIV E). This version had additional fuel in the rear fuselage and an oblique F24 camera aft

of the cockpit. This version could also carry a single 250-lb bomb or a 500-lb bomb on a fuselage drop tank mounting rack, or there was provision for two 250-lb bombs to be carried under the wings on some versions.

The Spitfire Mark XIV was responsible for the destruction of more than 300 flying bombs.

Hawker Tempest Mark V
The Tempest was a development of the Hawker Typhoon and in appearance both aircraft look remarkably similar. They were both powered by Napier Sabre engines, but the Tempest had a much thinner wing than the Typhoon. They look similar because the intention was to use as many components as possible from the Typhoon to develop the Tempest. This was in order to save time to meet an in-service target date of December 1943. Because of the thin wing design a new fuel tank had to be incorporated into the fuselage of the Tempest in front of the cockpit, lengthening the Tempest fuselage by some 22 inches over the Typhoon.

On 18 November Hawker was awarded a contract for two Tempest prototypes. Sir Sidney Camm's design team at Hawker immediately got underway developing and designing the Tempest. The number of prototypes was increased to six. There were two Tempest Mark I prototypes with the Napier Sabre IV engine and radiators in the wing roots; two Tempest Mark Vs with the Sabre II engine and the chin radiator; and the Tempest Mark II with the Centaurus IV radial engine, which was currently being tested in the Tornado project.[47]

On paper and in trials the Tempest Mark I proved to be a success, going beyond the specifications of the initial requirements, so an order of 400 Tempest Mark Is was given to Hawker. This aircraft was sleek and very fast, achieving a top speed during trials of 472 mph with the Sabre IV engine. However, it was not the aircraft that went into production. The Tempest Mark V, which had reached a maximum speed in excess of 432 mph with an existing engine (the in-service Sabre Mark II engine used on the Typhoons) was the one that was developed. Trouble with the Sabre IV engine rated at 4,000 hp and its lack of reliability meant that the Mark I version was never developed. The time it would take for the new Sabre engine to be rid of its many faults and be reliable enough for front-line service was too long.

At the time in early 1943 few Allied fighters could match the excellent Fw 190 and Me 109G at heights above 20,000 feet. The pressing demand was for an aircraft capable of 430 mph at this altitude with four cannon. There were specifications for jet fighters with these qualities that were being issued at the time, but only the Tempest V was capable of meeting these requirements and that after only four months' of trials.

The Tempests were needed quickly so the order for 400 Tempest Is was switched to 400 Tempest Vs. In July 1943 Squadron Leader Beamont was seconded to Hawker after commanding 609 Squadron flying Typhoons for eight months. Beamont had a close association with the Tempest V and his experience in front-line service was invaluable in helping to develop the aircraft. This helped Sydney Camm's design team to gain a feel for the needs and preferences of Fighter Command.

By the end of December 1943 the first thirty-six Tempest Vs had been delivered to the Maintenance Units where all the necessary equipment such as armament, gunsights, radio etc were fitted. From that point on the aircraft began arriving from the Maintenance Units to the front-line squadrons and were available in time for the battle against the flying bomb.

The Tempest, along with the Typhoon, left a powerful mark on the pages of Second World War aviation history. To some degree the Tempest and certainly the Typhoon were aircraft that did not suffer fools gladly. But the Tempest endeared itself to the pilots faced with day by day struggles, danger and perilous missions low over the battlefields of Europe in the last two years of the war. Whether it was a ground attack mission or a vicious air battle with a desperate enemy in excellent fighters, the Tempest proved itself again and again as one of the premier fighters of its day. Fast, agile and capable of high speeds at high altitude, it packed a powerful punch with its four 20-mm cannon. With a later version capable of carrying twelve 60-lb rockets under its wings, the Tempest was truly a formidable aircraft.

For every one of the 600 flying bombs the pilots of the Tempest Wing at Newchurch destroyed they saved lives. It could be said of the Tempest pilots that so much is truly owed to so few.

Appendix 6

Directive for Air Defence of Great Britain

In a directive dated 17 November 1943 Air Marshal Sir Trafford Leigh-Mallory, then Air Commander-in-Chief Allied Expeditionary Air Force, authorised the set up of Air Defence of Great Britain, which brought together all the functions and organisations of Fighter Command for the purposes of the air defence of Great Britain.

The directive stated that the operational functions of ADGB were:

(a) To be responsible for the air defence of Great Britain and Northern Ireland.

(b) To operationally control the activities of AA Command, The Royal Observer Corps, Balloon Command and other static elements of air defence formerly controlled by Fighter Command.

(c) To conduct defensive and offensive operations which involve the use of Squadrons of both ADGB and TAF under instructions already issued to both Headquarters until fresh instructions are issued.

(d) To develop interception methods and apparatus for eventual use in ADGB and other theatres.

This directive is the one that Sir Roderick Hill talks about in his report on the Air Defence of Great Britain in Chapter One.

APPENDIX 7

Minutes of a Meeting Held at Headquarters ADGB at 1730 hrs, 13 July 1944

What follows are the minutes of the momentous meeting held on 13 July 1944 when Air Marshal Sir Roderick Hill chairing the meeting tabled the motion that the anti-aircraft guns should be moved from London to the coast.

Where they could have complete freedom of action against 'Diver' aircraft whilst fighters should operate both over the sea area in front of the guns under close control and over the land area between the guns and balloons under running commentary control.

The meeting had been called to support the proposal and decide how it would be put into effect.

General Sir Frederick A Pile was in complete agreement with the proposal while Air Vice Marshal Saunders was also in agreement stating it 'was the best plan that had yet been produced.'

He was assured that the balloon barrage would not be moved forward and that the fighters should patrol over the gun belt above 5,000 feet or just below cloud base if it was below that height which was agreed by AA Command.

Sir Robert Watson-Watt mentioned in the meeting that they could already control up to 20 aircraft out to sea and he took on the responsibility of improving equipment to control more aircraft. However, such equipment would take weeks to bring online.

216

The decisions taken at the meeting were that the perimeter of the balloon barrage would not change. The guns, however, should be moved from the gun belt protecting London to a coastal strip extending from St Margaret's Bay to Beachy Head extending 10,000 yards out to sea and 5,000 yards inland. It was also decided that the fighters would not operate inside the gun belt but could operate in front of it, seawards and between the gun belt and the barrage balloons.

Restrictions on gunfire from the AA guns were also decided. 'Gaps should be made in the layout of the AA guns so as to avoid shooting down "Diver" aircraft onto the main towns on the coasts,' the minutes recorded. 'Such gaps should be utilised as corridors for fighters and aircraft in distress to fly over the AA gun strip.'

One last restriction was that those guns deployed should not fire above 8,000 feet even though orthodox hostile aircraft often flew above that height.

An Eight Year Old Boy Designs a Defence Against the Flying Bomb

In a letter dated 28 September 1944 an eight year old boy, Roy Law, sent a letter to the War Office, which was then passed onto the Ministry of Aircraft Production, that included an idea to combat the flying bombs. In his letter he stated that he wanted to return to the South so he suggested that the Ministry should 'try putting up helicopter machines with strong steel wires joining them.'

He then suggested they should be electronically controlled to save men having to go up in the helicopters.

Men could parachute down after setting the helicopters at the right height. 20 helicopters would be needed for each section and a lot of these would explode anything.

Included with the letter were detailed sketches of how the system would work. He then wrote a subsequent letter dated 1 October 1944, adding to his original letter 'If you think it ok I can send you details of my ideas to keep the thing in the air without it coming down or men going up during a long war.' Law believed the idea would work. 'I can fix this I think, if the thing can be put up at the angle on the sketch.'

Included with the sketch was a newspaper cutting. In it, Roy Law was listed as being from Borth near Aberystwyth and was a

London evacuee who was being tutored by his mother. She was quoted in the cutting as saying that his mathematical abilities were frightening.

The official reply from the Director of Scientific Research was that there were numerous proposals along similar ideas that were being carefully considered by the Department. 'The general idea is very well known and for your information it can be stated that aircraft of this type are not available for this purpose.'[48]

The letter then continued by saying that no further action would take place with regards Roy's idea.

You are to be congratulated on the ingenuity displayed, which, in a boy of your age, is quite remarkable. In thanking you for your efforts to be of assistance, the Department hope it will not be long before you can return to the South.

In a subsequent letter, dated 19 August 1945, Law asked if the Bristol factory making helicopters would be closed or would continue. Mentioning his earlier invention of using helicopters connected with cables to stop flying bombs, he had since refined the invention. 'I had a better scheme of an attraction station. But as this also needed helicopters I did not send this in.'

He then said he was very interested in the atom. 'I hope that America hangs tight to atom bomb secrets until we get someone like Churchill back.'

An official reply assured him that research and development in the field of aviation would continue and that his former suggestion was on file.

A year later Roy Law wrote again to the Ministry in a letter dated 9 December 1946, stating that he was back in the South and was still interested in helicopters.

I always knew that they would be useful for many purposes. They could be used to build an attraction station which I have had in my mind a long time. This station could draw things like the V2.

The last sentence of the letter from this remarkable boy then asked for more information on the atom bomb. 'I am trying to work out perpetual motion – it must be possible.'

He was ten years old when this letter was written.

Number of Flying Bombs Destroyed

Week ending at sunrise on:	Total bombs reported	Bombs in the target area	Percentages	Total bombs brought down	4 to 1 percentages	Bombs brought down by fighters	Bombs brought down by AA guns	Bombs brought down by balloons	Bombs brought down by naval guns
17.6.44	218	104	47.7	58	26.6	15	43		
24.6.44	650	315	48.5	250	38.5	195½	52	2½	
1.7.44	711	305	42.9	284	39.9	199½	74	10½	
8.7.44	820	369	45.0	367	44.8	295⅚	45⅚	25⅓	
15.7.44	535	177	33.1	282	52.7	218½	46½	17	
22.7.44	563	247	43.9	229	40.7	131	64	34	
29.7.44	674	199	29.5	379	56.2	213	142½	23½	
5.8.44	777	293	37.7	365	47.0	139½	177	48½	
12.8.44	457	101	22.1	300	65.6	139½	129½	31	
19.8.44	487	79	16.2	373	76.6	104½	251	17½	
26.8.44	497	114	22.9	313	63.0	51	248	14	
2.9.44	336	37	11.0	263	78.3	68½	186½	8	
Totals for first phase	6,725	2,340	34.8	3,463	51.5	1,771⅓	1,459⅚	231⅚	

Week ending at sunrise on:	Total bombs reported	Bombs in the target area	Percentages	Total bombs brought down	4 to 1 percentages	Bombs brought down by fighters	Bombs brought down by AA guns	Bombs brought down by balloons	Bombs brought down by naval guns
30.9.44	80	14	17.5	23	28.8	10	10½		2½
14.10.44	69	12	17.4	38	55.1	13	23		2
28.10.44	124	11	8.9	102	82.3	25½	76½		1½
11.11.44	120	7	5.8	88	73.3	13	73½		1½
25.11.44	77	7	9.1	58	75.3	2	54½		2
9.12.44	29	1	3.4	26	89.7	4	20		
23.12.44	58	3	5.2	39	67.2	4	35		
6.1.45	63	5	15.4	21	66.7		21		
20.1.45	18	7	38.9	8	44.4		7		1
Totals for second phase	638	67	10.5	403	63.2	71½	321		10½
17.3.45	41	8	19.5	26	63.4	1	24½		½
31.3.45	84	5	6.0	65	77.4	3	62		
Totals for third phase	125	13	10.4	91	72.8	4	86½		½
Totals for whole campaign	7,488	2,420	32.3	3,957	52.8	1,846⅚	1,867⅓	231⅚	11

APPENDIX 10

List of Fighter Units Used Against Flying Bombs with Successes Claimed 1944–5

Squadron No.:	Equipment	V1s Claimed
1	Spitfire IX LF	36
3	Tempest V	258
25	Mosquito XVII	27½
41	Spitfire XII	41⅓
56	Tempest V	63
68	Mosquito XVII	18
74	Spitfire IX LF	2
80	Tempest V	
85	Mosquito XVII	32½
91	Spitfire XIV	150
96	Mosquito XIII	181
125	Mosquito XVII	4
129	Mustang III	66½
130	Spitfire XIV	6
137	Typhoon	30
157	Mosquito XVII	32¾
165	Spitfire IX LF	48¾
219	Mosquito XXX	30
264	Mosquito XIII	16
274	Tempest V	16
277	Spitfire V	4
306	Mustang III	57⅓

Squadron No.:	Equipment	V1s Claimed
310	Spitfire IX LF	2
315	Mustang III	51
316	Mustang III	73 1/2
322	Spitfire XIV	94
350	Spitfire XIV	3 1/4
402	Spitfire XIV	3 3/4
409	Mosquito XII & XIII	10
456	Mosquito XVII	23 1/2
486	Tempest V	223 1/2
501	Tempest V	74 1/2
605	Mosquito VI	67 1/2
610	Spitfire XIV	43 2/5
616	Meteor I	8 1/2
Fighter Interception Unit	Various	70
Pilots not attached to squadrons	Various	29 1/4

APPENDIX 11

No. 486 Squadron Pilots and Their Scores

Below is a list of individual scores against flying bombs for pilots of 486 Squadron:

Warrant Officer OD Eagleson (21)
Flying Officer RJ Cammock (20½)
Flight Lieutenant JH McCaw DFC (19½)
Flight Lieutenant JR Cullen (16)
Flying Officer RJ Dansey (11)
Flight Lieutenant HN Sweetman DFC (10½)
Flight Sergeant BJ O'Connor (9½)
Flight Lieutenant SS Williams (8)
Pilot Officer JH Stafford (8)
Flying Officer WA Kalka (8)
Pilot Officer KA Smith (8)
Pilot Officer BM Hall (7½)
Warrant Officer CJ Sheddan (7½)
Flying Officer WA Hart (7)
Flight Lieutenant WL Miller (7)
Pilot Officer RD Bremner (7)
Flying Officer K McCarthy (6)
Pilot Officer WA Trott (6)
Flying Officer HN Mason (5½)
Flight Lieutenant NJ Powell (5)
Pilot Officer SJ Short (5)
Flight Lieutenant NW Tanner (4)
Flight Lieutenant LJ Appleton (3½)
Flying Officer JG Wilson (2½)

Flight Lieutenant V Cooke (2)
Flight Sergeant J Steedman (2)
Squadron Leader JH Iremonger (1½)
Flying Officer TM Kenton (1)
Pilot Officer RJ Wright (1)
Flight Sergeant WJ Campbell (1)
Flight Sergeant J Ferguson (1)
Flight Lieutenant KG Taylor-Cannon DFC (1)

Bibliography

The Years Flew Past, Roland Beamont, Airlife Publishing Ltd (2002)

The Men Who Flew the Mosquito, Martin W Bowman, Leo Cooper (2003)

War Diaries 1939–1945, Field Marshal Lord Alanbrooke, edited by Alex Danchev and Daniel Todman, Weidenfeld & Nicholson (2001), ISBN 1 84212 526 5

The Official History of the Royal Air Force, Volume Two, Her Majesty's Stationary Office

Air Operations by Air Defence of Great Britain and Fighter Command in connection with the German Flying Bomb and Rocket Offensives, 1944–1945, Air Chief Marshal Sir Roderick Hill, National Archives, Kew, London

The Hawker Typhoon and Tempest, Francis K Mason, Aston Publications Limited (1988), ISBN 0 946627 19 3

The Memoirs of Field Marshal The Viscount Montgomery of Alamein, KG, Collins (1958)

Official History and Combat Reports of 1 Squadron, National Archives, Kew, London

Official History and Combat Reports of 3 Squadron, National Archives, Kew, London

Official History and Combat Reports of 96 Squadron, National Archives, Kew, London

Official History and Combat Reports of 486 Squadron, National Archives, Kew, London

Official History and Combat Reports of 501 Squadron, National Archives, Kew, London

Official History and Combat Reports of 605 Squadron, National Archives, Kew, London

Typhoon and Tempest at War, Arthur Reed and Roland Beamont, Ian Allan Ltd (1974), ISBN 0 7110 0542 7

With Prejudice, The War Memoirs of Marshal of the Royal Air Force Lord Tedder GCB, Cassell and Company Ltd (1966)

Notes

1. This is the term used in Sir Roderick's report
2. The Allies called these sites 'ski sites' because on each site lay a number of buildings shaped like a ski laid on its side. The buildings, the Allies felt, were meant to provide blast-proof shelters for the missiles while they were being stored and sheltered.
3. These figures are outlined in Hill's report
4. More than 528 and 804 respectively.
5. Sir Roderick states that the Germans gave this information to the Allies after the armistice.
6. This is according to Sir Roderick Hill in his report.
7. It was code-named Diver because the V1 would simply dive to the ground the moment its engine cut out.
8. According to Sir Roderick's report 'the Germans meant the bombs to fly higher, doubtless so as to minimise the effect of light AA fire. This proved impracticable, and without the knowledge of the Air Ministry they changed their plans.'
9. This is according to Sir Roderick Hill's report on the flying bombs to the Air Ministry (page 13, paragraph 63).
10. Eighteen fighters were badly damaged and five pilots and one navigator killed in this way in the first six weeks of the battle, so even though the flying bomb could not fight back, destroying them was not without risk.
11. These steel mattresses were called 'Pile Mattresses' and were developed by the REME detachment of Anti-Aircraft Command.
12. The double parachute link was a device designed so that when a balloon cable was struck it would automatically break near the top and bottom so the aircraft that struck it would carry

away the central portion. Parachutes then opened at each end to provide enough drag to make the aircraft stall.

13. From Beamont's book *The Years Flew Past* published by Airlife Publishing Ltd, page 38, which is the beginning of his criticism of the AA command.

14. This is an assertion by Beamont but is not necessarily shown in either Tedder's memoirs or those of Alanbrooke.

15. An excerpt from *The Doodlebugs* by Norman Longmate, published by Hutchinson

16. Published in the *Aeronautical Review* of June 1990

17. One of the airfields where modified Heinkel 111 bombers designated He 111 H-22 were stationed. These bombers were V1 air launchers.

18. The facts of Berry's death were taken from an entry on the BBC website, the People's War.

19. It must be noted here that at low speeds the Tempests while manoeuvring behind the V1s invariably had to start weaving from side to side in order to avoid overshooting the V1 and enable them to stay behind.

20. As the V1 was flying at 100 feet, one has to assume that Birbeck was as well, which could mean that pieces from the crash hit his Tempest.

21. This was later to be sunk by rocket-firing Typhoons according to the 3 Squadron Operational History.

22. This is the code name for the standing patrols the squadrons flew to catch flying bombs coming in over Britain.

23. This airspeed is classified as 'indicated', which means the airspeed shown on the airspeed indicator of the Tempest or whatever aircraft the pilot was flying at the time of the attack.

24. Presumably it was not completely pitch black for him to identify the other aircraft as a Mustang.

25. In this combat report Barckley states no other claim was received but he writes that he didn't see the flying bomb go down, although it was later confirmed by Biggin Hill.

26. In fact he had taken off from Newchurch ten minutes before Dredge.

27. RAF slang for enemy aircraft.

28. There are several reports of Spitfires attacking V1s that were about to crash. One wonders if this was out of desperation or an RAF policy.

29. In Chapter 1 reference was made to the report by Air Marshal Sir Roderick Hill who stated that on average the patrol height for the fighters was between 5,000 and 7,000 feet.
30. There is no indication of what this could be but the Squadron diarist refers to it as being 'a somewhat larger diver'.
31. There is no reference given to Dansey's landing ten minutes after his wingman but one can assume that this was due to his second engagement with a flying bomb. Alternatively, it could be that they were staggering the arrival and departure times of the fighters so aircraft could come and go relatively safely.
32. Most likely this was Flight Sergeant Vassie, although there is no record of this.
33. This is from a report, 'A/C Report No. A.685 27/4/45 He 111', found on Kohlenbissen Airfield, which confirms the technical information provided by the unnamed Germans detailed in Air Ministry Report '579/44 He 111 with FZG 76'.
34. All this information comes from the secret report ADI K 579/44 dated 23 October 1944 entitled 'He 111 with FZG 76'.
35. Referred to as a 'Diver Box' while the gun belt was referred to as the 'Diver Belt'.
36. The exact wording in the Combat Report states 'exploded on sea after fuel tank had burst in the air.'
37. Although it's not stated anywhere, we must assume that after each attack the Mosquito crews would climb their aircraft as quickly as possible back up to their normal patrol height, as they did not have the speed the Tempests had to engage the V1s without diving on them.
38. Although these figures are published in their Consolidated Diver Reports, they are approximates only.
39. One has to assume that these times are approximates only, as only five minutes elapsed from the destruction of one flying bomb to the other according to Squadron Leader Chudleigh's combat report.
40. The Squadron's hundreth V1 destroyed.
41. This is from the Squadron history.
42. Taken from the BBC website 'The People's War'.
43. Taken from the letter Air Vice Marshal Ambler wrote to TCG James at the Air Ministry on 14 September 1945 where he outlined the events that led up to the redeployment of the anti-aircraft guns at the height of the battle against the flying bomb.

44. Taken from a letter from TCG James 5 November 1945 to Sir Robert Watson-Watt.
45. From *Mosquito Profile* by Stuart Howe published in 1984 by Ian Allen Ltd.
46. Taken from *Jane's Fighting Aircraft of World War II* published by Tiger Books International 1998 and originally published by Jane's Publishing Company as *Jane's All the World's Aircraft 1940/41/42/43/44/45*.
47. The Tornado was a Hawker project that was designed for testing three different engines, which included the Centaurus radial engine that eventually became the main engine for the Hawker Sea Fury and Hawker Tempest Mark II.
48. Taken from the official response dated 10 October 1944, reference R.Inv/49150/SR2/EB, which was in reply to Roy Law's initial letter.

Index